# HEIRS AND ORPHANS

## Anne Arundel County
## Maryland

## Distributions

## 1788–1838

*Walter E. Arps, Jr.*

HERITAGE BOOKS
2011

# HERITAGE BOOKS
*AN IMPRINT OF HERITAGE BOOKS, INC.*

## Books, CDs, and more—Worldwide

For our listing of thousands of titles see our website
at
www.HeritageBooks.com

Published 2011 by
HERITAGE BOOKS, INC.
Publishing Division
100 Railroad Ave. #104
Westminster, Maryland 21157

Other Heritage Books by Walter E. Arps, Jr.:

*Before the Fire: Genealogical Gleanings from the* Cambridge Chronicle, *1830–1855*

*Departed This Life: Death Notices from* The Baltimore Sun, *Volume 1: 1851–1853*

*Departed This Life: Death Notices from* The Baltimore Sun, *Volume 2: 1854–56*

*Departed This Life: Death Notices from* The Baltimore Sun, *Volume 4: 1859–60*

*Heirs and Orphans: Anne Arundel County Distributions, 1788–1838*

*Maryland Mortalities, 1876–1915, from the (Baltimore)* Sun Almanac

International Standard Book Numbers
Paperbound: 978-1-58549-086-8
Clothbound: 978-0-7884-8880-1

Heirs & Orphans consists of abstracts of the first four volumes of the
Distributions of the personal estates of Anne Arundel County intestates:
JG#1 (1788-1798), JG#2 (1803-1811), JG#3 (1812-1820), and TH#1 (1820-1838).
When a Marylander failed to leave a will, the pertinent county stepped
in to insure that his real property was divided as equitably as possible.
Such divisions were by fractional proportions, which are useful to the gene-
alogist in determining family relationships.

The legal structure devised for handling intestacies was in effect by
the early 18th century. Its provisions are succinctly summarized in the in-
dex of the Reverend Thomas Bacon's compilation of The Laws of Maryland, as
published (1765) in Annapolis by Jonas Green, Provincial Printer:

> After a full Account made by an Administrator of any Intestate's
> Estate, the Commissary-General shall make Distribution Surplusage,
> in Manner following, viz.

I One third Part to the Widow.

II The Residue, by equal Portions among the Children, and their legal
Representatives if any such Children be dead.

III Except such Children as have received Portions, by Settlement of
the Intestate in his Life Time, equal to the Share allotted by such
Distribution to the other Children.

IV Such Children as have received Settlements, from the Intestate in
his Life Time, not equal to the Share due by the Distribution to
the other Children, shall have so much of the Surplusage, as shall
make the Estate of all the Children, as equal as can be estimated.

V But the Heir at Law, notwithstanding any Lands he may have by Des-
cent, or otherwise, from the Intestate, shall have an equal share
with the other Children in the Distribution.

VI In case there be no Children, nor legal Representatives of them, the
Widow shall have one Moiety; and the Rest be divided among the next
of Kindred, in equal Degree, and their legal Representatives. But
no Representatives shall be admitted among Collaterals, after Brothers and Sisters Children.

VII If there be no Widow, then the Estate shall be equally divided among
the Children; and if no Children, then among the next of Kindred in
equal Degree, or their legal Representatives as aforesaid. [1715]

VIII In case the Administrator (where there are no nearer Collaterals) be
of Kin to the Deceased, within the 5th Degree, either of Consan-
guinity or Affinity; he, and all other as nearly Related, shall have
the same Right to the Residue as Brothers and Sisters Children. [1719,
1729]

IX But if there be a Widow, no other Collaterals shall be admitted than
those directed by this Act; and she shall have the whole Residue.
[1719, 1729]

The following provisions pertained to Orphans:

I Orphans entitled to any Portion in the Distribution of an Intestate's
Estate, if capable of chusing (sic) Guardians, shall be called into
Court, then and there to chuse their Guardians, into whose Hands their
Estates shall be committed. [1715]

II But if such Orphans be not at Age then shall the County Court appoint
fit Persons, to whom shuch Orphans and their Estates shall be committed, taking Bond with Two sufficient Sureties in the Names of the Orphans, for securing and delivering the same to the Orphans or their
Guardians, when thereunto lawfully called, etc. [Also 1715]

  _Liber_ JG#1 was previously abstracted in typescript form by Robert W. Barnes (with the assistance of Robert K. Headley) and deposited in the Library of the Maryland Historical Society. Then, this typescript was later published (1974) by Raymond B. Clark, Jr., in his magazine, _Maryland & Delware Genealogist._

  The genealogical value of Distributions was brought home to this compiler while trying to determine the father of Jesse Brashears (p. 12), who lived in the southern part of Anne Arundel County in the early 19th Century. The relationship of Waymack Brashears to his son, Jesse, appears to be revealed in the Distribution herein but in no other extant public document. That discovery triggered this compilation.

  Users of _Heirs & Orphans_ are urged to consult the original books, for verification.

JG#1/1: Mr. RICHARD HARRISON who intermarried with MARY NORRIS executrix of THOMAS NORRIS late of Anne Arundel Co. deceased. 5 February 1788 (final account passed 1 May 1783). Sureties: JOSEPH COWMAN + PHILIP THOMAS, Jr. MARY NORRIS, widow's third; fourths of the remaning balance to: ROBERT NORRIS, THOMAS NORRIS, SARAH NORRIS + MARY NORRIS.

JG#1/1: THOMAS COOK executor of WILLIAM SIMPSON late of Anne Arundel Co. deceased. 3 January 1788. Sureties: THOMAS PHILLIPS + ROBERT TEVIS. One third to the widow, who is unnamed; residue to daughter MARY SIMPSON.

JG#1/1: Mrs. SARAH GARDINER administratrix of JOHN GARDINER late of Anne Arundel Co. deceased. 26 November 1787. Sureties: GEORGE GARDINER + WILKERSON BRASHEARS. Widow SARAH GARDINER, one third; fifths of the remaining balance to ELIZABETH GARDINER, JAMES GARDINER, GEORGE GARDINER, WILLIAM GARDINER + MARY GARDINER.

JG#1/2: Mr. VACHEL STEVENS administrator of ELIZABETH STEVENS late of Anne Arundel Co. deceased. 8 March 1788. Sureties JOHN HOWARD + ABRAHAM CLAUDE. Fifths to: VACHEL STEVENS; SARAH THORP; ELIZABETH KINGSBURY; the three children of NANCY CLAUDE: JOHN CLAUDE, DENNIS CLAUDE + ABRAHAM CLAUDE; + KITTY STEVENS, d/o DENNIS STEVENS.

JG#1/2: Mrs. ELIZABETH HOPKINS executrix of JOHNS HOPKINS late of Anne Arundel Co. deceased. 15 April 1788. Sureties: JOSEPH HOPKINS + RICHARD HOPKINS. ELIZABETH HOPKINS, widow's third; fifths of the remainder of the balance to: MARY HOPKINS, MARGARET HOPKINS, ELIZABETH HOPKINS, ANNE HOPKINS, + RACHEL HOPKINS.

JG#1/2: Mr. HENRY ASHBAW executor of RICHARD JOYCE late of Anne Arundel Co. deceased. 28 April 1788. Sureties: JOSEPH MAYO + JOHN KILLMAN. A third to the widow (unnamed); thirds of the remainder of the balance to RICHARD JOYCE, WILLIAM JOYCE + ELIJAH JOYCE.

JG#1/3: Mr. LEONARD FOREMAN administrator of JACOB MATTOCKS late of Anne Arundel Co. deceased. 13 May 1788. Sureties: JOHN GRAY + JOHN FOREMAN. A third to the widow (unnamed); fourths of the remainder of the balance to: JONATHAN MATTOCKS, CHARLES MATTOCKS, CHARITY MATTOCKS + SUSANNAH MATTOCKS.

JG#1/3: Mr. EDWARD TIMMONS administrator of THOMAS BROWN late of Anne Arundel Co. deceased. 19 May 1788. Sureties: GEORGE PECKER + RICHARD GARDENER. The entire balance to the legal representative: WILLIAM BROWN.

JG#1/3: Mr. JOHN MERRIKEN administrator of JOSEPH MERRIKEN late of Anne Arundel Co. deceased. 9 June 1788. Sureties: WILLIAM WILKENS + GEORGE PECKER. Sixths to ANN MERRIKEN, SARAH MERRIKEN, JOSEPH MERRIKEN, ROBERT MERRIKEN, THOMAS MERRIKEN + JOHN MERRIKEN.

JG#1/4: Messrs JOSHUA MAYO, JOHN MAYO + ISAAC MAYO executors of JOSEPH MAYO late of Anne Arundel Co. deceased. 9 June 1788. Sureties: CHARLES STEWART + THOMAS STOCKETT. One third to widow HENRIETTA MAYO; thirds of the remainder of the balance to JOSHUA MAYO, JOHN MAYO + ISAAC MAYO.

JG#1/4: Mrs. DELILAH MOSS administratrix of NATHAN MOSS late of Anne Arundel Co. deceased. 13 June 1788. Sureties: JAMES LITTLE + ZACHARIAH ASHLEY. A third to widow DELILAH MOSS; fourths of the remainder of the balance to:

RACHEL MOSS, WILLOBY MOSS, RICHARD MOSS + SARAH MOSS.

JG#1/4: Mrs. MARY PACKER administratrix of GEORGE PACKER late of Anne Arundel Co. deceased. 25 April 1788. Sureties: CHARLES ROBINSON + ABSALOM RIDGELY. One half of the balance of the estate to widow MARY PACKER; the other half to MARY EVITT, m/o of the deceased, according to law.

JG#1/5: Mrs. SARAH GREEN administratrix with will annexed of ELIJAH GREEN late of Anne Arundel Co. deceased. 27 June 1788. Sureties: JACOB GREEN + ZACHARIAH MCCAULEY. Widow SARAH GREEN one third; remainder of balance in fifths to: LANCELOT GREEN, JACOB GREEN, ANNE MACCALLEY (sic), ELIZABETH GREEN + SARAH WARFIELD.

JG#1/5: Mr. JOSEPH SELBY administrator of BENJAMIN SELBY late of Anne Arundel Co. deceased. 27 July 1788. Sureties: GIDEON GRAY + ZACHARIAH DUVALL. Entire estate in sevenths to JOSEPH SELBY, BENJAMIN SELBY, POLLY SELBY, REBECCA SELBY, ANN SELBY, JEMIMA SELBY + ELIZABETH SELBY.

JG#1/5: Mrs. ELIZABETH YIELDHALL executrix of JOSHUA RIDGELY (d. testate) late of Anne Arundel Co. deceased. 22 October 1788. Sureties: THOMAS BIGNALL + ZACHARIAH CADLE. To SARAH RIDGELY d/o of the deceased the entire balance.

JG#1/6: Mrs. ANN STOCKETT executrix...LEWIS STOCKETT late of Anne Arundel Co. deceased. 7 November 1788. Sureties: Dr. THOMAS NOBLE STOCKETT + THOMAS STOCKETT. Widow ANN STOCKETT on half of the balance; sixths of the remainder to: MARY STOCKETT, REBECCA STOCKETT, JOHN STOCKETT, RICHARD STOCKETT, ANN STOCKETT + WILLIAM IJAMS STOCKETT.

JG#1/6: Mrs. FRANCES WHITE administratrix of JOSEPH WHITE late of Anne Arundel Co. deceased. 11 December 1788. Sureties: GRIFFITH WHITE + FRANCIS FREELAND. Widow FRANCES WHITE one third; fifths of the remainder of the balance to: JOSEPH WHITE, ROBERT WHITE, FRANCES FREELAND WHITE, ALFRED WHITE + ROENA WHITE.

JG#/6: Messrs BENJAMIN + NATHAN HATHERLY executors of JOHN HATHERLY late of Anne Arundel Co. deceased. 25 August 1785. Sureties: JAMES FROST + JOSHUA BROWN. Widow (unnamed) a third after deduction of a legacy left by the testator to BENJAMIN + NATHAN HATHERLY, each of whom receive a negro + one half each of the remainder of the balance.

JG#1/7: Mr. VACHEL JOHNSON executor...ROBERT JOHNSON late of Anne Arundel Co. deceased. 10 March 1789. Sureties: ABRAHAM CLAUDE + ZACHARIAH DUVALL. Money, personalty, or negroes to: ROBERT JOHNSON, Jr., VACHEL JOHNSON (of SAMUEL), ANN DAVIS, CATHARINE JAMES, HENRY JOHNSON (of HENRY) + ZACHARIAH JOHNSON; thirds of the balance plus a third each of RACHEL JOHNSON's proportion to: HENRY JOHNSON, ZACHARIAH JOHNSON + HENRIETTA JOHNSON.

JG#1/7: Mr. MOSES MACCUBBIN administrator of MARY MACCUBBIN late of Anne Arundel Co. deceased. 17 March 1789. Surety: ABRAHAM CLAUDE. ELIZABETH MACCUBBIN, one half of the balance; MOSES MACCUBBIN, the other half.

JG#1/8: Mrs. SARAH MACGILL administratrix of the Reverend JAMES MACGILL late of Anne Arundel Co. deceased. 16 June 1789. Sureties: HENRY GRIFFITH, Jr. + EDWARD SPURRIER. Widow SARAH MACGILL, one third; sevenths of the remainder of the balance to: heirs of THOMAS MACGILL, heirs of JOHN MACGILL,

SARAH RIDGELY, MARY MACGILL, ANNE MACGILL, MARGARET MACGILL + DELILAH
MACGILL.

JG#1/8: Mr. JOSEPH SELBY administratrix of BENJAMIN SELBY late of Anne
Arundel Co. deceased. 26 May 1789. Sureties: None indicated. Sixths of
the estate balance to: MARY SELBY (Mrs. LANCELOT GREEN), JOSEPH SELBY,
REBECCA SELBY, ANN SELBY (Mrs. EDWARD STEWART), JEMIMA SELBY + ELIZABETH
SELBY.

JG#1/9: Mrs. RACHEL BROWN administratrix of NICHOLAS BREWER late of Anne
Arundel Co. deceased. 5 October 1784 (sic; indicated twice here). Sure-
ties: DANIEL SMITH + JOHN MERRIKEN. Widow, one third; eighths of the re-
mainder of the balance to: NICHOLAS BREWER, JOHN BREWER, ANN BREWER,
ELIZABETH BREWER, heirs of SARAH JOYCE: SARAH JOYCE + CAROLINE JOYCE,
JOSEPH BREWER, LOT BREWER + ROADY BREWER.

JG#1/9: Mr. THOMAS ELLIOTT surviving executor of SARAH ELLIOTT late of
Anne Arundel Co. deceased. 15 April 1789. Sureties: JOSHUA LACKLAND +
JOSHUA HALL. Sevenths of the estate balance to: THOMAS ELLIOTT, ROBERT
ELLIOTT, WILLIAM ELLIOTT, ANN ELLIOTT, heirs of JAMES ELLIOTT, heirs of
SARAH ELLIOTT,+ heirs of ELIZABETH CADEL.

JG#1/10: Mrs. ELIZABETH WATERS executrix of JACOB WATERS late of Anne Arundel Co. deceased. 15 December 1788. Sureties: VACHEL STEVENS + JOSEPH
STEVENS. Widow ELIZABETH WATERS, one third, having renounced provisions
in the deceased's will; thirds of the remainder of the balance to: CHARLES
WATERS, JACOB WATERS + MARY WATERS.

JG#1/10: Mr. JOHN BASFORD administrator of THOMAS BASFORD late of Anne
Arundel Co. deceased. 6 March 1789. Sureties: LEONARD SELLMAN + WILLIAM
FRENCH. Eighths of the balance to: JOHN BASFORD, THOMAS BASFORD, RICHARD
BASFORD, FREDERICK BASFORD, ZACHARIAH BASFORD, BENJAMIN BASFORD, JEMIMA
BASFORD + RACHEL BASFORD (Mrs. ISAAC NICHOLS).

JG#1/11: Mrs. DEBORAH LUSBY administratrix of ROBERT LUSBY late of Anne
Arundel Co. deceased. 19 June 1789. Sureties: BENJAMIN WELCH + RICHARD
RAWLINGS. Widow DEBORAH LUSBY, one third; sevenths of remainder of the
estate balance to: SUSANNAH LUSBY, EDWARD LUSBY, SAMUEL LUSBY, JAMES LUSBY,
POLLY LUSBY, HENRY LUSBY + WILLIAM LUSBY.

JG#1/11: Mrs. ARTRIDGE ALLEIN executrix of JOSEPH ALLEIN late of Anne Arun-
del Co. deceased. 22 June 1786. Sureties: EZEKIEL GOTT + JACOB FRANKLIN.
Widow ARTRIDGE ALLEIN, one third + one fifth of the bequest to RACHEL AL-
LEIN (deceased); the remainder of RACHEL ALLEIN's share pro-rated and added
to the following fourths: MARY ALLEIN, ANN ALLEIN, JACOB ALLEIN + BENJAMIN
ALLEIN.

JG#1/12: Mr. JOSIAS CROSBY + JOSIAS CROSBY, Jr., executors of JOHN CROSBY
late of Anne Arundel Co. deceased. 5 September 1789. Sureties: JOHN CARR,
Jr. + WILLIAM POWELL. Widow RACHEL CROSBY, one third; remainder of the estate balance to: RICHARD CROSBY.

JG#1/12: Mr. VACHEL CONAWAY + AREA CONAWAY executors of RACHEL CONAWAY late
of Anne Arundel Co. deceased. 8 October 1789. Sureties: STEPHEN HANCOCK +
STEPHEN MCCOY. Legacy to DELILAH MOSS; fourths of the estate remainder to:
VACHEL CONAWAY, AMELIA CONAWAY, AREA CONAWAY + GEORGE CONAWAY.

JG#1/13: Mrs. SARAH TALBOT (now Mrs. WILLIAM MERRIKEN) + Mr. THOMAS TALBOT administrators of BENJAMIN TALBOT late of Anne Arundel Co. deceased. 16 October 1789. Sureties: ROBERT JOHN SMITH + WILLIAM EDWARDS. Widow SARAH TALBOT, one third; one half of the estate residue to THOMAS TALBOT, the other half to ANN TALBOT (Mrs. ELIJAH ROBINSON).

JG#1/13: Mrs. SARAH WATKINS administratrix of NICHOLAS WATKINS late of Anne Arundel Co. deceased. 6 November 1789. Surety: RICHARD WATKINS. Widow SARAH WATKINS, one third; one half of the estate residue to JAMES WATKINS, the other half of the residue to NICHOLAS WATKINS.

JG#1/13: Mr. JACOB CUTTER administrator of ELIZABETH GENNERS late of Anne Arundel Co. deceased. 9 November 1789. Sureties: JOHN NORRIS + WILLIAM HARRIS. The whole balance to MARY GONNERS (sic) d/o deceased.

JG#1/14: Mrs. SUSANNAH BREWER executrix JOHN BREWER late of Anne Arundel Co. deceased. 23 March 1790. Sureties: NICHOLAS BREWER + NATHANIEL BREWER. Widow SUSANNAH BREWER, one third of the balance "agreeably to will of the deceased"; thirds of the remainder of the balance to ANN ODLE BREWER, JOSEPH NATHANIEL BREWER + MARY NEWTON BREWER.

JG#1/14: Mr. THOMAS COOLEY administrator of ELEANOR BARRETT late of Anne Arundel Co. deceased. 25 March 1790. Sureties: JOHN WELCH + HENRY PLUMMER. Memorandum: Balance reflects estate and property of WILLIAM BARRETT, and left agreeably by his will to ELEANOR BARRET during her natural life. Legacies to children of HANBURY JONES: ISAAC JONES, HANBURY JONES, SUSANNAH JONES, RACHEL JONES + ESTHER JONES; children of NICHOLAS NICHOLSON: ESTHER NICHOLSON + ELEANOR NICHOLSON; children of WILLIAM TAYLOR: RICHARD TAYLOR + BENJAMIN TAYLOR; sixths of the remaining estate balance to: MARY NICHOLSON, ESTHER TAYLOR, ANN COOLEY, MARGARET COOLEY, JOHN BARRETT + JOSEPH BARRETT.

JG#1/15: Mrs. SOPHIA GRAY (now Mrs. NATHANIEL HANCOCK) administratrix of ZACHARIAH GRAY late of Anne Arundel Co. deceased. 9 April 1790. Sureties: RICHARD CHENEY + WILLIAM MARSH. Widow SOPHIA GRAY, one third; ninths of the remainder of the balance to: WILLIAM GRAY, ELIZABETH GRAY, ZACHARIAH GRAY, ANN GRAY, REBECCA GRAY, REUBIN GRAY, JULIANNA GRAY, REAH GRAY + JOHN GRAY.

JG#1/15: Mrs. RACHEL HOWARD (now Mrs. JOSEPH BEALL, of Frederick Co.) executrix of JOSEPH HOWARD late of Anne Arundel Co. deceased. 14 April 1790. Sureties: None indicated. Widow RACHEL HOWARD, one third + plus one quarter of the shares of CORNELIUS + WILLIAM HOWARD (both presumably deceased), whose pro-rated shares are added to the thirds of: JOSEPH HOWARD, RACHEL HOWARD + SARAH HOWARD.

JG#1/16: Mr. LEONARD SELLMAN one of the executors of GIDEON GARY late of Anne Arundel Co. deceased. 20 April 1790. Sureties: ELIJAH GREEN + THOMAS HENRY HALL. Unnamed widow, one third; fifths of the remainder of the estate balance to: MARY GARY, LLOYD GARY, LEONARD GARY, DEBORAH GARY + EVERARD GARY.

JG#1/16: Mr. JAMES MAYO executor of JOHN MAYO late of Anne Arundel Co. deceased. 21 April 1790. Sureties: EDWARD LEE + SAMUEL LUSBY. JAMES MAYO, livestock; HENRIETTA MAYO, residue of the balance, representing 10 times the value of the above livestock.

-4-

JG#1/16: Mr. WILLIAM MACCUBBIN (of JOHN) administrator with will annexed of JAMES MEEK late of Anne Arundel Co. deceased. 3 July 1790. Sureties: VACHEL CONAWAY + ZACHARIAH ASHLEY. Thirds of the estate balance to MARY MEEK, JAMES MEEK + WASTAL MEEK; personalty to SAMUEL GREEN.

JG#1/17: Mrs. SARAH GRAY executrix of JOHN GRAY late of Anne Arundel Co. deceased. 21 July 1790. Sureties: JOHN MERRIKEN, Jr. + JOSHUA MERRIKEN. Widow SARAH GRAY, one third; fifths of the remainder of the estate balance to: ANN GRAY, ELIZABETH GRAY, SARAH GRAY, JOHN GRAY + ZACHARIAH GRAY.

JG#1/17: Mr. RICHARD WEEDON administrator of JOHN WEEDON late of Anne Arundel Co. deceased. 19 November 1789. Sureties: WILLIAM SEEDERS + DAN-IEL WEEDON. The whole of the balance to ANN WEEDON + SAMUEL WEEDON, "children of the deceased."

JG#1/18: Mr. JAMES MOSS executor of CORNELIUS CHARD, late of Anne Arundel Co. deceased. 11 August 1790. Sureties: JOSHUA MERRIKEN + EDWARD TIMMONS. Unnamed widow, one third; one third + personalty to OLIVER CHARD; one third to REBECCA CHARD.

JG#1/18: Mrs. MARY LEWIS (Mrs. PEREGRINE RIDGELY) administratrix with will annexed of WILLIAM LEWIS late of Anne Arundel Co. deceased. 29 September 1790. Sureties: RICHARD WEEDON + ZACHARIAH GRAY. Widow MARY LEWIS, one third; thirds of the remainder of the estate balance to: ELIZABETH LEWIS, NICHOLAS LEWIS + REBECCA LEWIS.

JG#1/18: Mrs. ANN FAIRBROTHER administratrix of FRANCIS FAIRBROTHER late of Anne Arundel Co. deceased. 7 October 1790. Sureties: ARCHIBALD CHIS-HOLM + VACHEL YATES. Widow ANN FAIRBROTHER, one third; remainder of the estate balance to ELFRIDA FAIRBROTHER (Mrs. JOHN KER).

JG#1/19: Mrs. SARAH LEWIS administratrix of THOMAS LEWIS late of Anne Arundel Co. deceased. 25 September 1790. Sureties: JOHN MERRIKEN + JOSEPH FOREMAN. Widow SARAH LEWIS, one third; fifths of the remainder of the estate balance to: ELIZABETH LEWIS (Mrs. THOMAS SAPPINGTON), SARAH LEWIS, THOMAS WILLIAM HENRY LEWIS, ANN LEWIS + HELLEN LEWIS. N.B. Note due to the estate from JAMES PEARCE.

JG#1/19: Mr. MARTIN FISHER administrator of SARAH CHALK late of Anne Arundel Co. deceased. 14 October 1792. Surety: THOMAS HINTON. Thirds of the estate balance to REBECCA CHALK (Mrs. MARTIN FISHER), MINAH CHALK + ALEX-ANDER CHALK.

JG#1/20: Mr. PHILEMON DORSEY executor of PHILEMON DORSEY late of Anne Arundel Co. deceased. 25 October 1792. Sureties: JOHN DORSEY + CALEB DORSEY. Widow RACHEL DORSEY, one third; ninths of the remainder of the estate balance to: PHILEMON DORSEY, ANN DORSEY, CATHERINE DORSEY, ELIZABETH DORSEY, SARAH DORSEY, AMELIA DORSEY, JOSHUA DORSEY, HENRIETTA DORSEY, + ARIANA DORSEY.

JG#1/20: Mr. THOMAS BEARD, ELIZABETH BEARD + LURANAH BEARD executors of RICHARD BEARD late of Anne Arundel Co. deceased. 11 December 1790. Sureties: JONATHAN BEARD + WILLIAM HARWOOD. Widow MARY BEARD, one third; one shilling each to: RICHARD BEARD, STEPHEN BEARD, THOMAS BEARD, JONATHAN BEARD, REBECCA WATTS + RUTH WATKINS; one half of the balance to ELIZABETH BEARD; the other half to LURANAH BEARD.

JG#1/21: Mr. WILLIAM SANDERS administrator of JOHN HOUGHTON late of Anne Arundel Co. deceased. 24 December 1790. Surety: FREDERICK GREEN. Whole of the estate balance to SARAH HOUGHTON d/o the deceased.

JG#1/21: Mrs. MARGARET CONAWAY administrator of JOHN CONAWAY late of Anne Arundel Co. deceased. 1 February 1791. Sureties: CADWALEDER EDWARDS + THOMAS TALBOTT. Whole of the estate balance to widow MARGARET CONAWAY during her natural life; then to be sold + equally divided among the deceased's unnamed children.

JG#1/22: Mrs. SARAH TODD administratrix of NATHAN TODD late of Anne Arundel Co. deceased. 26 March 1791. Sureties: THOMAS ROCKHOLD + WILLIAM HENWOOD. Widow SARAH TODD, one third; remainder of the estate balance to daughter ELIZABETH TODD.

JG#1/22: Mr. WILLIAM SIMMONS administrator of LEWIS LEWIN late of Anne Arundel Co. deceased. 9 April 1791. Sureties: None indicated. Elevenths of the estate balance to: ELIZABETH LEWIN, m/o of the deceased; MARY LEWIN (Mrs. WILLIAM ____); RICHARD LEWIN; heirs of ANN LEWIN (Mrs. JOHN CARTER); heirs of ELIZABETH LEWIN (Mrs. ABRAHAM FISHER); HENRIETTA LEWIN (Mrs. JOHN STEELE); MARGARET LEWIN (Mrs. JOHN DEALE); KITTY LEWIN (Mrs. JACOB BRICE); heirs of FANNY LEWIN (Mrs. PETER CLARKE); SARAH LEWIN (Mrs. SAMUEL SADLER); + SAMUEL LEWIN (of SAMUEL).

JG#1/22: Mr. JOHN HAYWARD executor of HENRY PIERPOINT late of Anne Arundel Co. deceased. 12 April 1791. Sureties: WILLIAM HAYWARD + WILLIAM DILLWORTH. The whole of the estate balance to FAITHFUL PIERPOINT.

JG#1/23: Mr. ROBERT LUSBY executor of BALDWIN LUSBY late of Anne Arundel Co. deceased. 9 April 1791. Sureties: CALEB BURGESS + THOMAS MACCAULEY. Widow ELIZABETH LUSBY, one third; five shillings to ELEANOR RAWLINGS + NANCY MACCAULEY; fifths of the remainder of the estate balance to: ROBERT LUSBY, JOHN LUSBY, DEBRA LUSBY, SUSANNAH LUSBY + PEGGY LUSBY.

JG#1/24: Mr. LANCELOT DORSEY administrator de bonis non of MICHAEL DORSEY late of Anne Arundel Co. deceased. No date indicated. Sureties: EPHRAIM HOWARD + NICHOLAS WATKINS. Mostly equal shares to: HELLEN + PROVIDENCE ELDER granddaughters of the deceased, heirs of JOHN DORSEY, ELIZABETH BURGESS, SARAH BERRY, RUTH DORSEY, heirs of LYDIA TALBOTT + NANCY DORSEY.

JG#1/24: Mrs. ANN MACCAULEY executrix of FRANCIS MACCAULEY late of Anne Arundel Co. deceased. 6 May 1791. Sureties: JOSEPH SELBY + SAMUEL ELLIOTT. Widow ANN MACCAULEY whole of the balance during her natural life + after her death to be divided between JEHOSOPHAT MACCAULEY + DELIA MACCAULEY.

JG#1/25: Mr. THOMAS NORMAN administrator de bonis non of WILLIAM NORMAN late of Anne Arundel Co. deceased. 3 June 1791. Sureties: BENJAMIN CARR + WILLIAM DEALE. Unnamed widow, one third; fifths of the remainder of the estate balance to: ELIZABETH NORMAN (w/o JOHN WOODFIELD), RICHARD NORMAN, JANE NORMAN (w/o ABRAHAM FURGUSON), JOSEPH NORMAN + JOHN NORMAN.

JG#1/25: Mr. WILLIAM COE administrator of JOHN BEVERIDGE late of Anne Arundel Co. deceased. 16 June 1791. Sureties: RICHARD OWENS + JOHN SHAW. ANN BEVERIDGE, the widow's third; half of the remainder of the estate balance to JOHN BEVERIDGE; the other half to FRANCES BEVERIDGE.

JG#1/26: Mr. SAMUEL YEALDHALL executor of ANN POMPHREY [PUMPHREY] late of Anne Arundel Co. deceased. 30 June 1791. Sureties: THOMAS CROMWELL + SOLOMON JOHNSON. Personalty to ELIZABETH RIDGELY; one shilling to WILLIAM POMPHREY; sixths of the remainder of the estate balance to REZIN POMPHREY, JOSEPH POMPHREY, ZACHARIAH POMPHREY, EDWARD POMPHREY, FRANCES YEALDHALL + granddauthers AMINTY POMPHREY + ELIZABETH RIDGELY.

JG#1/26: Mr. LANCELOT DORSEY executor of JOHN DORSEY late of Anne Arundel Co. deceased. 13 April 1791. Sureties: EPHRAIM HOWARD + NICHOLAS WATKINS. Widow ANN DORSEY, on third + proportion of ELIZABETH DORSEY [who presumably is deceased]; equal shares to RUTH DORSEY, CHARLES WARFIELD (h/o CATHERINE DORSEY), BAZIL BURGESS (h/o ELEANOR DORSEY), PHILEMON DORSEY + VACHEL DORSEY; major heir: MICHAEL DORSEY "in full for his part of the deceased's estate."

JG#1/27: Mr. EDWARD TIMMONS administrator of JOHN GIVENS late of Anne Arundel Co. deceased. 9 April 1791. Sureties: ABSOLOM RIDGELY + CORNELIUS CHARD. The whole of the balance to WILLIAM GIVENS of South Carolina brother of the deceased.

JG#1/27: Mr. JOHN STEVENS administrator of ELIZABETH DAVIS late of Anne Arundel Co. deceased. 24 December 1791. Sureties: WILLIAM HENWOOD + JOHN BURTON. Thirds of the remainder of the estate balance to HENRY DAVIS, SARAH DAVIS + NANCY DAVIS.

JG#1/27: Mr. WILLIAM JOICE administrator de bonis non of FRANCIS RIDGELY late of Anne Arundel Co. deceased. 3 February 1792. Sureties: WILLIAM WOODWARD Jr. + STEPHEN BEARD. Fourths of the estate balance to ELIZABETH RIDGELY m/o the deceased; SARAH RIDGELY (legal representative of JOSHUA RIDGELY); WILLIAM RIDGELY; + SARAH + ELIZABETH YEALDHALL (legal representatives of GILBERT YEALDHALL).

JG#1/28: Mr. JOHN WILLIAMS administrator of AMINTA POMPHREY [PUMPHREY] late of Anne Arundel Co. deceased. 9 March 1792. Sureties: ABRAHAM WILLIAMS + BRYAN WILLIAMS. Fourths of the estate balance to: FREDERICK POMPHREY, NACKY POMPHREY, MARY POMPHREY + ELIZABETH POMPHREY.

JG#1/28: Mr. JOHN WILLIAMS executor of JOHN WILLIAMS late of Anne Arundel Co. deceased. 9 March 1792. Sureties: JOSEPH POMPHREY + MARMADUKE WILLIAMS. One shilling: BRYAN WILLIAMS; negroes to MARMADUKE WILLIAMS, ABRAHAM WILLIAMS + MINTY WILLIAMS; personalty to: SARAH WILLIAMS; + remainder of the estate balance to: JOHN WILLIAMS, the major heir.

JG#1/28: Mr. JAMES PATTISON executor of THOMAS PATTISON late of Anne Arundel Co. deceased. 20 March 1792. Sureties: ABRAHAM CLAUDE + ALEXANDER FRAZIER. Halves of the estate balance to: JEREMIAH PATTISON + JACOB PATTISON.

JG#1/29: Mr. WILLIAM FISH executor of BENJAMIN FISH late of Anne Arundel Co. deceased. 9 November 1791. Sureties: ZACHARIAH JACOB + JOSHUA MERRIKEN. Unnamed widow, one third of balance; RICHARD FISH, one third; + WILLIAM FISH, one third.

JG#1/29: Mr. THOMAS BATSON administrator of JOHN BATSON (d. testate) late of Anne Arundel Co. deceased. 17 April 1792. Sureties: THOMAS WHITTINGTON + SAMUEL PEACO. Widow ELIZABETH BATSON remainder of balance after the

deduction of legacies to: THOMAS BATSON, granddaughter MARY JONES, SARAH
DOWEL, daughter SUSANNA CANADY, daughter MARGARET MEGUINES, + granddaughters ELIZABETH FISHER, FANNY FISHER + ELEANOR FISHER. Final item: a legacy
to the unspecified children of MARY STALLINGS.

JG#1/30: Mrs. HELLENDER SMALL executrix of THOMAS SMALL late of Anne Arun-
del Co. deceased. 3 May 1792. Sureties: JOSHUA MERRIKEN + THOMAS STINCH-
COMB. Thirds of the estate balance to: widow HELLENDER SMALL, THOMAS SMALL
+ SARAH SMALL.

JG#1/30: Mrs. MARY SEEDERS administratrix of WILLIAM SEEDERS late of Anne
Arundel Co. deceased. 3 May 1792. Sureties: RICHARD WEEDON + BENNETT
SEEDERS. Widow MARY SEEDERS, one third; fourths of the remaining balance
to: BENNETT SEEDERS, MARTHA SEEDERS, RUTH SEEDERS + WILLIAM SEEDERS.

JG#1/31: Mrs. ELEANOR RAWLINGS (now Mrs. ZACHARIAH TUCKER) administratrix
of STEPHEN RAWLINGS. 12 May 1792. Sureties: RICHARD RAWLINGS + THOMAS
MACCAULEY. Widow ELEANOR RAWLINGS, one third; thirds of the remaining estate balance to THOMAS RAWLINGS, LURANA RAWLINGS + ELEANOR RAWLINGS.

JG#1/31: Mrs. MARY PENN administratrix of JOSEPH PENN late of Anne Arun-
del Co. deceased. 29 May 1792. Sureties: JOSEPH PENN + THOMAS IJAMS.
Widow MARY PENN, one third; sixths of the remaining estate balance to:
RACHEL PENN, MARY PENN, JOSHUA PENN, SARAH PENN, JOSEPH PENN + PEGGY PENN.

JG#1/32: Mr. JOHN MARRIOTT executor of SAMUEL MEEK late of Anne Arundel Co.
deceased. 1 June 1792. Sureties: WILLIAM YEALDHALL + LUKE WARFIELD.
Fourths of the estate balance to the following negroes: TOBY, CHARLES,
SOLOMON + THOMAS (L9..7..10 each).

JG#1/32: Mrs. SARAH MACCUBBIN (now Mrs. JAMES CLEARY) executrix of NICHO-
LAS MACCUBBIN. 22 August 1792. Sureties: VACHEL STEVENS + ABRAHAM CLAUDE.
Widow SARAH MACCUBBIN, one third; the remainder of the balance NICHOLAS
ZACHARIAH MACCUBBIN.

JG#1/32: Mr. DANIEL SOWARD, Jr. administrator of JOHN CROUCH late of Anne
Arundel Co. deceased. 23 August 1792. Sureties: JOHN SMITH + SOLOMON SO-
WARD. Halves to JOHN CROUCH + ANN CROUCH.

JG#1/33: ZACHARIAH CHILDS administrator of ELIZABETH CHILDS late of Anne
Arundel Co. deceased. 4 September 1792. Sureties: WILLIAM FISHER + LEWIS
FISHER. Eighths of the estate balance to: ANN CHILDS (w/o ISAAC SIMMONS),
SARAH CHILDS, ZACHARIAH CHILDS, the children of ELIZABETH CHILDS (w/o
WILLIAM FISHER), SEPHAS CHILDS, MARY CHILDS (w/o LEWIS FISHER), NELLY
CHILDS + BARBARY CHILDS.

JG#1/33 + 34: NICHOLAS NORMAN + THOMAS NORMAN executors of BENJAMIN NORRIS
late of Anne Arundel Co. deceased. 13 June 1791. Sureties: JOHN NORRIS +
SAMUEL HARRIS. Sevenths of the estate balance to: EDWARD HALE, WALTER NOR-
MAN, HORATION NORMAN, ELIJAH NORMAN, NICHOLAS NORMAN, ELEANOR NORMAN + ELIZA-
BETH NORMAN.

JG#1/34: Mrs. MONICA MOSS (w/o JAMES MOSS) administratrix of SAMUEL SKID-
MORE MOSS. 8 September 1792. Sureties: JAMES MOSS + CHARLES GREENWELL.
Widow, one third; fourths of the remainder of the estate balance to: SAMUEL
SKIDMORE MOSS, ELIZABETH MOSS, JOHN THOMAS MOSS + THOMAS MOSS.

JG#1/34: Mr. SAMUEL JACOB administrator de bonis non of THOMAS TOFT late
of Anne Arundel Co. deceased. 2 September 1792. Sureties: WILLIAM PEARCE
+ FRANCIS GUINN. Unnamed widow, one third; thirds of the remainder of the
estate balance to: JOHN TOFT, MARY TOFT + ELEANOR TOFT (w/o CALEB FENNELL).

JG#1/35: Mrs. SARAH CORD administratrix of JAMES CORD late of Anne Arundel
Co. deceased. 10 October 1792. Sureties: JOHN BROWN (of JOSHUA) + AQUILLA
RANDALL. Widow SARAH CORD, one third; tenths of the remainder of the estate
balance to REBECCA CORD, SARAH CORD, JOHN CORD, HENRY CORD, HELLEN CORD,
ANN CORD, CATHERINE CORD, SOPHIA CORD, GEORGE CORD + JESSE CORD.

JG#1/36: Messrs. ROBERT PHELPS + GEORGE PHELPS executors of DEBORAH PHELPS,
late of Anne Arundel Co. deceased. 20 October 1792. Sureties: BAZIL
PHELPS + ZACHARIAH PHELPS. Livestock to MARY PHELPS (w/o HENRY PURDY),
legacy to the children of DEBORAH PHELPS, and halves of the estate remainder
to ROBERT PHELPS + GEORGE PHELPS.

JG#1/36 + 37: ABRAHAM SHEKELL + FRANCIS SHEKELL + BENJAMIN BASFORD execu-
tors of JOHN SHEKELL late of Anne Arundel Co. deceased. 9 December 1792.
Sureties: WILLIAM SIMMONS + BENJAMIN CHENEY. Eighths to FRANCIS SHEKELL,
ELIZABETH SHEKELL (w/o BENJAMIN BASFORD), ABRAHAM SHEKELL, REBECCA MAGRUDER,
MARY SHEKELL, SUSANNAH RAY, DEBORAH DOWLEY + RICHARD SHEKELL.

JG#1/37 + 38: Mrs. SARAH DOVE administratrix of WILLIAM DOVE late of Anne
Arundel Co. deceased. 19 December 1792. Sureties: ISAAC SIMMONS + HENRY
PLUMMER. Widow SARAH DOVE, one third; sevenths of the estate remainder to
ELIZABETH DOVE, JOSEPH DOVE, THOMAS DOVE, SARAH DOVE, JAMES STEWARD (h/o
ALICE DOVE) + JOHN HOOPER (h/o MARY DOVE).

JG#1/38: Mr. JOHN GRAY executor of SARAH GRAY late of Anne Arundel Co. deceased. 2 January 1793. Sureties: JOSHUA CROMWELL + ZACHARIAH ASHLEY.
Widow SARAH GRAY a negro woman and her increase; a negro lad plus remaining
balance of the estate to JOHN GRAY.

JG#1/38: Mr. JAMES COLLINS administrator de bonis non OF THOMAS ATKINSON
late of Anne Arundel Co. deceased. 29 January 1796. Sureties: DANIEL
HOLLWAY + RICHARD COLLINS. Sixths of the estate balance to: NATHAN ATKIN-
SON, RACHEL ATKINSON, CATHARINE ATKINSON, ELIZABETH ATKINSON, THOMAS AT-
KINSON + FRANCIS ATKINSON.

JG#1/39: Mr. WILLIAM ELLIOTT administrator of ROBERT ELLIOTT late of Anne
Arundel Co. deceased. 11 Mary 1793. Sureties: JAMES CADLE + WILLIAM HAYS.
Halves of the balance of the estate to JOHN ELLIOTT + SAMUEL ELLIOTT.

JG#1/39: Mr. BRICE JOHN GASSAWAY executor of CATHERINE GASSAWAY late of
Anne Arundel Co. deceased. 2 March 1790. Sureties: ZACHARIAH ALDRIDGE
+ CHARLES GASSAWAY. Beneficiaries: BRICE JOHN GASSAWAY, THOMAS GASSAWAY,
CHARLES GASSAWAY, ANN ROGERS, SARAH WARFIELD, NICHOLAS ROGERS + SAMUEL
ROGERS.

JG#1/40: Mr. ABEL CHENEY administrator of RICHARD CHENEY late of Anne Arundel
Co. deceased. Sureties: CHARLES JOHNSON + THOMAS CHENEY. Tenths to: THOMAS
ROWLES, HEZEKIAH CHENEY, NATHANIEL HANCOCK (h/o SOPHIA CHENEY), MICHAEL DUNN
(h/o ELIZABETH CHENEY), ABEL CHENEY, JAMES HOLMES (h/o DELILAH CHENEY),
THOMAS CHENEY, GREENBURY GRAY (h/o SUSANNA CHENEY).+ DENNIS ROBINSON (h/o
ANN CHENEY). N.B. Only nine of the "tenths" enumerated.

JG#1/40: Mr..ROBERT JOHN SMITH administrator of JOHN CARVILL late of Anne Arundel Co. deceased. 23 March 1793. Sureties: RICHARD WELLS + EDMUND WAYMAN. Halves of the estate balance to ELIZABETH CARVILL + MARY CARVILL.

JG#1/41: Mr. JOSEPH BREWER executor of RACHEL BREWER late of Anne Arundel Co. deceased. 4 April 1793. Sureties: DANIEL SMITH + JAMES HAWKINS. Thirds to: RHODA BREWER, LOT BREWER + JOSEPH BREWER.

JG#1/41: ELEANOR HEWITT + THOMAS WILLIAM HEWITT executors of JANE HEWITT late of Anne Arundel Co. deceased. 8 April 1793. Sureties: SAMUEL HUTTON + JOHN CHAMBERS. The two executors share the entire estate equally.

JG#1/42: Mrs. ELIZABETH ROBOSON administratrix of VACHEL ROBOSON late of Anne Arundel Co. deceased. 6 June 1793. Sureties: CHARLES JOHNSON + THOMAS ROBOSON. Widow ELIZABETH ROBOSON, one third; fourths of the remainder of the balance to: JOHN ROBOSON, SARAH ROBOSON, VACHEL ROBOSON + DORSEY ROBOSON.

JG#1/42: Mrs. ALLISON TROTT administratrix of THOMAS TROTT late of Anne Arundel Co. deceased. 11 June 1793. Sureties: BENJAMIN CHILD + THOMAS PARROTT. Widow ALLISON TROTT, one third; eighths of the remainder of the balance to: ELIZABETH TROTT, JAMES TROTT, SARAH TROTT, NANCY TROTT, ESTER TROTT, THOMAS TROTT, ALLISON TROTT + REBECCA TROTT.

JG#1/43: Mr. BAZIL PHELPS administrator of GEORGE STALKER late of Anne Arundel Co. deceased. 13 July 1793. Sureties: MATHEW BEARD + RICHARD PHELPS. Thirds of the balance to: ELEANOR STALKER, ROBERT STALKER + JOHN STALKER.

JG#1/43: Mr. CHARLES RIDGELY administrator of THOMAS PIPER late of Anne Arundel Co. deceased. 2 August 1793. Sureties: ABSALOM RIDGELY + JAMES CHALMERS. Thirds of the balance of the estate to ANN PIPER, ELIZABETH PIPER + MARY PIPER.

JG#1/43: Mr. EPHRAIM DUVALL administrator of HUSLEY BURGESS late of Anne Arundel Co. deceased. 6 August 1793. Sureties: ZACHARIAH DUVALL + ENOS DUVALL. The whole of the balance agreeably to the deceased's will to: SARAH DUVALL.

JG#1/44: Mrs. SARAH TODD administratrix de bonis non of CLARK ROCKHOLD late of Anne Arundel Co. deceased. 11 September 1793. Sureties: JOHN REED + CHARLES ROBINSON. Negroes to THOMAS CLARKE ROCKHOLD + RACHEL ROCKHOLD; ₺ 15 to THOMAS FIELDS ROCKHOLD; fifths of the remainder of the estate balance to: CHARLES ROCKHOLD, JOHN ROCKHOLD, SARAH ROCKHOLD, SOLORAH ROCKHOLD + MARY ROCKHOLD.

JG#1/45: Mr. PEREGRINE RIDGELY administrator of WILLIAM GRAY late of Anne Arundel Co. deceased. 14 September 1793. Sureties: ABSALOM RIDGELY + GEORGE CONAWAY. Deceased's sister ANN GRAY, sorrel horse + ₺ 10; residue of the estate to the deceased's brother, ZACHARIAH GRAY.

JG#1/45: Mr. JOHN ROBINSON administrator of THOMAS TUCKER late of Anne Arundel Co. deceased. 21 September 1793. Sureties: CHARLES JOHNSON + HAMPTON ROBINSON. Widow JANE TURNER (now ROBINSON), one third; remainder of the balance to: SARAH TURNER.

JG#1/45: Mr. WILLIAM EDWARDS administrator of EDWARD EDWARDS late of Anne Arundel Co. deceased. 23 September 1793. Sureties: THOMAS BICKNELL + JONA-

THAN EDWARDS. Tenths of the balance of the estate to: Children of JEMIMA
EVANS, Children of CATHERINE LUSBY, WILLIAM ANDERSON (h/o ELIZABETH EDWARDS),
SARAH EDWARDS, CEPHAS WATERS (h/o MARY EDWARDS), JOHN LINTHICUM (h/o MARY
EDWARDS, sic), JOHN FONERDON (h/o MARGARET EDWARDS), WILLIAM EDWARDS, CAD-
WALLADER EDWARDS + JONATHAN EDWARDS.

JG#1/46: Mr. BENJAMIN PHILIPS executor of JOHN PHILIPS late of Anne Arundel
Co. deceased. 3 October 1793. Sureties: EDWARD MARSHALL + ZACHARIAH ASHLEY.
Fifths of the balance of the estate to: RUTH PHILIPS, w/o ZACHARIAH ANGLING;
JOHN PHILIPS; SARAH PHILIPS: MARY PHILIPS + DELILAH PHILIPS.

JG#1/47: Mr. JOHN CHAMBERS administrator de bonis non of EDWARD OWENS late
of Anne Arundel Co. deceased. 11 October 1793. Sureties: WILLIAM GOLD-
SMITH + GILBERT MIDDLETON. Halves of the balance to: JAMES OWENS + ELIZA-
BETH OWENS.

JG#1/47: Mr. ANDREW MERCER executor of JOHN HAWKINS late of Anne Arundel
Co. deceased. 28 October 1793. Sureties: JOHN SHIPLEY + ROBERT HUDSON.
Ninths of the balance to: PRISCILLA HUDSON, grandson JOHN MERCER, THOMAS
HAWKINS, WILLIAM HAWKINS, REZIN HAWKINS, NICHOLAS HAWKINS, CHARLES HAWKINS,
CALEB HAWKINS, RUTH HAWKINS + REBECCA HAWKINS.

JG#1/48: Mrs. MARY WATSON administratrix of WILLIAM WATSON late of Anne Arundel Co. deceased. 13 November 1793. Sureties: JOHN LONG + RICHARD DORSEY.
Widow MARY WATSON, "half of the balance per marriage articles entered into between the said deceased and Mary Watson"; thirds of the remainder of the balance to CHARLES WATSON, WILLIAM WATSON + MARY WATSON.

JG#1/49: Mr. JOHN ROBINSON administrator of CHARLES ROCKHOLD late of Anne
Arundel Co. deceased. 16 November 1793. Sureties: CHARLES JOHNSON + HAMP-
TON ROBINSON. Widow JANE ROCKHOLD (now w/o JOHN ROBINSON), one third;
thirds of the remainder of the balance to: THOMAS ROCKHOLD, CHARLES ROCK-
HOLD + ELIZABETH ROCKHOLD.

JG#1/49: Mr. EDWARD LUSBY administrator of WILLIAM ALLEN late of Anne Arundel Co. deceased. 13 September 1793. Sureties: CALEB WARFIELD + THOMAS
WARFIELD. Unnamed widow, one third; remainder of balance to LINDY ALLEN.

JG#1/49 + 50: MARY GAMBRILL + WILLIAM GAMBRILL executors of WILLIAM GAM-
BRILL late of Anne Arundel Co. deceased. 10 December 1793. Sureties: DOR-
SEY JACOB + ZACHARIAH JACOB. Widow MARY GAMBRILL, one third; sixths of the
remainder of the balance to: MARGARET JOHNSON, MARY GAMBRILL, WILLIAM GAM-
BRILL, JOHN GAMBRILL, AUGUSTUS GAMBRILL + THOMAS GAMBRILL.

JG#1/50 + 51: Mrs. MARTHA MARRIOTT executrix of EMANUEL MARRIOTT late of
Anne Arundel Co. deceased. 30 December 1793. Sureties: THOMAS WARFIELD
+ STEVENS GAMBRILL. Widow MARTHA MARRIOTT, legacies and one third; sixths
of the remainder of the balance to: AUGUSTINE GA (?) MARRIOTT, JOSEPH MAR-
RIOTT, CALEB MARRIOTT, MARY MARRIOTT, ELIZABETH MARRIOTT + RACHEL MARRIOTT
(w/o SAMUEL MILLER).

JG#1/51: Mr. CORNELIUS SHRIVER administrator of JACOB SHRIVER late of Anne
Arundel Co. deceased. 19 March 1795. Sureties: NATHANIEL HALL + JOHN
CROMWELL. Ninths of the balance to: FREDERICK SHRIVER, LAWRENCE SHRIVER,
LEWIS SHRIVER, SAMUEL SANDERS (h/o CHRISTINA SHRIVER), JESSE MILLER (h/o
ELIZABETH SHRIVER), HENRY SHRIVER, WILLIAM SIBEL, WILLIAM CROMWELL + COR-
NELIUS SHRIVER.

JG#1/52: Mr. JOSEPH MACCUBBIN administrator of MARY BRAY late of Anne Arundel Co. deceased. 20 March 1794. Sureties: THOMAS CALLAHAN + JAMES MACCUBBIN. Thirds of the estate balance to: ELLIN BRAY, JOSEPH BRAY + JOHN BRAY.

JG#1/52: Mrs. LYDIA GILLHAM administratrix of ROBERT JACKSON late of Anne Arundel Co. deceased. 14 April 1794. Sureties: JOHN NORRISS + JESSE CRUCHLEY. LYDIA GILHAM, widow's third; fourths of the remainder of the estate balance to: SARAH JACKSON (Mrs. JAMES or JOSEPH MACE), SUSANNA JACKSON (Mrs. JOHN PHIPS), ELIZABETH JACKSON + MATILDA JACKSON.

JG#1/53: Mr. JOHN STEVENS administrator of TOPPIN SMITH late of Anne Arundel Co. deceased. 26 April 1794. Sureties: WILLIAM HENWOOD + THOMAS GOODWIN. One half of the estate balance to MILCAH SMITH; one half to the seven unnamed children of NANCY HENWOOD.

JG#1/53: Mr. ZACHARIAH JACOB administrator de bonis non of DENNIS STEVENS late of Anne Arundel Co. deceased. 19 May 1794. Sureties: STEVENS GAMBRILL + THOMAS BICKNELL. The whole of the balance to KITTY STEVENS d/o the deceased.

JG#1/53: Mrs. ELIZABETH BOONE + JOHN MERRIKEN Jr. administrators of BURLE BOONE late of Anne Arundel Co. deceased. 20 May 1794. Sureties: JOHN MERRIKEN Sr. + EPHRAIM DUVALL. ELIZABETH BOONE, widow's third; halves of the reremainder of the estate balance to deceased's daughters ELIZABETH BOONE + CHARLOTTE BURLE BOONE.

JG#1/54: Mr. JOHN S. (? initial unclear) RAY administrator of STEPHEN BEARD late of Anne Arundel Co. deceased. 9 July 1794. Sureties: JOSEPH BEARD + THOMAS KNOTT Jr. One half of the estate balance to JOSEPH BEARD, deceased's bro; one half to CATHERINE BEARD (now RAY), deceased's sister.

JG#1/54: Mr. PEREGRINE RIDGELY + Mr. JOHN ASHPAW administrators of ZACHARIAH GRAY late of Anne Arundel Co. deceased. 20 August 1794. Sureties: HENRY ASHPAW + FRANCIS CROMWELL. Fourths of the estate balance to MARY RIDGELY, ANN ASHPAW, REBECCA GRAY + LINCH GRAY.

JG#1/55: Mrs. PATIENCE HALL administratrix of JESSE HALL late of Anne Arundel Co. deceased. 18 September 1794. Sureties: ELISHA HALL + CHARLES BOONE. PATIENCE HALL, widow's third; fifths of the remainder of the estate balance to: JOHN HALL, DANIEL HALL, RICHARD JACOB HALL, ELIZABETH HALL + SARAH HALL.

JG#1/55: Messrs BENJAMIN + GEORGE WHIPS executors of SARAH LUCRESE WHIPS late of Anne Arundel Co. deceased. 14 October 1794. Sureties: SAMUEL WHIPS + WALTER PEARCE. Executors are the major heirs; other legatees: JOHN WHIPS (of GEORGE), JOHN WHIPS POOLE (of PETER) + SARAH LUCRESE WHIPS.

JG#1/56: Messrs LEVI + JESSE BRASHEARS administrators of WAYMACK BRASHEARS late of Anne Arundel Co. deceased. 13 November 1794. Sureties: LEONARD GRAY + JOSIAS CROSBY. Sixths of the estate balance to: MARGERY BRASHEARS, JUDSON BRASHEARS, JESSE BRASHEARS, LEVI BRASHEARS, LILBURN BRASHEARS + NANCY BRASHEARS.

JG#1/56 + 57: Messrs EBENEZER + WILLIAM PUMPHREY executors of EBENEZER PUMPHREY late of Anne Arundel Co. deceased. 4 March 1795. Sureties: CHARLES STEWART + EBENEZER STEWART.

JG#1/57: Mr. DORSEY JACOB + Mrs. PATIENCE DORSEY executors of RICHARD DORSEY late of Anne Arundel Co. deceased. 20 May 1795. Sureties: JOSEPH MAYO + SAMUEL JACOB. PATIENCE JACOB, widow's third; halves of the remainder of the balance to: JOSEPH JACOB + DORSEY JACOB.

JG#1/58: Mr. JUNINGHAM DRURY administrator of ZABEDEE WOOD late of Anne Arundel Co. deceased. 22 August 1795. Sureties: SAMUEL WARD + ISAAC SIMMONS. Widow ANN WOOD, one third; all of the remainder of the balance to the deceased's daughter ANN WOOD.

JG#1/58: Mrs. CHARITY COLLINS (sic) administratrix of EDWARD COLLINSON late of Anne Arundel Co. deceased. 22 December 1795. Sureties: NATHANIEL CHEW + ARNOLD WATERS. CHARITY COLLINSON, widow's third; sevenths of the remainder of the estate balance to: ALSE COLLINSON, JOHN COLLINSON, EDWARD COLLINSON, WILLIAM COLLINSON, SARAH COLLINSON, BENJAMIN COLLINSON + MARY COLLINSON.

JG#1/59: Mrs. ELIZABETH HOOD + Mr. JOHN HOOD executors of JOHN HOOD late of Anne Arundel Co. deceased. 9 April 1795. Sureties: THOMAS CORNELIUS HOWARD + BRICE HOWARD. ELIZABETH HOOD, widow's third; fifths of the remainder of the balance to grandsons: JAMES HOOD, JOHN HOOD, BENJAMIN HOOD, THOMAS HOOD + JOSHUA HOOD.

JG#1/59 + 60: Messrs RICHARD + JOHN BROWN executors of JOHN BROWN late of Anne Arundel Co. deceased. 14 October 1795. Sureties: ADAM CRANDALL + WILLIAM DRURY. Legatees: JOHN BROWN, REBECCA LANE, RICHARD BROWN (of RICHARD), ANN + RACHEL BROWN (of RICHARD), ALLEY BROWN (of RICHARD), JOHN BROWN (of son JOHN), JENNETT BROWN (of JOHN), HARRIET BROWN (of JOHN) + JOHN LANE.

JG#1/60: Mr. BENJAMIN PHILLIPS administrator of EDWARD MARSHALL late of Anne Arundel Co. deceased. 16 October 1795. Sureties: None indicated. SARAH MARSHALL the deceased's daughter the whole of the estate balance.

JG#1/61 + 62: Mr. JOSEPH STANSBURY administrator of ELIZABETH STANSBURY late of Anne Arundel Co. deceased. 7 December 1795. Sureties: CHARLES BOONE + JOSHUA MERRIKEN. Fifths of the estate balance: PATIENCE HALL, JOSEPH STANSBURY, the children of EZEKIEL STANSBURY, the children of EMANUEL STANSBURY + CHARLES BOONE (who m. ELIZABETH STANSBURY); legacies to: DANIEL STANSBURY, JOSEPH JACOB, WILLIAM STANSBURY, SARAH HALL + GEORGE PRESTMAN, apparent widower of CHARITY STANSBURY.

JG#1/61: Mr. LANCELOT GREEN administrator of JACOB GREEN late of Anne Arundel Co. deceased. 16 October 1795. Sureties: JOHN WELCH + ROBERT ISRAEL. Fourths of the estate balance to: ANN GREEN (w/o WILLIAM BIRD), LANCELOT GREEN, ELIZABETH GREEN (w/o THOMAS TALBOTT) + SARAH WARFIELD.

JG#1/62: Mrs. ELIZABETH SIMMONS administratrix of JEREMIAH CHAPMAN SIMMONS. late of Anne Arundel Co. deceased. 3 March 1796. Sureties: WILLIAM SIMMONS + BENJAMIN WARD SIMMONS. ELIZABETH SIMMONS, widow's third; fifths of the remainder of the estate balance to: JEREMIAH CHAPMAN SIMMONS, ELIZABETH SIMMONS, RICHARD SIMMONS, MARGARET SIMMONS + WILLIAM SIMMONS.

JG#1/63: Mr. CHARLES ROBINSON administrator of JOHN HAMMOND late of Anne Arundel Co. deceased. 24 March 1796. Sureties: ABSOLAM RIDGELY + JONATHAN EDWARDS. The whole of the estate balance to SOPHIA MINSHIE [whose relationship to the deceased is unstated].

JG#1/63: Mr. JOHN CHENEY executor of THOMAS BENSON late of Anne Arundel Co. deceased. 7 April 1796. Sureties: WALTER T. WORTHINGTON + JOHN MARRIOTT Jr. Legacies to: RICHARD BENSON, THOMAS BENSON, JOHN BENSON, ELIZABETH BENSON, SARAH BENSON, JOHN MILLER, ANN WARFIELD; halves of the remainder of the estate balance to: WILLIAM BENSON + RACHEL BENSON.

JG#1/64: Messrs JAMES HOOD + WALTER TOLLY WORTHINGTON executors of ELIZABETH HOOD late of Anne Arundel Co. deceased. 14 April 1796. Sureties: None indicated. Halves of the remainder of the estate balance to: granddaughter SARAH WORTHINGTON + granddaughter ELIZABETH HOOD; legacy to ggrandson JOHN TOLLY HOOD WORTHINGTON.

JG#1/64: Mr. DORSEY JACOB administrator of JOHN TROTMAN late of Anne Arundel Co. deceased. 9 June 1796. Sureties: FRANCIS CROMWELL + CHARLES STEWART. The whole of the estate balance to: JEAN DUNN.

JG#1/65: Mr. CHARLES ROGERS administrator of JOHN ROGERS late of Anne Arundel Co. deceased. 15 June 1796. Sureties: SAMUEL ROGERS + BRICE JOHN GASSAWAY. Sevenths of the balance of the estate to: NICHOLAS G. ROGERS, SAMUEL ROGERS, ANN ROGERS (w/o JOHN WARFIELD), CHARLES ROGERS, MARY ROGERS, JOHN ROGERS + CATHERINE ROGERS.

JG#1/65: Mr. CHARLES STEWART executor of ELIZABETH BASIL late of Anne Arundel Co. deceased. 19 July 1795. Sureties: JOSEPH EVANS + JOSEPH BURNESTON. Fourths of the remainder of the estate to: the heirs of JAMES SANDERS Sr., ROBERT SANDERS, REBECCA REED + SARAH COLLINS.

JG#1/66: Mr. HENRY LEEKE executor of JOSEPH LEEKE late of Anne Arundel Co. deceased. 9 August 1796. Sureties: BRICE JOHN GASSAWAY + GEORGE COOPER. The whole of the balance "agreeably to the deceased's will + testament" to: ANNE LEEKE + HENRY LEEKE.

JG#1/66 + 67: Mr. ROBERT LUSBY administrator of JOHN LUSBY late of Anne Arundel Co. deceased. 30 September 1796. Sureties: SIMON RETALLIE + THOMAS LINTHICUM. Sixths of the remainder of the estate to: HELLENDER LUSBY (w/o ZACHARIAH TUCKER), NANCY LUSBY (w/o THOMAS MACAULEY), ROBERT LUSBY, DELIA LUSBY (w/o JOHN JOHNSON), SUSANNA LUSBY (w/o WILLIAM JAMES) + PEGGY LUSBY.

JG#1/66: Mr. CHARLES ROBINSON + Mr. CHARLES STEWART executors of Mr. CHARLES ROBINSON late of Anne Arundel Co. deceased. 17 August 1796. Sureties: CHARLES ROBINSON + CHARLES JOHNSON. Thirds of the balance of the estate to: HANNAH STEWART, RACHEL ROBINSON + CHARLES ROBINSON.

JG#1/67: Mr. THOMAS MAYO executor of MARY MAYO late of Anne Arundel Co. deceased. 5 October 1796. Sureties: ZACHARIAH DAVIS + NATHAN ATWELL. Halves + legacies to: THOMAS MAYO + GEORGE M. SELLMAN.

JG#1/67 + 69 (no p. 68): Mrs. MARY MARSH administratrix of WILLIAM MARSH late of Anne Arundel Co. deceased. 8 October 1796. Sureties: DORSEY JACOB + JOHN MERRIKEN. MARY MARSH, widow's third; fifths of the remainder to: ELIZABETH MARSH, MARY MARSH, ANN MARSH, CHARITY MARSH + WILLIAM MARSH.

JG#1/70: Mr. PHILIP WILLIAMS executor of PAUL PHILLIPS late of Anne Arundel Co. deceased. 8 November 1796. Sureties: SETH SWEETZER + JAMES REED. Legacy to SOLOMON LUSBY (of EDWARD); HENRIETTA PHILLIPS the deceased's widow the remainder of balance representing the major part of the estate.

JG#1/70: Mrs. KEZIAH RUSSELL administratrix of BENJAMIN RUSSELL late of Anne
Arundel Co. deceased. 5 November 1796. Sureties: JAMES RUSSELL + HENRY POW-
ELL. KEZIAH RUSSELL, widow's third; sevenths of the balance of the estate to:
JAMES RUSSELL, JANE RUSSELL (w/o SAMUEL CARR), SARAH RUSSELL (w/o JOSEPH WHIT-
TINGTON), MARY RUSSELL (w/o VANSANT SCREVENER), PROVIDENCE RUSSELL, RICHARD
RUSSELL + JEMIMA RUSSELL.

JG#1/70: Mr. NATHAN ALLWELL executor of WILLIAM ALLWELL late of Anne Arundel
Co. deceased. 9 January 1797. Sureties: ZACHARIAH JACOB + NATHAN MEWSHAW.
SARAH ALLWELL, widow's third; thirds to: NICHOLAS ALLWELL + REBECCA ALLWELL;
MARY RODWELL to receive livestock and personalty.

JG#1/71: Mr. NATHAN ALWELL administrator of SARAH ALWELL late of Anne Arundel
Co. deceased. 9 January 1797. ZACHARIAH JACOB + THOMAS ROBOSON, sureties.
Sevenths of the balance of the estate to: NICHOLAS + REBECCA ALWELL (of WIL-
LIAM), NATHAN ALWELL (of JACOB), SARAH + MARY RODWELL (of ELIZABETH RODWELL),
SARAH HEATH (of MARY), JOHN ALWELL (of STEPHEN), SAMUEL BUTCHER (of SARAH
BUTCHER) + NATHAN ALWELL.

JG#1/71: Mr. THOMAS ROBINSON executor of RICHARD GOODWIN late of Anne Arundel
Co. deceased. 19 January 1797. Sureties: JOHN BURTON + CHARLES ROBINSON.
MARY GOODWIN, widow's third plus legacies; THOMAS GOODWIN, ELIZABETH JOHNSON
(one third), JOHN GOODWIN, RICHARD GOODWIN (one third), ARA GOODWIN, ELLINDER
GOODWIN + AMELIA + ELIZABETH HENSHAW.

JG#1/72: Mr. CHARLES DRURY administrator of HESTER DRURY late of Anne Arundel Co. deceased. 26 January 1797. Sureties: JUNINGHAM DRURY + ABEL HILL.
Ninths of the estate balance to: SARAH HODGE, WILLIAM DRURY, the two children
of ELIZABETH COWLEY (unnamed), MARGARET PINDELL, MARY SIMMONS, ANN BROWN,
CHARLES DRURY, SAMUEL DRURY + JUNINGHAM DRURY.

JG#1/72: Mr. JOHN BURTON administrator of JOHN STEVENS late of Anne Arundel
Co. deceased. 28 January 1797. Sureties: CHARLES JOHNSON + THOMAS ROBINSON.
Halves of the balance to the deceased's daughters: ELIZABETH STEVENS + MARY
HENWOOD.

JG#1/73: Mr. JOHN BURTON administrator of WILLIAM HENWOOD late of Anne Arun-
del Co. deceased. 20 February 1797. Sureties: CHARLES JOHNSON + THOMAS
ROBINSON. MARY HENWOOD, widow's third; tenths of the balance of the estate to:
RACHEL HENWOOD (w/o JOHN BURTON), ROBERT HENWOOD, NANCY BURTON, CHARLES HENWOOD,
ELIZABETH HENWOOD, SARAH HENWOOD, JOSHUA HENWOOD, VACHEL HENWOOD, MERTILDA
HENWOOD + WILLIAM HENWOOD.

JG#1/73 + 74: Mr. PHILIP H. WATTS executor of STEPHEN MCKAY late of Anne
Arundel Co. deceased. 25 February 1797. Sureties: CHARLES MOSS + WILLIAM
HAYS. Thirds + negroes to: GREENBURY LARK, STEPHEN LARK + MARY LARK.

JG#1/74: Mrs. MARIAM BALDWIN (now GAMBRILL) administratrix of HENRY BALDWIN
late of Anne Arundel Co. deceased. 29 March 1797. Sureties: JAMES BALDWIN +
THOMAS BICKNELL. Widow, one third; thirds of the remainder of the balance to:
SARAH BALDWIN, ELIZABETH BALDWIN + WILLIAM BALDWIN.

JG#1/74: Mrs. ELIZABETH MOSS (now w/o GEORGE ADAM) administratrix of ROBERT
MOSS late of Anne Arundel Co. deceased. 31 Mary 1797. Sureties: CHARLES
MOSS + RICHARD KELLY. Widow, one third; thirds of the remainder of the es-
tate to: JOSEPH MOSS, RICHARD MOSS + SARAH MOSS.

JG#1/75: Mrs. ELIZABETH WOOD (now w/o MARSHALL POOLE) administratrix of WIL-
LIAM WOOD Jr. late of Anne Arundel Co. deceased. 12 June 1797. Sureties:
THOMAS SULLIVAN + MORGAN WOOD. ELIZABETH WOOD POOLE, widow's third; fourths
of the remainder of the balance: MARGARET WOOD, CASSANDRA WOOD, MORGAN WOOD +
WILLIAM WOOD.

JG#1/75 + 76: Mrs. RACHEL ATWELL administratrix of BENJAMIN ATWELL late of
Anne Arundel Co. deceased. 15 June 1797. Sureties: THOMAS NORRIS + MARTIN
NORRIS. RACHEL ATWELL, widow's third; sixths of the remainder of the estate
balance to: JOSEPH ATWELL, WILLIAM ATWELL, MARGARET ATWELL, JOHN ATWELL, BEN-
JAMIN ATWELL + SARAH ATWELL.

JG#1/76: Mrs. POLLY DORSEY administratrix of AMOS DORSEY late of Anne Arundel Co. deceased. 9 August 1797. Sureties: JOHN WORTHINGTON (of JOHN) +
JOHN SAPPINGTON (of JOHN). POLLY DORSEY, widow's third; fourths of the estate balance to: DEBORAH DORSEY, ELIZABETH DORSEY, AMOS DORSEY + MARY ANN
DORSEY.

JG#1/77: Mrs. SARAH PARISH administratrix of AARON PARISH late of Anne Arundel Co. deceased. 10 August 1797. Sureties: THOMAS NORRIS (of THOMAS) +
NATHANIEL FOSTER. SARAH PARISH, widow's third; thirds of the estate balance
to JOHN PARISH, ISAAC PARISH + SUSANNA PARISH.

JG#1/77 + 78: Mrs. _____ HOPKINS administratrix of RICHARD HOPKINS late of
Anne Arundel Co. deceased. 29 August 1797. Sureties: BARZILLA SIMMONS +
BENJAMIN MCCENEY. Unnamed widow, one third; ninths of the remainder of the
balance to: PHILIP HOPKINS, ELIZABETH HOPKINS, MARGARET HOPKINS, SAMUEL HOP-
KINS, WILLIAM HOPKINS, JOSEPH HOPKINS, JOHNSEY HOPKINS, SARAH HOPKINS + ED-
WARD HOPKINS.

JG#1/78: Mr. SOLOMON SPARROW surviving administrator of EDWARD LEE late of
Anne Arundel Co. deceased. 4 September 1797. Sureties: MORDICA STEWART +
JOSEPH CLARKE. MARY LEE, widow's third; thirds of the remainder of the balance to DEBORAH LEE (w/o ROBERT LUSBY), SARAH LEE ( w/o BENJAMIN WELCH) +
the deceased's grandchildren EDWARD LEE + STEPHEN LEE.

JG#1/79: Mr. JOHN WELCH administrator of JAMES BRUCE late of Anne Arundel
Co. deceased. 19 September 1797. Surety: JOHN HURST. The whole of the balance to the deceased's daughter AFFA BRUCE.

JG#1/79: Mrs. SUSANNA GASTON (now WELLS) administratrix of THOMAS GASTON
late of Anne Arundel Co. deceased. 25 September 1797. Sureties: None indicated. SUSANNAH GASTON (now WELLS), widow's third; remainder of the estate
balance to NANCY GASTON.

JG#1/79: Mrs. CATHERINE HANDS administratrix of WILLIAM HANDS late of Anne
Arundel Co. deceased. 17 January 1798. Sureties: JOHN RIDGELY + GREENBURY
RIDGELY. CATHERINE HANDS, widow's third; ninths of the estate balance to:
WILLIAM HANDS, JOHN HANDS, MARGARET HANDS, ACHSAH HANDS, SARAH HANDS, LANCE-
LOT HANDS, EPHRAIM HANDS, NICHOLAS HANDS + MARY HANDS.

JG#1/80 + 81: Mrs. RACHEL CARR executrix of JOHN CARR Jr., who was administrator with will annexed of JOHN CARR Sr. late of Anne Arundel Co. deceased.
Sureties: LEONARD GARY (Anne Arundel Co.) + SAMUEL MEAD (Calvert Co.). One
shilling each to WILLIAM CARR + granddaughter ANN HOLLIDAY. Negro to ELIZA-
BETH LAMBETH. Fifths of the estate balance to: JOHN CARR, CATHERINE CARR,

MARY CARR, PAMELIA CARR + MARTHA CARR.

JG#1/81: Mr. CHARLES GRAY surviving executor of JOHN GRAY (of JOSHUA) late of Anne Arundel Co. deceased. 5 Mary 1798. Sureties: None indicated. The whole of the balance as willed by the deceased to JOSHUA RIGHT, s/o ELLEN RIGHT.

JG#1/81: Messrs RICHARD SHEKELL + THOMAS PARKER executors of SAMUEL SHEKELL late of Anne Arundel Co. deceased. 9 April 1798. Sureties: BARZILLA SIMMON + GEORGE CALVERT. One shilling each to: ANN CARTER + AGNES GRIFFITH; fourths of the remainder of the balance to: RICHARD SHEKELL, SURRANCE NUTWELL, MARY PARKER + DEBORAH ESSEX.

JG#1/82: Mr. REZIN HAMMOND administrator of JOHN HAMMOND late of Anne Arundel Co. deceased. 10 April 1798. Sureties: PHILIP HAMMOND + BARRUCK FOWLER. Fourths of the remainder to: CHARLES HAMMOND, PHILIP HAMMOND, REZIN HAMMOND + HANNAH HAMMOND (w/o RICHARD HOPKINS).

JG#1/83: Mr. LANCELOT GREEN executor of SARAH GREEN late of Anne Arundel Co. deceased. 12 April 1798. Sureties: THOMAS WOODFIELD + WILLIAM BIRD. Thirds of the balance to daughter ANN BIRD, granddaughter SARAH WARFIELD + grandchildren SARAH TALBOT, MARY TALBOT + BENJAMIN TALBOT (children of ELIZABETH TALBOT).

JG#1/83: Mrs. SARAH ANN MAYO (now w/o JONATHAN WATERS) executrix of ISAAC MAYO late of Anne Arundel Co. deceased. 14 April 1798. Sureties: JOSEPH JENIFER + JOSHUA LINTHICUM. SARAH ANN MAYO WATERS, widow's thirds; remainder of the balance to: SARAH MAYO + GEORGE MAYO.

JG#1/84: Mrs. ANN DORSEY (now GRIFFITH) and Mr. LUKE POOL administrators of VACHEL DORSEY (of JOHN) late of Anne Arundel Co. deceased. 25 April 1798. Sureties: ANDREW MERCER (Anne Arundel Co.) + BEAL GAITHER (Montgomery Co.). ANN DORSEY, widow's third; remainder of the balance to HARRIET DORSEY + JOHN HENRY DORSEY.

JG#1/84: Mr. THOMAS DRANE administrator of LANCELOT TODD late of Anne Arundel Co. deceased. 1 May 1798. Sureties: JOHN DUNHAM + JOSHUA WRIGHT. Thirds of the remainder to: THOMAS DRANE; JAMES DRANE; and REZIN TODD + MARY TODD, the representatives of JOHN TODD.

JG#2/1 + 2: Mr. SAMUEL WARFIELD executor of JOSEPH DANIELSON late of Anne Arundel Co. deceased. 12 February 1803. Sureties: EDWARD ANDERSON + EPHRAIM MARRIOTT. Personalty to JOSEPH DANIELSON (of SAMUEL); remainder of estate during her lifetime to ELIZABETH DANIELSON, then to be shared equally by SUSANNA WARFIELD (w/o SAMUEL WARFIELD) + ELEANOR WILLIAMS.

JG#2/1 + 2: Mr. DAVID STEWART executor of ROBERT SANDERS late of Anne Arundel Co. deceased. 2 February 1803. Sureties: BENJAMIN WATKINS + MORDECAI HALE. ELIZABETH STEWART (d/o EDWARD STEWART), JANE ALLEN + MARTHA ALLEN (daughters of WILLIAM ALLEN + DINAH his wife), WILLIAM HARWOOD, ELEANOR REED (REECE?), JOHN IGLEHART + DAVID STEWART; major beneficiaries: heirs of JAMES SANDERS, heirs of WILLIAM SANDERS (of the Island of Barbadoes), REBECCA REED + SARAH COLLINS.

JG#2/1 + 2: Mr. FRANCIS CROMWELL administrator de bonis non of ANN MACCUBBIN late of Anne Arundel Co. deceased. 29 January 1803. Sureties: DORSEY JACOB + JOHN MERCER STEVENS. The whole of the balance as willed to HENRY GRAY.

JG#2/3 + 4: Mrs. ANN MILLS administratrix of FREDERICK MILLS late of Anne Arundel Co. deceased. 20 April 1803. Sureties: RICHARD RICHARDSON + JOHN THOMAS RICHARDSON. Fourths of the remainder of the balance to: ACHSAH MILLS, ANN MILLS, ELIZABETH MILLS + FREDERICK MILLS.

JG#2/3 + 4: Mr. PHILIP ROGERS of Baltimore Co. administrator of REBECCA YOUNG late of Anne Arundel Co. deceased. 12 July 1803. Sureties: None indicated. Thirds of the remainder of the balance to: REBECCA WOODWARD ("who intermarried with the accountant"), ACHSAH WOODWARD + HARRIET WOODWARD (w/o WILLIAM MURRAY).

JG#2/3 + 4: Dr. HENRY HOWARD of Baltimore Co. administrator with the will annexed of ACHSAH HOWARD late of Anne Arundel Co. deceased. 12 July 1803. Sureties: RICHARD RIDGELY + WILLIAM DORSEY. Major portion to ELIZABETH HOWARD; legatees: HENRY HOWARD, BRUTUS HOWARD, EPHRAIM HOWARD, SALLY ELDER + JOSEPH HILL.

JG#2/5 + 6: Mr. JOHN PHIPS administrator of PAUL BUSY late of Anne Arundel Co. deceased. 30 August 1803. Sureties: BENJAMIN HARRISON + WILLIAM JOHNSON. SARAH BUSY, widow's third (now w/o JOHN PHIPS); sevenths of the remainder of the balance to: WILLIAM BUSY, BENJAMIN BUSY, SAMUEL BUSY, SARAH BUSY, JANE BUSY, JOSEPH BUSY + MARY BUSY.

JG#2/5 + 6: Mrs. SARAH COALE surviving executor of THOMAS COALE late of Anne Arundel Co. deceased. 6 September 1803. Sureties: None indicated. SARAH COALE, widow's third; fourths of the remainder of the balance to: CHARLES RIDGELY COALE, ALFRED COALE, HARRIET COALE + ANNA MARIA COALE.

JG#2/7 + 8: Mrs. ELIZABETH TALBOT (now w/o HENRY TAYMAN) executrix of THOMAS TALBOT. 11 October 1803. Sureties: LANCELOT GREEN + JOHN LINTHICUM. ELIZABETH TALBOT, widow's third; thirds of the remainder of the balance to: SARAH TALBOT, MARY TALBOT + BENJAMIN TALBOT.

JG#2/7 + 8: Mrs. ELIZABETH W. RAWLINGS administratrix of RICHARD RAWLINGS late of Anne Arundel Co. deceased. 2 November 1803. Sureties: JOHN DUVALL + NATHAN RAWLINGS. ELIZABETH W. RAWLINGS, widow to receive half; remaining half of the balance to: MARY RAWLINGS, JOHN RAWLINGS, AARON RAWLINGS, MOSES RAWLINGS, SUSANNA RAWLINGS, ELIZA RAWLINGS (now ATTWELL), MARY RAWLINGS (now LUSBY) + REBECCA RAWLINGS (now DUVALL).

JG#2/7 + 8: Mr. CHARLES DRURY executor of MARY ANN WOOD late of Anne Arundel Co. deceased. 22 November 1803. Sureties: CEPHAS CHILDS + JUNINGHAM DRURY. ANN BROWN, legacy of a negro; the remainder of the balance to MARGARET PINDELL (d/o JOHN PINDELL).

JG#2/7 + 8: Mr. HENRY DEAVER executor of STEPHEN DEAVER late of Anne Arundel Co. deceased. 30 November 1803. Sureties: JOSHUA PENN + JOHN BRICE BURGESS. Sevenths of the remainder of the estate balance to: HENRY DEAVER, STEPHEN DEAVER, ELEANOR DEAVER (now BEALL), SARAH DEAVER (now WATERS), ANN DEAVER, LUCY DEAVER + MARGARET DEAVER.

JG#2/9 + 10: Mrs. ANN JOHNSON executrix of CHARLES JOHNSON late of Anne Arundel Co. deceased. 7 December 1803. Sureties: CHARLES POLTON + JOHN BURTON. Fourths + legacies to: ONEAL JOHNSON, ANN JOHNSON, CHARLES JOHNSON, ARCHIBALD JOHNSON; ANN JOHNSON, widow's third.

JG#2/9 + 10:  Mr. SAMUEL DEALE administrator de bonis non of THOMAS DEALE late of Anne Arundel Co. deceased. 11 December 1802. Sureties: NATHAN DEALE + JOHN WELCH. RACHEL DEALE (now w/o THOMAS PURNALL), widow's third; sixths of the remainder of the balance to: SAMUEL DEALE; NATHAN DEALE; JAMES DEALE; RACHEL DEALE (now HARRISON); JOSEPH COWLEY the legal representative of ELIZABETH DEALE, who married CHARLES COWLEY + SARAH DEALE (w/o WILLIAM JOHNSON).

JG#2/9 + 10:  Mr. RICHARD MARRIOTT executor of JOHN MARRIOTT late of Anne Arundel Co. deceased. 16 February 1802. Sureties: JOHN SEWELL Jr. + THOMAS HALL DORSEY. Fifths of the estate balance to: RICHARD MARRIOTT, JOHN MARRI-OTT, RACHEL MARRIOTT, RUTH MARRIOTT + ELIZABETH MARRIOTT.

JG#2/11 + 12:  Mr. WILLIAM WARD Jr. administrator de bonis non of ROBERT WARD Jr. late of Anne Arundel Co. deceased. 19 Feburary 1802. Sureties: WILLIAM WARD Sr. + JACOB PATTISON. SARAH WARD, widow's third; eighths of the remainder of the balance to: ELIZABETH PATTISON, WILLIAM WARD Jr, ROBERT WARD, JOHN WARD, SARAH WARD, ELEANOR WARD, RICHARD WARD + SAMUEL WARD.

JG#2/11 + 12:  Mrs. ANN STEWART administratrix of MORDECAI STEWART late of Anne Arundel Co. deceased. 6 March 1802. Sureties: JOSEPH WATKINS + ROBERT WELCH. ANN STEWART, widow's third; tenths of the remainder to: MARY BECK, SARAH ROBINSON, RICHARD STEWART, CHARLES STEWART, RACHEL STEWART, MORDECAI STEWART, ELIZABETH STEWART, SUSANNA STEWART, ELEANOR STEWART + CHARLES CHEN-EY (of WILLIAM), grandson.

JG#2/13 + 14:  Mrs. ELIZABETH CLAUDE administratrix of ABRAHAM CLAUDE late of Anne Arundel Co. deceased. 9 March 1802. Sureties: ALLEN QUYNN + JOHN WELCH. ELIZABETH CLAUDE, widow's third; thirds of the remainder to: JOHN CLAUDE, DENNIS CLAUDE + ABRAHAM CLAUDE.

JG#2/13 + 14:  Mrs. SUSANNA FOSTER administratrix of NATHANIEL FOSTER late of Anne Arundel Co. deceased. 31 March 1802. Sureties: JOSEPH MACE + JO-SEIPH JENNIFER. SUSANNA FOSTER, widow's third; thirds of the remainder to: SARAH MACE, MARY ANN CRUTCHERY (sic) + the heirs of JOSEPH FOSTER "four in number" (unnamed).

JG#2/15 + 16:  Mr. GEORGE HOWARD administrator de bonis non of BRICE HOWARD late of Anne Arundel Co. deceased. 31 March 1802. Sureties: HENRY HOWARD + BENJAMIN H. MULLIKEN. ANN HOWARD, widow's third; eighths of the remainder to: WILLIAM _ HOWARD, HARRIET HOWARD, MARGARET HOWARD, GEORGE HOWARD, THOMAS W. HOWARD, JEREMIAH B. HOWARD, ANN HOWARD + BRICE W. HOWARD.

JG#2/15 + 16:  Mr. GEORGE HOWARD executor of ANNE HOWARD late of Anne Arun-del Co. deceased. 4 May 1802. Sureties: HENRY HOWARD (of EPHRAIM) + BEN-JAMIN HALL MULLIKEN (of Baltimore Co.). Sevenths of the estate balance to: HARRIET HOWARD, MARGARET HOWARD, GEORGE HOWARD, THOMAS WORTHINGTON HOWARD, JEREMIAH BRICE HOWARD, ANN HOWARD, BRICE WORTHINGTON HOWARD.

JG#2/17 + 18:  Mr. AMZI BATEMAN administrator of HENRY BATEMAN late of Anne Arundel Co. deceased. 25 May 1802. Sureties: ABNER LINTHICUM + JOHN JARVIS. Sixths of the estate balance to: BENJAMIN BATEMAN, AMZI BATEMAN, ELIZABETH BATEMAN, ANN BATEMAN, RACHEL BATEMAN + LEMUEL BATEMAN.

JG#2/17 + 18:  Mrs. ELIZABETH THOMPSON (now w/o JASON JONES) administratrix of JOHN JOHNSON late of Anne Arundel Co. deceased. 25 May 1802. Sureties: JAMES BALDWIN + JOHN SEWELL Jr. ELIZABETH THOMPSON, widow's third; thirds of the estate balance to: JOHN TOMPSON, MARGARET THOMPSON + SARAH THOMPSON.

JG#2/17 + 18: Mr. GEORGE HOWARD administrator of CORNELIUS HOWARD late of
Anne Arundel Co. deceased. 4 May 1802. Sureties: HENRY HOWARD (of EPHRAIM),
Anne Arundel Co. + BENJAMIN HALL MULLIKEN, Baltimore Co. Sevenths of the
estate balance to: HARRIET HOWARD, MARGARET HOWARD, GEORGE HOWARD, THOMAS
WORTHINGTON HOWARD, JEREMIAH BRICE HOWARD, ANNE HOWARD, BRICE WORTHINGTON
HOWARD.

JG#2/19 + 20: Mrs. MARY MILES (now w/o WILLIAM SMITH) executrix of RICHARD
MILES late of Anne Arundel Co. deceased. 14 July 1802. Sureties: JUNING-
HAM DRURY + JOSIAS CROSBY. MARY MILES, widow's third; the whole of the re-
mainder of the balance to daughter MARGARET MILES.

JG#2/19 + 20: Mr. DAVID ROBINSON administrator with will annexed of WILLIAM
ROBINSON late of Anne Arundel Co. deceased. 14 July 1802. Sureties: LUKE
ROBINSON + EPHRAIM DUVALL. Legacies to JOHN ROBINSON, RICHARD ROBINSON +
ANN HAZEL; remainder of the balance to DAVID ROBINSON.

JG#2/19 + 20: Mr. ROBERT FRANKLIN administrator of JOSEPH GOTT late of Anne
Arundel Co. deceased. 10 August 1802. Sureties: BENJAMIN HARRISON + WILLIAM
DAVIDSON. "Sixths" (seven persons enumerated) to: ELIZABETH GOTT, RACHEL
DEALE, HENRIETTA DEALE, MARY CONNOR, PRISCILLA CRANDALL, ELIZABETH FRANKLIN
+ RISPA GOTT.

JG#2/21 + 22: Mr. RICHARD JACOB Jr. administrator of JOHN MERRIKEN late of
Anne Arundel Co. deceased. 21 September 1802. Sureties: JOHN ASHLAND +
CHARLES MERRIKEN. SARAH MERRIKEN, widow's third; fourths of the balance to:
ANN MERRIKEN, JACOB MERRIKEN, ELIZABETH MERRIKEN + JOHN DORSEY MERRIKEN.

JG#2/21 + 22: Mr. LYDE GRIFFITH administrator of JOHN H. DORSEY late of
Anne Arundel Co. deceased. 10 August 1802. Sureties; HENRY WAYMAN + EPH-
RAIM WARFIELD. Halves of the estate balance to the deceased's mother ANN
GRIFFITH + sister HARRIET DORSEY.

JG#2/21 + 22: Mrs. DORCAS MACCUBBIN administratrix of JOSEPH MACCUBBIN late
of Anne Arundel Co. deceased. 14 August 1802. Sureties: THOMAS ROCKHOLD +
LLOYD JOHNSON. Thirds of the estate balance to: DORCAS MACCUBBIN (widow),
CHARLOTTE MACCUBBIN + NICHOLAS MACCUBBIN.

JG#2/23 + 24: Mrs. SUSANNA S(?) GOTT + BENJAMIN ALLEIN executors of EZE-
KIEL GOTT late of Anne Arundel Co. deceased. 28 September 1802. Sureties:
CEPHAS CHILDS + SAMUEL DRURY. SUSANNA S. GOTT, widow's third; fourths of
the balance to: SAMUEL GOTT (+ a large legacy), EDWIN GOTT, ELIEL GOTT +
ELIZABETH GOTT.

JG#2/23 + 24: Mrs. ACHSAH FRIZELL administratrix of JOHN FRIZELL late of
Anne Arundel Co. deceased. 2 October 1802. Sureties: BASIL SMITH + ABNER
LINTHICUM. ACHSAH FRIZELL, widow's third; thirds of the balance to: ELIZA-
BETH FRIZELL, CHARLES FRIZELL + NELLY FRIZELL.

JG#2/23 + 24: Mrs. JOHANNA TURNER administratrix of ZACHARIAH TURNER late
of Anne Arundel Co. deceased. 15 October 1802. Sureties: THOMAS PARROTT +
ABRAHAM TURNER. JOHANNA TURNER, widow's third; fourths of the balance to:
ABRAHAM TURNER, WILLIAM TURNER, JOHN TURNER + RICHARD TURNER.

JG#2/25 + 26: Mr. WILLIAM TUCKER administrator of THOMAS TUCKER late of Anne
Arundel Co. deceased. 18 October 1802. Sureties: RICHARD DORSEY + ZACHARIAH
TURNER. Tenths of the estate balance to: WILLIAM TUCKER, JOHN TUCKER, ABEL
TUCKER, NANCY TUCKER, FRANCIS TUCKER, JAMES TUCKER, ENOCH TUCKER, SAMUEL TUCK-
ER, JOSEPH TUCKER + SELEY TUCKER.

JG#2/25 + 26: Dr. WILLIAM MURRAY administrator de bonis non of JOHN FRANKLIN
late of Anne Arundel Co. deceased. 19 November 1802. Surety: WALTER DULANY.
MARY FRANKLIN, widow's third; remainder of the balance to JOHN FRANKLIN.

JG#2/25 + 26: Mrs. LYDIA HOBBS administratrix of WILLIAM HOBBS late of Anne
Arundel Co. deceased. 30 November 1802. Sureties: LANCELOT DORSEY + VACHEL
DORSEY Jr. LYDIA HOBBS, widow's third; sevenths of the remainder to: ELEANOR
TALBOT, LANCELOT HOBBS, SAMUEL (LEMUEL ?) HOBBS, RUTH HOBBS, MARIA HOBBS,
WILLIAM HOBBS + RACHEL HOBBS.

JG#2/27 + 28: Mrs. ANN CHESTON administratrix of JAMES CHESTON late of Anne
Arundel Co. deceased. 2 February 1801. Sureties: JOHN GALLOWAY + BENJAMIN
GALLOWAY. ANN CHESTON, widow's third; thirds of the balance to: ANN CHESTON,
FRANCINA AUGUSTINA CHESTON + JAMES CHESTON.

JG#2/27 + 28: Mr. RICHARD + Mr. JAMES SEFTON executors of JOHN SEFTON late
of Anne Arundel Co. deceased. 4 or 9 February 1801. Sureties: WILLIAM BROG-
DEN + JOHN CRAIGGS. Legacies to RICHARD SEFTON, JAMES SEFTON, THOMAS SEFTON,
CHARLES SEFTON, SARAH SEFTON (daughter-in-law) + granddaughters ELIZABETH +
MARIA SEFTON.

JG#2/27-30: Mr. JOHN SHELHAMER executor of GEORGE SHELHAMER late of Anne
Arundel Co. deceased. 11 February 1801. Sureties: SAMUEL PEARCE + GEORGE
SHELHAMER. Houses + lots at Elk Ridge Landing to: JOHN SHELHAMER, CATHERINE
SHELHAMER + ELIZABETH SHELHAMER PEARCE; legacies to: granddaughter ANN BUR-
GESS, granddaughter MARY COOGLE + granddaughter ELIZABETH BURGESS, as well as
GEORGE SHELHAMER, ROSANNA COOGLE + ELIZABETH BURGESS.

JG#2/29 + 30: Mrs. SARAH WHITE + Mr. GIDEON WHITE administrators of FRANCIS
WHITE late of Anne Arundel Co. deceased. 13 February 1801. Sureties: THOMAS
MACCAULEY + THOMAS BICKNELL. SARAH WHITE, widow's third; eighths of the bal-
ance to: GIDEON WHITE, ELIZABETH WHITE, ELISHA WHITE, REUBEN WHITE, SARAH
WHITE, CALEB WHITE, ISAAC WHITE + SUSANNA HOPPER.

JG#2/29 + 30: Mr. JOSEPH MARRIOTT executor of AUGUSTINE MARRIOTT late of
Anne Arundel Co. deceased. 13 March 1801. Sureties: THOMAS WARFIELD + NA-
THANIEL SAPPINGTON. MARTHA MARRIOTT, a legacy; thirds of the balance to:
MARY MARRIOTT, RACHEL MILLER + ELIZABETH ANN MILLER.

JG#2/31 + 32: Mr. THOMAS WARFIELD administrator of KITTY MARRIOTT late of
Anne Arundel Co. deceased. 19 March 1801. Sureties: JOHN WELCH + STEVENS
GAMBRILL. Eighths of the balance to: ACHSAH MARRIOTT, JOSEPH MARRIOTT, THOM-
AS MARRIOTT, RUTHY WHITE, ELIZABETH MARRIOTT, MARY MARRIOTT, HENRIETTA MAR-
RIOTT + ACHSAH MARRIOTT (2d listing).

JG#2/31 + 32: Mrs. BETHRIDGE SIMMONS executrix of WILLIAM SIMMONS late of
Anne Arundel Co. deceased. 16 June 1801. Sureties: JOSEPH HILL + CHARLES
DRURY. BETHRIDGE SIMMONS, widow's third; fourths of the balance to: RICHARD
SIMMONS, DAVID SIMMONS, SARAH SIMMONS + SUSANNA SIMMONS. The deceased was
son of RICHARD SIMMONS.

JG#2/31 + 32: Mr. SAMUEL BUSEY administrator of ZACHARIAH HOWSE late of Anne
Arundel Co. deceased. 14 July 1801. Sureties: HENRY BUSEY + CHARLES DRURY.
ELIZABETH HOWSE, widow's third; sevenths of the estate balance to: MARY HOWSE,
JONATHAN HOWSE, WILLIAM HOWSE, SARAH HOWSE, ELIZABETH HOWSE, ELLENDER HOWSE +
THOMAS HOWSE.

JG#2/33 + 34: Mr. JESSE LEWIS administrator of ISAAC LEWIS late of Anne Arundel Co. deceased. 18 August 1801. Sureties: SAMUEL LEWIS + JOHN LEWIS. Sevenths of the estate balance to: ELIZABETH NIXON, JESSE LEWIS, MARY LOWMAN,
CATHARINE LEWIS, SAMUEL LEWIS, JOHN LEWIS + ISAAC LEWIS.

JG#2/33 + 34: Mrs. MARGARET DONALSON administratrix of RICHARD DONALSON
late of Anne Arundel Co. deceased. 27 August 1801. Sureties: MARK FOWLER +
THOMAS EARLE. MARGARET DONALSON, widow's third; fourths of the estate balance
to: FRANCIS DONALSON, RICHARD DONALSON, HEZEKIAH DONALSON + SARAH DONALSON.

JG#2/33 + 34: Mr. WILLIAM + Mr. SAMUEL DRURY administrators of RUTH IJAMS
late of Anne Arundel Co. deceased. 10 November 1801. Sureties: WILLIAM
COWLEY + EDWARD ROBERTS. Thirds of the estate balance to: WILLIAM DRURY,
SAMUEL DRURY + the children of PLUMMER IJAMS--five unnamed individuals.

JG#2/35 + 36: Mr. VACHEL GAITHER + Mr. THOMAS BICKNELL administrators de
bonis non of THOMAS FOWLER (of JOHN) late of Anne Arundel Co. deceased. 14
November 1801. Sureties: WILLIAM HAMMOND + THOMAS PRICE. PRISCILLA FOWLER,
widow's third; remainder of the estate balance to ACHSAH FOWLER (w/o NINIAN
RIGGS).

JG#2/35 + 36: Mr. AARON WELCH administrator of AARON WELCH late of Anne
Arundel Co. deceased. 3 December 1801. Sureties: JOHN WELCH (of ROBERT) +
ROBERT WELCH. ELIZABETH WELCH, widow's third; fifths of the remainder to:
AARON WELCH, CATHARINE WELCH, JOHN WELCH, RACHEL WELCH + BENJAMIN WELCH.

JG#2/35 + 36: Mr. ELIJAH JOHNSON administrator of MARY JOHNSON late of Anne
Arundel Co. deceased. 18 December 1801. Sureties: JOSHUA JOHNSON + JOHN
JOHNSON. Thirteenths of the estate balance to: MARY JOHNSON, JOSHUA JOHNSON,
ELIJAH JOHNSON, ORLANDO JOHNSON, RUTH CHENEY, PATIENCE RIDGELY, LLOYD JOHNSON,
CHRISTOPHER JOHNSON, JOHN JOHNSON, ELIZABETH JOHNSON, ZACHARIAH JOHNSON,
NANCY JOHNSON + RACHEL LINTHICUM.

JG#2/37 + 38: Mrs. ELIZABETH THOMPSON administratrix of EDWARD THOMPSON
late of Anne Arundel Co. deceased. 29 April 1800. Sureties: ABSOLAM RIDGE-
LY + RICHARD FRAZIER. ELIZABETH THOMPSON, widow's third; fourths of the balance to: ALITIA THOMPSON, HENRY THOMPSON, JOHN THOMPSON + CHARLES THOMPSON.

JG#2/37-40: Mrs. MARY JOHNSON + Mr. JOSHUA JOHNSON administrators with will
annexed of SOLOMON JOHNSON late of Anne Arundel Co. deceased. Sureties:
CHARLES JOHNSON + WILLIAM FENNELL. MARY JOHNSON, widow's third; the 14 bene-
ficiaries: RUTH CHENEY, PATIENCE JOHNSON, MARY JOHNSON, ANN JOHNSON, RACHEL
JOHNSON, ELIZABETH JOHNSON, JOSHUA JOHNSON, ELIJAH JOHNSON, SOLOMON JOHNSON,
RINALDO JOHNSON, LLOYD JOHNSON, CHRISTOPHER JOHNSON, JOHN JOHNSON + ZACHARIAH
JOHNSON.

JG#2/39 + 40: Mrs. Mrs. MARY PRICE (now w/o PAUL HARTMAN, of Baltimore Co.)
administratrix of THOMAS PRICE late of Anne Arundel Co. deceased. 10 April
1800. Sureties: JOHN ADAM BOYER + JOHN KERR. MARY PRICE (now HARTMAN), widow's third; sixths of the balance to: ELIZABETH (married name unclear), ED-

-22-

WARD PRICE, LETTY (married name unclear), HARRIET PRICE, THOMAS PRICE + SO-PHIA PRICE.

JG#2/39 + 40: Mrs. RACHEL PLUMMER administratrix of HENRY PLUMMER late of Anne Arundel Co. deceased. 17 April 1800. Sureties: SAMUEL WARD + GASSAWAY WATKINS. RACHEL PLUMMER, widow's third; eighths of the balance to: ANN PLUMMER (now BASFORD), HENRY PLUMMER, MARGARET PLUMMER, RICHARD PLUMMER, RACHEL PLUMMER, SAMUEL PLUMMER, JAMES PLUMMER + ELIZABETH PLUMMER.

JG#2/41 + 42: Mr. PEREGRINE RIDGELY administrator of MORDECAI RIDGELY late of Anne Arundel Co. deceased. 24 May 1800. Sureties: STEPHEN HANCOCK + GEORGE CONAWAY. MARY RIDGELY, widow's third; halves of the remaining balance to: WILLIAM RIDGELY + RHOADY RIDGELY.

JG#2/41 + 42: Mr. ROBERT WELCH administrator of ELIZABETH FERGUSON late of Anne Arundel Co. deceased. 24 April 1800. Sureties: JOHN WELCH + WILLIAM BETHRAY (?). Thirds of the estate balance to: ROBERT WELCH, ISABELLA BEALL + the children of SOLOMON SPARROW.

JG#2/43 + 44: Mrs. ANN WILLSON administratrix of WILLIAM WILLSON late of Anne Arundel Co. deceased. 12 June 1800. Sureties: ADAM CRAWFORD + JOHN SMITH GIST. ANN WILLSON, widow's third; elevenths of the balance to: ANN WILLSON (now COALE), JOHN WILLSON, MARY WILLSON (now SIMPSON), DRUSILLA WILLSON, ELIZABETH WILLSON, WILLIAM WILLSON, SUSANNA WILLSON, LETHA (?) WILLSON, HENRY WILLSON, FIELDER WILLSON + OLIVER WILLSON.

JG#2/45 + 46: Mrs. PATIENCE GAITHER administratrix of JOSEPH JACOB late of Anne Arundel Co. deceased. 8 July 1800. Sureties: JOHN MERRIKEN + JOHN ASH-BAW. Sevenths of the estate balance to: PATIENCE GAITHER, DORSEY JACOB, JOHN HALL, DANIEL HALL, RICHARD HALL, ELIZABETH HALL + SARAH HALL.

JG#2/45 + 46: Mr. RICHARD DORSEY executor of JOHN PORTER late of Anne Arundel Co. deceased. 16 July 1800. Sureties: JOHN IJAMS + JOSHUA MARRIOTT Jr. Halves of the estate balance to ARRY DISNEY + MORDECAI DISNEY.

JG#2/45 + 46: Mrs. MARGARET JACOB executrix of ZACHARIAH JACOB late of Anne Arundel Co. deceased. 11 August 1800. Sureties: THOMAS WARFIELD + STEVENS GAMBRILL. MARGARET JACOB, slaves + one half of the deceased's personal estate; the other half to daughter SARAH JACOB.

JG#2/47 + 48: Messrs LEONARD ARMIGER + BENJAMIN ARMIGER executors of WILLIAM ARMIGER late of Anne Arundel Co. deceased. 13 August 1800. Sureties: JOSIAS CROSBY + ZACHARIAH TURNER. Five shillings each to: JOHN ARMIGER, MARY WHITTINGTON + WILLIAM ARMIGER; personalty + livestock to JESSE ARMIGER; halves of the remaining balance to LEONARD ARMIGER + BENJAMIN ARMIGER.

JG#2/47 + 48: Mrs. MARY RAWLINGS + JOHN RAWLINGS executors of AARON RAWLINGS late of Anne Arundel Co. deceased. 17 October 1800. Sureties: NATHAN RAWLINGS + THOMAS DAVIS. MARY RAWLINGS, the whole of the balance during her natural lifetime or widowhood or after her marriage, then to be divided among the deceased's children: JOHN RAWLINGS, AARON RAWLINGS, MOSES RAWLINGS, RICHARD RAWLINGS, NATHAN RAWLINGS, SUSANNA RAWLINGS, ANNE RAWLINGS, ELIZABETH RAWLINGS, MARY LUSBY + REBECCA RAWLINGS.

JG#/47 + 48: Mr. WILLIAM YOUNG administrator of WILLIAM YOUNG late of Anne

Arundel Co. deceased. 10 January 1799. Sureties: JOHN IJAMS + JOHN RIDGELY. RACHEL YOUNG, widow's third; ninths of the remaining balance to: LURANA YOUNG, WILLIAM YOUNG, RICHARD YOUNG, RACHEL YOUNG, MARY YOUNG, NATHAN YOUNG, COMFORT YOUNG, BENJAMIN YOUNG + JOSHUA YOUNG.

JG#2/49 + 50: Mr. NOBLE STOCKETT executor of WILLIAM THOMAS STOCKETT late of Anne Arundel Co. deceased. 11 January 1799. Sureties: STEPHEN BEARD + JOHN STOCKETT. Unnamed widow, one third; the remainder of the estate balance to: JOHN STOCKETT.

JG#2/49 + 50: Mrs. MARY HARRISON administratrix of RICHARD HARRISON late of Anne Arundel Co. deceased. 8 February 1799. Sureties: BENJAMIN HARRISON + THOMAS NORRIS (of THOMAS). MARY HARRISON, widow's third; remainder of the balance equally to: ELEANOR HARRISON + JOSEPH HARRISON.

JG#2/49 + 50: Mrs. ELIZABETH GOTT administratrix of JOSEPH GOTT Sr. late of Anne Arundel Co. deceased. 9 February 1799. No sureties indicated. Sixths of the estate balance to: RACHEL GOTT (now DEALE), HENRIETTA GOTT (now CONNOR), MARY GOTT (now CONNOR), PRISCILLA GOTT (now CRANDALL), RIZPAH GOTT + ELIZABETH GOTT (now FRANKLIN).

JG#2/51 + 52: Mrs. ELIZABETH WHITE administratrix of SUSANNA MILLER late of Anne Arundel Co. deceased. 20 February 1799. Sureties: WILLIAM DORSEY + RICHARD DISNEY. Eighths of the estate balance to: ELIZABETH WHITE (accountant), THOMAS BABBS, NANCY BABBS, SARAH WHITE, REGANCY WHITE, POLLY WHITE, CHARLES WHITE + NACKEY WHITE.

JG#2/51 + 52: Mr. NICHOLAS BALDWIN surviving executor of TYLER BALDWIN late of Anne Arundel Co. deceased. 21 December 1798. Sureties: GASSAWAY WATKINS + THOMAS WOODFIELD. Halves of the remaining balance to: REZIN BALDWIN + TYLER BALDWIN.

JG#2/51 + 52: Mr. WILLIAM HINCKS executor of JOSHUA FISHER late of Anne Arundel Co. deceased. 13 February 1799. Sureties: CHARLES A. WARFIELD + TALBOT SHIPLEY. Thirds of the remaining balance to JEMIMA HINCKS, MARY WOOD HINCKS + SARAH WOOD HINCKS.

JG#2/51 + 52: Mrs. JULIET BREWER administratrix of NICHOLAS BREWER late of Anne Arundel Co. deceased. 14 February 1799. Sureties: REZIN HAWKINS + NICHOLAS JOYCE. JULIET BREWER, widow's third; thirds of the remaining balance to: ELIZABETH BREWER, NICHOLAS BREWER + ELIAS BREWER.

JG#2/53 + 54: Mr. JOHN GALLOWAY surviving executor of SAMUEL GALLOWAY late of Anne Arundel Co. deceased. 20 March 1799. Sureties: JOSEPH GALLOWAY + UPTON SCOTT. Halves of the remaining balance to: JOHN GALLOWAY + ANN CHESTON.

JG#2/54 + 54: Mr. JAMES HOOD executor of JOHN HOOD late of Anne Arundel County deceased. 18 April 1799. Sureties: WALTER TOLLEY WORTHINGTON + RICHARD RIDGELY. ELIZABETH HOOD, widow's third; bequests of varying worth to: BENJAMIN HOOD, HANNAH HOOD, SARAH WORTHINGTON, ELIZABETH HOOD, JAMES HOOD, JOHN HOOD, THOMAS HOOD + HENRY GAITHER HOOD.

JG#2/55 + 56: Mrs. ANN TUCKER administratrix of JOHN TUCKER late of Anne Arundel Co. deceased. 14 August 1799. Sureties: SELE TUCKER + SAMUEL PEACO. ANN TUCKER, widow's third; fifths of the remaining balance to: THOMAS TUCKER, JOHN TUCKER, JAMES TUCKER, SUSAN TUCKER + WILLIAM TUCKER.

JG#2/55 + 56: Mr. WILLIAM WOOTTON BREWER administrator of RACHEL BREWER late of Anne Arundel Co. deceased. 23 July 1799. Sureties: JAMES WHARFE + JOSEPH N. BREWER. Thirds of the balance to: WILLIAM WOOTTON BREWER, ELEANOR BREWER (w/o JAMES WHARFE) + RACHEL BREWER.

JG#2/55 + 56: Mr. HENRY BUSY + Mr. DANIEL BUSY administrators de bonis non of CHARLES BUSY late of Anne Arundel Co. deceased. 25 June 1799. Sureties: SAMUEL MEAD + CHARLES DRURY. Fourths of the remaining balance to: HENRY BUSY, ANN BUSY, MARY BUSY + NELLY BUSY.

JG#2/55 + 56: Mrs. MARY ROBOSON + ELIZABETH ROBOSON + ANN ROBOSON (now GHISE-LIN) executors of ELIJAH ROBOSON late of Anne Arundel Co. deceased. 20 June 1799. Sureties: CHARLES WATERS LANCELOT WARFIELD. MARY ROBOSON, widow's third; remaining balance to ELIZABETH ROBOSON, ANN ROBOSON (w/o Dr. REVERDY GHISELIN) + ELIJAH ROBOSON.

JG#2/57 + 58: Mrs. MARY THOMPSON administratrix of THOMAS THOMPSON late of Anne Arundel Co. deceased. 29 October 1799. Sureties: GERRET S. CRAYCROFT of Anne Arundel Co. + JESSE DUVALL of Prince George's Co. MARY THOMPSON, widow's third; remainder of the balance to JOHN THOMPSON.

JG#2/57 + 58: NICHOLAS BALDWIN administrator of SAMUEL BALDWIN late of Anne Arundel Co. deceased. 10 September 1799. Sureties: WILLIAM GLOVER + JOHN YOUNG. Sixths of the remaining balance to: JOHN BALDWIN; THOMAS + RICHARD DAVIS, representatives of MARY DAVIS; THOMAS BALDWIN; ZACHARIAH BALDWIN; RE-ZIN + TYLER BALDWIN, representatives of TYLER BALDWIN; + NICHOLAS BALDWIN.

JG#2/57 + 58: Mr. THOMAS WOOTTON administrator of THOMAS WOOTTON late of Anne Arundel Co. deceased. 2 December 1799. Sureties: RICHARD DORSEY + RICHARD WHITE. ELIZABETH WOOTTON, widow's third; sevenths of the remainder to: THOMAS WOOTTON, WILLIAM WOOTTON, RICHARD WOOTTON, JOHN WOOTTON, ELIZA-BETH WOOTTON, ARTHUR WOOTTON + SAMUEL WOOTTON.

JG#2/57 + 58: Mr. JOHN MERRIKEN Jr. administrator with will annexed of JOHN SMALL late of Anne Arundel Co. deceased. 8 December 1794. Sureties: JOSHUA MERRIKEN + RICHARD MERRIKEN. Thirds of the remaining balance to: ANN SMALL, JOHN SMALL + ROBERT SMALL.

JG#2/59: Distribution of the estate of WILLIAM RAY Jr. per account of 26 September 1787. No sureties indicated. Widow (unnamed), one third; sevenths of the remaining balance to: ELIZABETH RAY, PRISCILLA RAY, NICHOLAS RAY, SARAH RAY, ANNE RAY, REBECCA RAY + MATTHEW RAY.

JG#2/59: Distribution of the estate of ONEAL JOHNSON. Undated. No sureties indicated. Widow (unnamed), one third; legacies to ONEAL JOHNSON, THOMAS JOHNSON (of LLOYD) + BENEDICT SEBORN (s/o ANN JOHNSON); fourths of the remaining balance to: THOMAS JOHNSON + BENEDICT SEBORN, SOLOMON JOHNSON, ONEAL JOHN-SON + CHARLES JOHNSON.

JG#2/59 + 60: Messrs NICHOLAS RIDGELY + HENRY RIDGELY administrators of WIL-LIAM RIDGELY late of Anne Arundel Co. deceased. Undated. Sureties: JOHN RIDGELY + GREENBURY RIDGELY. Remaining balance to be dispersed to the deceased's eight children: MORDECAI RIDGELY, PEREGRINE RIDGELY, CHARLES RIDGELY, ABSALOM RIDGELY, AIRY RIDGELY, DELILAH RIDGELY, LINDA RIDGELY + ELIZABETH RIDGELY.

JG#2/60: Distribution of the estate of WILLIAM RAY Sr. 12 May 1785. No ad-ministrator, executor, or sureties indicated. Fifths to be distributed among

the following representatives: JOHN RAY, JOSEPH RAY, the heirs of WILLIAM
RAY, NICHOLAS RAY + ANN RAY.

JG#2/60: Distribution of the estate of JAMES CAREY. No administrator, executor, or sureties named. 17 October 1783. Personalty to infant PHILIP MAYO;
ELIZABETH BREWER is, in effect, sole legatee.

JG#2/60: Distribution of the estate of JOSEPH PUMPHREY. No administrator,
executor, or sureties named. Undated. Widow (unnamed), one third; remaining balance to: SILVANUS PUMPHREY, REZIN PUMPHREY, WILLIAM PUMPHREY, ZACHA-
RIAH PUMPHREY, JOSEPH PUMPHREY, the eight children of MARY ANN RIDGELY, FRAN-
CES YEALDHALL + ELIZABETH PUMPHREY.

Mrs. ANN ARMIGER (w/o JAMES PRICE) administratrix of BENJAMIN ARMIGER late
of Anne Arundel Co. deceased. 11 December 1804. Sureties: LEONARD ARMIGER
+ BENJAMIN CARR. ANN ARMIGER, widow's third; fifths of the remaining balance
to: JOSEPH ARMIGER, REZIN ARMIGER, JAMES ARMIGER, BENJAMIN ARMIGER + LEONARD
ARMIGER.

JG#2/61 + 62: Mr. JAMES CLEARY administrator de bonis non of CATHARINE STE-
VENS late of Anne Arundel Co. deceased. 5 January 1804. Sureties: NICHOLAS
MACCUBBIN + JOHN _ SIBELL. Thirds of the balance to: administrator JAMES
CLEARY in right of his wife, S____ CLEARY; S____ STEVENS (daughter) +
three CLAUDEs.

JG#2/61 + 62: Mr. HORATIO RIDOUT administrator of SARAH WEEDON late of Anne
Arundel Co. deceased. 1 February 1804. Sureties: RICHARD WEEDON + SAMUEL
RIDOUT. Thirds of the remaining balance to: JONATHAN WEEDON, JULIAN WEEDON
+ ELIZA WEEDON.

JG#2/61 + 62: Mr. FREDERICK GREEN surviving executor of WILLIAM SANDERS (d.
testate) late of Anne Arundel Co. deceased. 8 February 1804. Sureties:
ROBERT DENNY + RUTH DAVIS. ELIZABETH GASSAWAY SANDERS ( w/o RICHARD CONTEE),
widow's third; halves of the remaining balance to WILLIAM SANDERS + JOHN
SANDERS.

JG#2/63 + 64: Mrs. SARAH SPURRIER administratrix of THOMAS HAWKINS late of
Anne Arundel Co. deceased. 20 February 1804. Sureties: OLIVER CROMWELL +
JOSEPH HAWKINS. SARAH SPURRIER, widow's third; thirds of the remaining bal-
ance to: RALPH HAWKINS, JOSEPH HAWKINS + THOMAS HAWKINS.

JG#2/63 + 64: Mrs. PRISCILLA PARKER administratrix of ISAAC PARKER late of
Anne Arundel Co. deceased. 20 March 1804. Sureties: JOSHUA MAYO + MARK
FOWLER. PRISCILLA PARKER, widow's third; daughter ELIZABETH PARKER the rest.

JG#2/63 + 64: Mr. ENNION WILLIAMS + Mr. JOSEPH TOWNSEND of Baltimore Co.
executors of ISAAC VORE late of Anne Arundel Co. deceased. Sureties: JOHN
PURVIANCE + JAMES P. BOYD. REBECCA VORE, widow's third; sixths of the remaining balance to children: SARAH VORE, RACHEL VORE (w/o SAMUEL MILLS),
BENJAMIN VORE, JACOB VORE, ISAAC VORE + REBECCA VORE.

JG#2/65 + 66: Mrs. ACHSAH GWINN of Baltimore Co. executrix of CALEB DORSEY
(of CALEB) late of Anne Arundel Co. deceased. 6 April 1804. Sureties:
JOHN DORSEY + WILLIAM DORSEY. ACHSAH GWINN, widow's third; legacies to:
JOHN DORSEY, WILLIAM DORSEY, SALLY LAWRENCE + REBECCA DORSEY; fourths of
the remaining balance to: ANN GWINN, CALEB GWINN, EDWARD GWINN + ACHSAH

GWINN. A REBECCA GWINN, one of the deceased's legatees, died before this date.

JG#2/65 + 66: Mr. BENJAMIN HALL MULLIKEN administrator of BELT MULLIKEN late of Anne Arundel Co. deceased. 7 April 1804. Sureties: VACHEL GAITHER + AR-NOLD WATERS. MARY MULLIKEN, widow's third; tenths of the remaining balance to: BENJAMIN H. MULLIKEN, MARTHA WATERS, SOPHIA DUCKETT, MARGARET MULLIKEN, RICH-ARD D. MULLIKEN, ANN D. MULLIKEN, BASIL D. MULLIKEN, KITTY D. MULLIKEN, RIGAL MULLIKEN + BARRUCH MULLIKEN.

JG#2/67 + 68: Mr. LUKE ROBINSON + Mr. DAVID ROBINSON administrators of JOHN ROBINSON late of Anne Arundel Co. deceased. 12 April 1804. Sureties: THOMAS ROCKHOLD + HAMPTON ROBINSON. Fifths of the remaining balance to: LUKE ROBIN-SON, HAMPTON ROBINSON, EPHRAIM DUVALL (m. JEMIMA HAZELL), CHARLOTTE JOHNSON the representative of REBECCA JOHNSON + DAVID ROBINSON.

JG#2/67 + 68: Mrs. BARBARA WOOD executrix of JOHN JONAS WOOD late of Anne Arundel Co. deceased. 17 April 1804. Sureties: SAMUEL TROTT + THOMAS PARROTT. BARBARA WOOD, widow's third; halves of the remaining balance to: JOHN WOOD + MATILDA BURGESS WOOD.

JG#2/69 + 70: Mr. CALEB DORSEY surviving executor of THOMAS BEALL DORSEY late of Anne Arundel Co. deceased. 18 April 1804. No sureties indicated. Fourths of the remaining balance to: CALEB DORSEY, JOHN WORTHINGTON DORSEY, THOMAS BEALL DORSEY + SARAH MERREWEATHER.

JG#2/69 + 70: Mrs. PATIENCE JACOB (now CROMWELL) administratrix of DORSEY JACOB late of Anne Arundel Co. deceased. 24 April 1804. Sureties: JOSEPH LOWREY + RICHARD DORSEY. Sixths of the remaining balance to: PATIENCE JA-COB (now CROMWELL) and siblings JOHN HALL, DANIEL HALL, RICHARD HALL, ELIZA-BETH HALL + SARAH HALL.

JG#2/69 + 70: Mr. STEPHEN CRAMLICK administrator de bonis non of JOHN CRAM-LICK (d. testate) late of Anne Arundel Co. deceased. 13 June 1804. ANDREW CRAMLICK + JOHN CRAMLICK, sureties. Legacies to MARY CHAMBERS + MICHAEL CRAMLICK; eighths of the remaining balance to: ANDREW CRAMLICK, JOHN CRAM-LICK, ELIZABETH CRAMLICK, JACOB CRAMLICK, STEPHEN CRAMLICK, FREDERICK CRAM-LICK, NANCY HOWARD + grandchildren THOMAS + ELIZABETH CRAMLICK.

JG#2/71 + 72: Messrs HENRY EVANS + JOSEPH EVANS executors of ELIZABETH EVANS late of Anne Arundel Co. deceased. 14 June 1804. Sureties: CADWALLADER ED-WARDS + GEORGE W. HIGGINS. Fourths of the remaining balance to: HENRY EVANS, JOSEPH EVANS, ANN SOPER + the heirs of WILLIAM MERRIKEN: SARAH MERRIKEN, ELIZABETH DUVALL + WILLIAM MERRIKEN.

JG#2/71 + 72: Mr. BRUCE RANDALL executor of AQUILLA RANDALL late of Anne Arundel Co. deceased. Sureties: JOHN FROST Sr. + ELY BROWN. Fifths of the remaining balance to: NATHAN RANDALL, CHRISTOPHER RANDALL, JOHN RANDALL, AQUILLA RANDALL + BRICE RANDALL.

JG#2/73 + 74: Mr. MARTIN NORRIS executor of JOHN NORRIS late of Anne Arundel Co. deceased. 15 June 1804. Sureties: WILLIAM NORRIS + JACOB FRANKLIN. Eighths of the remaining balance to: MARTIN NORRIS, THOMAS NORRIS, WILLIAM NORRIS, SARAH SANDS, the heirs of CLAIR HARRIS: JAMES + JOHN LEGG, RICHARD NORRIS, ELEANOR GOTT + ANN DEALE.

JG#2/73 + 74: Mr. ABEL HILL administrator of SARAH HILL (d. testate) late of Anne Arundel Co. deceased. 3 July 1804. Sureties: MARTIN FISHER + LEWIS FISHER. Fourths of the remaining balance to: PRISCILLA SIMMONS, BETHRIDGE SIMMONS, ABEL HILL + the children of JOSEPH HILL: ABEL HILL, JOSEPH HILL + MORGAN HILL.

JG#2/73 + 74: Mrs. SARAH MARSH (w/o DANIEL LINSEY) administratrix of RICHARD MARSH late of Anne Arundel Co. deceased. 14 August 1804. No sureties indicated. SARAH MARSH (now LUSBY, sic), widow's third; remainder of the balance to RICHARD MARSH.

JG#2/75 + 76: Mrs. MARY WEEMS administratrix de bonis non with will annexed of ELIZABETH MAGOWAN late of Anne Arundel Co. deceased. 15 October 1804. Sureties: JOHN HALL + RICHARD DORSEY. Sixths of the remaining balance to: JOHN BEAL WEEMS, WILLIAM WEEMS, the children of RICHARD JOHNS in right of their mother SARAH JOHNS, ALEXANDER MCPHERSON in right of unnamed wife, MARY WEEMS + NANCY WEEMS. An ELIZABETH WEEMS is deceased.

JG#2/75 + 76: Mr. JAMES NUTWELL administrator of ELIAS NUTWELL late of Anne Arundel Co. deceased. 24 October 1804. Sureties: GEORGE HERBUTT + ABEL JOYCE. Sevenths of the remaining balance to: JAMES NUTWELL, ELIZABETH NUTWELL, AGNES NUTWELL, SAMUEL NUTWELL, PATSEY NUTWELL, LEVI NUTWELL + SARAH NUTWELL.

JG#2/75 + 76: Mrs. ELIZABETH WAYBILL administratrix of ADAM WAYBILL late of Anne Arundel Co. deceased. 26 November 1804. Sureties: WILLIAM WAYBILL + FREDERICK SCOTT. ELIZABETH WAYBILL, widow's third; fourths of the remaining balance to: MARY WAYBILL, WILLIAM WAYBILL, ADAM WAYBILL + HANNAH WAYBILL.

JG#2/77 + 78: Mr. STEPHEN MOCKABEE executor of RACHEL NICHOLS late of Anne Arundel Co. deceased. 11 December 1804. Sureties: CHARLES A. WARFIELD + HENRY NELSON. Legacy to RACHEL DORSEY, d/o of VACHEL DORSEY; residue of the balance to SARAH MOCKABEE.

JG#2/77 + 78: Mr. JOHN BURTON administrator of WILLIAM BURTON late of Anne Arundel Co. deceased. 24 December 1804. Sureties: CHARLES ROBINSON + CHARLES POULTON. Fifths of the remaining balance to: JOHN BURTON, MARY BURTON (w/o PAUL RICHARDS), SARAH BURTON (w/o CHARLES POULTON), NANCY BURTON (w/o LANCELOT JOHNSON) + EDWARD BURTON's heirs: ELIZABETH + CHARLES BURTON.

JG#2/77 + 78: Miss SARAH MERRIKEN + JOSEPH EVANS executors of WILLIAM MERRIKEN late of Anne Arundel Co. deceased. 16 February 1805. Sureties: HENRY EVANS + JAMES P. SOPER. Halves of the remaining balance to daughters: SARAH MERRIKEN + ELIZABETH DUVALL.

JG#2/79 + 80: Mrs. RACHEL RIDGELY administratrix of HENRY RIDGELY late of Anne Arundel Co. deceased. 14 February 1805. Sureties: JOHN RIDGELY + CHARLES GRIFFITH. RACHEL RIDGELY, widow's third; remainder of the balance to: ACHSAH CLARIDGE, CHARLES RIDGELY, ANN MACCUBBIN, ELEANOR MACCUBBIN, HENRIETTA RIDGELY, WILLIAM RIDGELY, RACHEL RIDGELY, SARAH RIDGELY, NICHOLAS RIDGELY + DAVID G. RIDGELY.

JG#2/79 + 80: Mr. BENJAMIN CLARK of Prince George's Co. administrator with will annexed of BENJAMIN CLARK. 19 February 1805. Sureties: AUGUSTINE GAMBRILL + WILLIAM GAMBRILL. RACHEL CLARK, widow's third; legacies to BENJAMIN CLARK, DORCAS CLARK, HENNY CLARK, JOSIAH CLARK, AMOS CLARK + JACOB CLARK.

JG#2/81 + 82: Dr. CHARLES ALEXANDER WARFIELD administrator of AZEL WARFIELD late of Anne Arundel Co. deceased. 9 April 1805. Sureties: JOHN SNOWDEN + HENRY GRIFFITH. SUSANNA WARFIELD, widow's third; eighths of the remaining balance to: CHARLES ALEXANDER WARFIELD, DINAH GASSAWAY, CATHARINE GRIFFITH, WALTER WARFIELD, NANCY WATERS, ZACHARIAH WARFIELD, GEORGE A(?) WARFIELD + SALLY WATERS.

JG#2/81 + 82: Mr. HUMPHREY PHILLIPS administrator of JOHN ALLEN late of Anne Arundel Co. deceased. 2 April 1805. Sureties: JOHN MERRIKEN + ZACHARIAH AUGLIN. SUSANNA ALLEN, widow's third; halves of the remaining balance to: RUTH ALLEN + AZEL ALLEN.

JG#2/83 + 84: Mr. BRICE HOWARD + Mr. JOHN ROWAN executors of THOMAS COR- NELIUS HOWARD late of Anne Arundel Co. deceased. 29 July 1805. Sureties: GASSAWAY WATKINS + HENRY CORNELIUS HOBBS. Elevenths of the remaining bal- ance to: HENRY HOWARD, CHARLES HOWARD, MARY HOWARD, RACHEL DUVALL and her unnamed children, REBECCA YOUNG, ANN HOWARD, THOMAS HOWARD (of CHARLES), THOMAS DUVALL, THOMAS WORTHINGTON HOWARD, BRICE HOWARD,+ ELIZABETH ROWAN.

JG#2/85 + 86: Mr. JOHN STOCKETT administrator of VINCENT LUSBY late of Anne Arundel Co. deceased. 24 August 1805. Sureties: WILLIAM J. STOCKETT + JAMES DAVIDSON. Whole of the balance to ANN LUSBY, the deceased's only child.

JG#2/85 + 86: Mr. LLOYD M. LOWE administrator of JOSEPH MACCUBBIN late of Anne Arundel Co. deceased. 30 August 1805. Sureties: RICHARD H. HARWOOD + NICHOLAS BREWER. Legacies to DORCAS MACCUBBIN (now ROBINSON), mother of the deceased; LLOYD M. LOWE in right of his (unnamed) wife; CHARLOTTE MAC- CUBBIN, the deceased's sister + his brother, NICHOLAS MACCUBBIN.

JG#2/85 + 86: Mrs. MARGARET DORSEY administratrix of JOHN DORSEY late of Anne Arundel Co. deceased. 23 October 1805. Sureties: RICHARD DORSEY + RICHARD RIDGELY. MARGARET DORSEY, widow's third; remainder of the balance to: STEPHEN BOONE DORSEY, CALEB DORSEY, RICHARD DORSEY, CHARLES DORSEY, HUMPHREY DORSEY + MARGARET DORSEY.

JG#2/86 + 87: Mr. FRANCIS BELMEAR Jr. administrator with will annexed of FRANCIS BELMEAR Sr. late of Anne Arundel Co. deceased. 23 November 1805. Sureties: RICHARD GAMBRILL + THOMAS BICKNELL. Sevenths of the remaining balance to: ANN ANDERSON, JOHN BELMEAR, SARAH ANDERSON, CATHARINE VIERS, LEWIS BELMEAR, SAMUEL BELMEAR + FRANCIS BELMEAR.

JG#2/87: Mr. FRANCIS BELMEAR administrator with will annexed of ELIZABETH BELMEAR late of Anne Arundel Co. deceased. 14 December 1805. Sureties: RICHARD GAMBRILL + THOMAS BICKNELL. Sevenths of the remaining balance to: ANNE ANDERSON, JOHN BELMEAR, SARAH ANDERSON, CATHARINE VIERS, LEWIS BELMEAR, SAMUEL BELMEAR + FRANCIS BELMEAR.

JG#2/88: Dr. CHARLES ALEXANDER WARFIELD executor of SARAH DORSEY late of Anne Arundel Co. deceased. 14 December 1805. Sureties: JOHN SHIPLEY Jr. + CHARLES HAMMOND. Personalty to SARAH RIDGELY; thirds of the remaining bal- ance to: Major THOMAS SNOWDEN (and ANN his wife + their heirs), Dr. CHARLES ALEXANDER WARFIELD (and ELIZABETH his wife + their heirs) + POLLY SAPPING- TON + her heirs.

JG#2/88 + 89: Mr. JOSEPH MCCENEY administrator of JOHN HARDESTY late of Anne Arundel Co. deceased. 24 October 1806. Sureties: CHARLES D. HODGES +

EDWARD HALL. AGNES HARDESTY (now SIMMONS), widow's third; fifths of the remaining balance to: MARY HARDESTY, HARRIET HARDESTY, RICHARD HARDESTY, ELIZA-
BETH HARDESTY + ELIAS HARDESTY.

JG#2/89 + 90: Mr. RICHARD OWINGS administrator of JOSEPH CRAYCROFT late of
Anne Arundel Co. deceased. 1 January 1806. Sureties: THOMAS WORTHINGTON
(of JOHN) + NICHOLAS WORTHINGTON (of JOHN). SARAH CRAYCROFT, widow's third;
elevenths of the remaining balance to: CHARLES CRAYCROFT, JOSEPH CRAYCROFT,
BLADEN CRAYCROFT, MARY CRAYCROFT, ANDREW CRAYCROFT, ELEANOR CRAYCROFT, ELIZA-
BETH CRAYCROFT, SUSANNA CRAYCROFT, RICHARD CRAYCROFT, SARAH CRAYCROFT + SAM-
UEL CRAYCROFT.

JG#2/90 + 91: Mrs SARAH MERRIWEATHER, widow's third; sevenths of the remaining balance to: THOMAS BEALL DORSEY MERRIWEATHER, SALLY MERRIWEATHER, NICHO-
LAS MERRIWEATHER, POLLY MERRIWEATHER, ELIZABETH MERRIWEATHER, ELEANOR MERRI-
WEATHER + LOUISA MERRIWEATHER. [It is noted that this estate reflects in-
heritance from "the estate of Lord Baltimore."] REUBEN MERRIWEATHER's estate.

JG#2/91 + 92: Mr. THOMAS NORRIS administrator of JOSEPH MACE late of Anne
Arundel Co. deceased. 22 March 1806. Sureties: JOHN MUNROE + RICHARD MACE.
SARAH MACE, widow's third; fourths of the remaining balance to: LYDIA MACE,
ELIZABETH MACE, HARRIET MACE + AMELIA MACE.

JG#2/92: Mrs. ANN ARMIGER administratrix of MATTHEW ERRICKSON late of Anne
Arundel Co. deceased. 1 April 1806. Sureties: LEONARD ARMIGER + THOMAS
SOLLARS. ANN ARMIGER (formerly ERRICKSON), one third; remainder of the bal-
ance to ELIZABETH ERRICKSON.

JG#2/92 + 93: Mr. RICHARD DORSEY executor of ELIZABETH DORSEY late of Anne
Arundel Co. deceased. 26 April 1806. Sureties: THOMAS HOBBS + STEPHEN MOCK-
ABEE. Major heir: RICHARD DORSEY; legacies to grandchildren: MORTIMER DORSEY,
CALEB DORSEY, ELLEN STRINGER, ELIZA ANN DORSEY + PEGGY DORSEY.

JG#2/93: Mr. NATHAN WARD administrator of SAMUEL WARD late of Anne Arundel
Co. deceased. 4 June 1806. Sureties: EDWARD HALL + JAMES NUTWELL. ELIZA-
BETH WARD, widow's third; remainder of the balance to daughter ELIZABETH WARD.

JG#2/93 + 94: Mrs. ANNE JACOB administratrix of EZEKIEL JACOB late of Anne
Arundel Co. deceased. 6 August 1806. Sureties: NICHOLAS BREWER + JOHN
BREWER. ANNE JACOB, widow's third; fourths of the remainder of the balance
to: PRISCILLA JACOB, ANNE JACOB, DAVID LOVE JACOB + ELIZABETH JACOB.

JG#2/94 + 95: Mr. BENJAMIN WINTERSON administrator of WILLIAM TUCKER late
of Anne Arundel Co. deceased. 12 August 1806. Sureties: RICHARD MACE +
JOHN TAYLOR. Division of estate among mother ANN WINTERSON + siblings
THOMAS TUCKER, JOHN TUCKER, JAMES TUCKER + SUSANNA TUCKER.

JG#2/95: Mrs. SARAH CORNISH WHEELER (w/o LEONARD SCOTT) executrix of JOHN
WHEELER late of Anne Arundel Co. deceased. 20 August 1806. Sureties: SMITH
PRICE + STEPHEN RUMMELS. Whole of the balance to SARAH CORNISH WHEELER (now
SCOTT).

JG#2/95 + 96: Messrs JOHN THOMAS RICHARDSON + WILLIAM RICHARDSON executors
of RICHARD RICHARDSON late of Anne Arundel Co. deceased. 21 August 1806.
Sureties: PHILIP PINDELL + GEORGE GARDNER. Legacies plus sixths of the remaining balance to: JOHN THOMAS RICHARDSON, REBECCA WILKINS, WILLIAM RICHARD-

SON, ANN MILLS, DEBORAH SHEKEL + SARAH RICHARDSON.

JG#2/96: Mr. THOMAS NORRIS (of THOMAS) administrator of SARAH MACE late of
Anne Arundel Co. deceased. 28 October 1806. Sureties: RICHARD HARWOOD +
JAMES MUNROE. Fourths of the remaining balance to daughters: LYDIA MACE,
ELIZABETH MACE, HARRIET MACE + AMELIA MACE.

JG#2/97: Mr. SNOWDEN ANKERS administrator with will annexed of JOSEPH DEA-
VER late of Anne Arundel Co. deceased. 20 September 1806. Sureties: WIL-
LIAM FOXCROFT + CHARLES ALEXANDER WARFIELD. Thirds of the remaining balance
to sons: JOSEPH DEAVER, BENJAMIN DEAVER + ANN DEAVER.

JG#2/97: Mr. WILLIAM JOHNSON administrator of THOMAS DAVIDSON late of Anne
Arundel Co. deceased. 24 September 1806. Sureties: WILLIAM JAMES + WILLIAM
TERRY. Halves of the remaining balance to: sister ANN CARTER + WILLIAM JOHN-
SON in right of his wife _____.

JG#2/98: Mr. JOHN HILTON administrator of EZEKIEL PIERCE late of Anne Arundel Co. deceased. 24 December 1806. Sureties: WILLIAM PIERCE + PHILIP R.
(or K.) WATTS. Thirds of the remaining balance to: son WILLIAM PIERCE; THOM-
AS IVORY in right of wife ELIZABETH, a daughter of the deceased; JOHN HILTON
in right of wife ELEANOR, a daughter of the deceased.

JG#2/98: Mrs. HANNAH FOWLER administratrix of JOHN FOWLER late of Anne Arundel Co. deceased. 1 January 1807. Sureties: JOHN JACOBS + WILLIAM H. HOGG.
Halves of the remaining balance to: widow HANNAH FOWLER + JUB(?), father of
the deceased.

JG#2/99: Mr. STEPHEN HANCOCK administrator with will annexed of ROBERT BOONE
late of Anne Arundel Co. deceased. 28 April 1807. Sureties: FRANCIS HAN-
COCK + STEPHEN HANCOCK. ANN BOONE (m. EBENEZER THOMAS), widow's third; other
thirds to STEPHEN BOONE + ROBERT BOONE; legacy and personalty to CHARLES BOONE.

JG2/99 + 100: Mr. JOHN WEEDON administrator de bonis non with will annexed
of EDWARD RICHARDS late of Anne Arundel Co. deceased. 13 January 1807. Sureties: THOMAS WEEDON + BASIL SHEPHERD. Fifths of the remaining balance to:
MARTHA SEEDERS (now WEEDON), WILLIAM RICKORD, ANN RICKORD, WILLIAM W. SEEDERS
+ MARY ANN SEEDERS, the legal representative of RUTH SEEDERS.

JG#2/100: Mr. REZIN SPURRIER surviving administrator of CALEB BURGESS late of
Anne Arundel Co. deceased. 21 January 1807. Sureties: ROBERT LUSBY + THOMAS
SPURRIER Jr. SUSANNA BURGESS, widow's third; children: DEBORAH BURGESS (now
SPURRIER), CALEB BURGESS, JOHN BURGESS, MATILDA BURGESS (now SIMPSON) + SAMUEL
BURGESS.

JG#2/101: Mr. JAMES ANDERSON + Mr. EDWARD E. ANDERSON executors of WILLIAM
ANDERSON Sr. late of Anne Arundel Co. deceased. 27 January 1807. Sureties:
JAMES H. MARRIOTT + EPHRAIM MARRIOTT. Legacies to: the heirs of MARY WIL-
LIAMS, DENNIS O'CONNOR, ELIZABETH CHENEY + ONEAL O'CONNOR; fourths of the re-
maining balance to: WILLIAM ANDERSON, SAMUEL ANDERSON JAMES ANDERSON + EDWARD
E. ANDERSON.

JG#2/101 + 102: Mrs. ANN WHITTLE administratrix of DAVID WHITTLE late of Anne
Arundel Co. deceased. 24 February 1807. Sureties: WILLIAM DISNEY + RICHARD
IGLEHART. Fifths of the remaining balance to: NICHOLAS WHITTLE, MARY WHITTLE,
NANCY WHITTLE, ELIZABETH WHITTLE + WILLIAM WHITTLE.

JG#2/102: Mr. RICHARD BATTEE administrator de bonis non of JAMES MAYO late of Anne Arundel Co. deceased. 27 February 1807. Sureties: RICHARD HARWOOD + JONATHAN SELLMAN. One third of RICHARD BATTEE, who intermarried with the deceased's widow _____; thirds of the remaining balance to: WILLIAM MAYO, HANNAH MAYO + JOHN MAYO.

JG#2/103: Mr. RICHARD BROWN executor of RICHARD BROWN Sr. late of Anne Arundel Co. deceased. 3 March 1807. Sureties: ABEL HILL + CHARLES DRURY. ANN BROWN, widow's third; remainder of the balance to: the heirs of ROBERT BROWN, grandson RICHARD CROSBY, grandson RICHARD BROWN (of RICHARD), RICHARD BROWN, OBADIAH BROWN, RACHEL BROWN + ALETHEA (?) BROWN.

JG#2/103 + 104: Mr. HENRY PURDY executor of FRANCIS WINN late of Anne Arundel Co. deceased. 10 April 1807. Sureties: JOHN JACOBS + SAMUEL DAVIS. ELIZABETH GWINN, widow's third; remainder of the balance to daughters: ESTHER GWINN (now PHELPS), ELIZABETH PEARCE, MARY PURDY, SUSANNA MEDCALF + SARAH GWINN (now DRAIN).

JG#2/104 + 105: Mrs. MARTHA P. CHILDS + Mr. CHARLES DRURY administrators of CEPHAS CHILDS late of Anne Arundel Co. deceased. 16 April 1807. Sureties: JOSEPH CHILDS + ROBERT CARR. MARTHA P. CHILDS, widow's third; fifths of the remaining balance to: HENRY CHILDS, JOHN CHILDS, BENJAMIN CHILDS, SAMUEL CHILDS + ANN CHILDS.

JG#2/105: Mr. ABRAHAM SIMMONS administrator of RICHARD SIMMONS late of Anne Arundel Co. deceased. 17 April 1807. Sureties: JOHN SIMMONS + JOHN LANE. SUSANNA SIMMONS, widow's third; thirds of the remaining balance to: MARGARET SIMMONS, GILBERT SIMMONS + JEREMIAH SIMMONS.

JG#2/106: Mr. AQUILA PUMPHREY administrator of EBENEZER PUMPHREY late of Anne Arundel Co. deceased. 20 April 1807. Sureties: RICHARD CROMWELL + THOMAS LEE. Thirds of the remaining balance to: AQUILLA PUMPHREY, PRISCILLA PUMPHREY + EBENEZER PUMPHREY.

JG#2/106: Mrs. ANN WATKINS administratrix of JOHN WATKINS late of Anne Arundel Co. deceased. 4 June 1807. Sureties: NICHOLAS WATKINS (of THOMAS) + STEPHEN BEARD (of STEPHEN). ANN WATKINS, widow's third; halves of the remaining balance to: daughter RACHEL WATKINS + daughter JULIANA WATKINS.

JG#2/107: Mrs. DELILAH WHITE administratrix of RICHARD WHITE late of Anne Arundel Co. deceased. 9 June 1807. Sureties: JOSEPH PIERCE + WILLIAM PURDY. DELILAH WHITE, widow's third; remainder of the balance to RICHARD THOMAS WHITE.

JG#2/107: Mr. THOMAS OWENS executor of ISAAC OWENS late of Anne Arundel Co. deceased. 9 June 1807. Sureties: GASSAWAY PINDLE + JOHN WELCH. Legacies to: the children of ANN CHILDS, PRISCILLA WELCH + the children of MARGARET LOWREY; fourths of the remaining balance to BETSY CHILDS, THOMAS OWENS, WILLIAM OWENS + NICHOLAS OWENS.

JG#2/108: Mr. SAMUEL GAITHER executor of EVAN GAITHER late of Anne Arundel Co. deceased. 10 June 1807. Sureties: VACHEL GAITHER + NATHAN SAPPINGTON. Legacies and fifths to: ZACHARIAH GAITHER, SAMUEL GAITHER, NANCY GAITHER, SARAH GAITHER + MARY GAITHER.

JG#2/109: Mr. JAMES ANDERSON surviving administrator of JAMES ANDERSON late of Anne Arundel Co. deceased. 10 June 1807. Sureties: ANDERSON WARFIELD +

JAMES BALDWIN. LYDIA ANDERSON, widow's third; fourths of the remaining balance to: WILLIAM ANDERSON, the heirs of LYDIA WARFIELD, ANDREW ANDERSON + JAMES ANDERSON.

JG#2/109 + 110: Messrs JOHN LUSBY + EBENEZER CROMWELL administrators of WILLIAM FENNEL late of Anne Arundel Co. deceased. 11 June 1807. Sureties: OLIVER CROMWELL + WILLIAM GAMBRILL. ANN FENNEL (now FREEBURGHER), widow's third; fourths of the remaining balance to: ELISHA FENNEL, ELEANOR FENNEL, ANN FENNEL + DORCAS FENNEL.

JG#2/110 + 111: Mr. GEORGE GARDINER administrator of JAMES GARDINER late of Anne Arundel Co. deceased. 23 June 1807. Sureties: WILLIAM GARDINER + JOHN THOMAS RICHARDSON. WILLAMINA GARDINER, widow's third; sixths of the remaining balance to: JOHN GARDINER, ANN GARDINER, GEORGE GARDINER, EDWARD GARDINER, MARTHA GARDINER + MARY GARDINER.

JG#2/111: Mr. SAMUEL HOPKINS administrator of THOMAS TROTT late of Anne Arundel Co. deceased. 23 June 1807. Sureties: JAMES P. WOOD + PHILIP HOPKINS. Sixths of the remaining balance to: sister ELIZABETH CANADY, brother JAMES TROTT, sister ANN CHILDS, sister HESTER HOPKINS, sister REBECCA BLUNT + the heirs of sister SARAH GRIFFITH.

JG#2/111 + 112: Mr. WILLIAM JOYCE administrator of SARAH JOYCE late of Anne Arundel Co. deceased. 1 July 1807. Sureties: THOMAS G. ADDISON + BENJAMIN D. CLARK. Legacy to HENRIETTA MARIA ADDISON; fourths of the remaining balance to: SALLY MALLONEE, WILLIAM JOYCE, ELIZABETH DEROCH(?) BROWN (sister) + PHILLIS JOYCE.

JG#2/112: Mrs. MARGARET LEE + Mr. JOSEPH JENIFER executors of EDWARD LEE late of Anne Arundel Co. deceased. 10 July 1807. Sureties: SAMUEL WATKINS + ROBERT WELCH (of BENJAMIN). MARGARET LEE, widow's third; thirds of the remaining balance to: JOSEPH EDWARD LEE, ELIZABETH LEE + HENRIETTA LEE.

JG#2/113: Mrs. RACHEL ROWLES administratrix of JACOB ROWLES lated of Anne Arundel Co. deceased. 14 August 1807. Sureties: LLOYD JOHNSON + JOSHUA JOHNSON. Fourths of the remaining balance to: DAVID ROWLES, JOSEPH ROWLES, LERASIA(?) ROWLES + JOHN ROWLES.

JG#2/113 + 114: Mr. JAMES ANDERSON administrator with will annexed of ABSALOM ANDERSON late of Anne Arundel Co. deceased. 1 October 1807. FRANCIS BELMEAR + GIDEON WHITE, sureties. Eighths of the remaining balance to: ROBERT ANDERSON, ABSALOM ANDERSON, JAMES ANDERSON, THOMAS ANDERSON, SAMUEL ANDERSON, ELIZABETH ANDERSON (now BELMEAR), JOSHUA ANDERSON + ANN ANDERSON (now HALL).

JG#2/114 + 115: Mrs. MARY HARRISON administratrix of JOSEPH HARRISON late of Anne Arundel Co. deceased. 6 October 1807. Sureties: BENJAMIN HARRISON Sr. + THOMAS NORRIS (of THOMAS). Fifths of the remaining balance to: THOMAS NORRIS, SARAH NORRIS, MARY NORRIS (w/o THOMAS DENNY), ELLEN HARRISON (w/o THOMAS ROWLAND) + MARY HARRISON, the deceased's mother.

JG#2/115 + 116: Messrs CHARLES GRIFFITH, ROBERT GRIFFITH + VACHEL WARFIELD executors of CHARLES GRIFFITH late of Anne Arundel Co. deceased. 13 October 1807. Sureties: GREENBURY PUMPHREY + GREENBURY RIDGELY. Legacy to grandson CHARLES BOONE; elevenths of remaining balance to: CHARLES GRIFFITH, ROBERT GRIFFITH, JOHN GRIFFITH, BASIL GRIFFITH, RACHEL RIDGELY, ANN RIDGELY, MARY

LINTHICUM, HENRIETTA GEORGEHEGEN [probably GEOGHEGAN], ELEANOR WARFIELD, MARGARET HOLLAND,+ SARAH BOONE.

JG#2/116 + 117: Mrs. ACHSAH RIZEL (now CHENEY) guardian to ELIZABETH FRIZEL. 13 October 1807. Sureties: ABNER LINTHICUM + NICHOLAS SANK. Thirds of the remaining balance to: ACHSAH FRIZEL (now CHENEY), mother of the deceased, one third; other thirds to the deceased's siblings, NELLY FRIZEL + CHARLES FRIZEL.

JG#2/117: Mr. HENRY WOOD + MR. THOMAS SULLIVAN Sr, administrators of WILLIAM WOOD deceased. 15 October 1807. Sureties: JAMES P. WOOD + LEONARD GARY. Elevenths of the remaining balance to: JOHN WOOD (son), HENRY WOOD (son), SAMUEL WOOD (son), ROBERT WOOD (son), SARAH SULLIVAN (daughter), MARY WHITTINGTON (daughter), DOROTHY SUNDERLAND (daughter), the heirs of WILLIAM WOOD, the heirs of SUSANNA WHITTINGTON, the heirs of ANN PARROTT + the heirs of JAMES WOOD.

JG#2/118: Mr. SAMUEL YEALDHALL executor of GASSAWAY YEALDHALL late of Anne Arundel Co. deceased. 17 October 1807. Sureties: BASIL SMITH + JOHN SANK. Legacy to WILLIAM YEALDHALL (of SAMUEL); halves of the remaining balance to: SAMUEL YEALDHALL + SAMUEL YEALDHALL (of BENJAMIN).

JG#2/118: Mr. EDWARD TIMMONS administrator of EDWARD TIMMONS late of Anne Arundel Co. deceased. 13 December 1807. Sureties: THOMAS GARDINER + GEORGE WATTS. Thirds of the remaining balance to: accountant EDWARD TIMMONS, MARY SIMMONS (sic; now WOODFIELD) + SARAH TIMMONS (now REES?).

JG#2/119: Mr. THOMAS SELLMAN administrator of JOSHUA SELBY late of Anne Arundel Co. deceased. 20 January 1807. Sureties: JAMES IGLEHART + JOHN BASSFORD. ELIZABETH SELBY, widow's third; sevenths of the remaining balance to: DEBORAH SELBY, ELIZABETH SELBY, JEMIMA SELBY, JOSEPH SELBY, HARRIET SELBY, MARIA SELBY + JOHN SELBY.

JG#2/119 + 120: Mr. THOMAS ROBINSON executor of RICHARD JACOB (of RICHARD) late of Anne Arundel Co. deceased. 18 February 1808. Sureties: CHARLES ROBINSON + JOHN BURTON. Legacy to RACHEL LINTHICUM; halves of the remainder to the children of ABNER LINTHICUM + the children of THOMAS ROBINSON.

JG#2/120: Mr. JOHN WEEDON administrator with will annexed of MARY RICORDS late of Anne Arundel Co. deceased. 15 March 1808. Sureties: THOMAS WEEDON + BASIL SHEPHERD. Legacies to: WILLIAM SEEDERS, MARY ANN SEEDERS, CAROLINE WEEDON + MARTHA WEEDON.

JG#2/121: Mr. RICHARD GREYHAM HUTTON administrator of HENRY HUTTON late of Anne Arundel Co. deceased. 22 March 1808. Sureties: CHARLES DRURY + THOMAS _ SIMMONS. Fifths of the remaining balance to: JOSHUA HUTTON, SARAH HUTTON, ANN HUTTON, MARY HUTTON + RICHARD HUTTON.

JG#2/121: Mrs. SARAH CHILDS administratrix of CEPHAS CHILDS (of WILLIAM) late of Anne Arundel Co. deceased. 29 March 1808. Sureties: CEPHAS CHILDS + THOMAS SMITH. SARAH CHILDS, widow's third; eighths of the remaining balance to: MARY CHILDS (now SCRIVENER), OBADIAH CHILDS, MORDECAI CHILDS, ELIJAH CHILDS, ELIZABETH CHILDS, ANN CHILDS, SARAH CHILDS + SOPHIA CHILDS.

JG#2/122: Mrs. PRISCILLA FARIS administratrix of WILLIAM FARIS late of Anne Arundel Co. deceased. 8 April 1808. Sureties: JOHN DAVIDSON + JOHN RANDALL.

PRISCILLA FARIS, widow's third; thirds of the remaining balance to: WILLIAM
FARIS, ANN PITT + ABIGAIL CARR.

JG#2/122 + 123: Mr. SAMUEL TROTT administrator de bonis non of LEWIS JONES
late of Anne Arundel Co. deceased. 12 April 1808. Sureties: BENJAMIN GRIF-
FIN + _____ MCCENEY. "Fourths" of the remaining balance to daughters: ELIZA-
BETH JONES, SARAH AUSTIN + NANCY SHEKELS.

JG#2/123: Mr. NICHOLAS OWENS + Mr. JAMES OWENS administrators of JAMES OWENS
late of Anne Arundel Co. deceased. 13 April 1808. Sureties: BENJAMIN OWENS +
ABRAHAM B. WOODWARD. Fourths of the remaining balance to: NICHOLAS OWENS,
JAMES OWNES, PRISCILLA WOODWARD + POLLY SHEPHERD.

JG#2/123 + 124: Mrs. ANNE MASH administratrix de bonis non with will annexed of
Mr. NICHOLAS WILLIAMS. Spring 1808. Sureties: BRYAN WILLIAMS + JOSEPH WILLIAMS.
Major legatees: BASIL WILLIAMS, ANNE MASH + RACHEL JACOB; other legatees:
MARY SMITH + the three (unnamed) children of JOHN WILLIAMS.

JG#2/124: Mrs. CHARITY FRANKLIN executrix of WILLIAM FRANKLIN late of Anne
Arundel Co. deceased. 17 May 1808. ʳ reties: THOMAS NORRIS (of THOMAS) +
JOHN COLLINSON. CHARITY FRANKLIN, widow's third; remainder to the deceased's
eight daughters: ANN OWENS, SARAH FRANKLIN, MARY FRANKLIN, RACHEL DEALE, RE-
BECCA BLACKISON, ISABELLA FRANKLIN, SUSAN FRANKLIN + ARTRIDGE FRANKLIN.

JG#2/125: Mr. JOHN SCRIVENER + Mr. JOHN WORTHINGTON executors of FRANCIS
SCRIVENER late of Anne Arundel Co. deceased. 15 June 1808. Sureties: CE-
PHAS CHILDS + LEWIS SCRIVENER. Sevenths of the remaining balance to the de-
ceased's children: ELIZABETH WHITTINGTON, MARY SCRIVENER, SARAH WARD, ANN
DOWELL, THOMAS SCRIVENER, JOHN SCRIVENER + GEORGE SCRIVENER.

JG#2/125 + 126: Mr. FRANCIS CROMWELL administrator of WILLOBY MOSS late of
Anne Arundel Co. deceased. 16 June 1808. Sureties: THOMAS ROCKHOLD + SAMUEL
CRANE. Thirds of the remaining balance to JOHN CRANE, REUBEN CRANE + SARAH
MOSS.

JG#2/126: Mr. FRANCIS CROMWELL administrator of RICHARD MOSS late of Anne
Arundel Co. deceased. 16 June 1808. Sureties: THOMAS ROCKHOLD + SAMUEL
CRANE. Thirds of the remaining balance to JOHN CRANE, SARAH MOSS + REUBEN
CRANE.

JG#2/126 + 127: SARAH DAVIS executrix of SARAH DAVIS late of Anne Arundel
Co. deceased. 22 June 1808. Sureties: WILLSON WATERS + NICHOLAS BREWER.
Legacies and halves of the remaining balance to: PRISCILLA JACOB + SARAH DAVIS.

JG#2/127: Mr. ABRAHAM SIMMONS administrator of SUSANNAH SIMMONS late of Anne
Arundel Co. deceased. 23 June 1808. Sureties: JOHN SIMMONS + JOHN LANE.
Thirds of the remaining balance to: MARGARET SIMMONS, GILBERT SIMMONS + JERE-
MIAH SIMMONS.

JG#2/127 + 128: Mr. ZACHARIAH CROMWELL administrator with will annexed of
SARAH GRAY late of Anne Arundel Co. deceased. 10 August 1808. Sureties:
FRANCIS CROMWELL + JOHN CROMWELL. Eighths of the remaining balance to: JOHN
HENRY MACCUBBIN, JOHN CROMWELL, SARAH CROMWELL, ZACHARIAH CROMWELL, WILLIAM
CROMWELL, ELIZABETH JONES, NANCY CHENEY + MARY CROMWELL.

JG#2/128 + 129: Mrs. SUSANNA WYVILL executrix of MARMADUKE WYVILL late of
Anne Arundel Co. deceased. 13 September 1808. Sureties: JOSEPH CHILDS +

THOMAS T. SIMMONS. SUSANNA WYVILL, widow's third; half of the remainder of the
balance to MARMADUKE WYVILL; residue divided among ANN WYVILL (now SIMMONS),
JANE WYVILL, ELIZABETH WYVILL, SUSANNA WYVILL, MARY WYVILL, HAIL WYVILL + PRIS-
CILLA WYVILL.

JG#2/129: Mr. GEORGE DORSEY administrator of PHILEMON DORSEY late of Anne Arun-
del Co. deceased. 23 September 1808. Sureties: SAMUEL BANKS + SAMUEL RIDGELY.
Sixths of the remaining balance to the deceased's children: JOHN DORSEY, ELIZA-
BETH STRINGER, ELEANOR BANKS, MARY GARDINER, ANNE DORSEY + CATHARINE DORSEY.

JG#2/129 + 130: Mr. SAMUEL MUSGROVE executor of SAMUEL MUSGROVE late of Anne
Arundel Co. deceased. 24 September 1808. Sureties: THOMAS HOBBS + BEALE GAI-
THER. Legacies of varying value to: SAMUEL MUSGROVE, MARY MUSGROVE, STEPHEN
MUSGROVE (grandson), ANTHONY MUSGROVE, STEPHEN MUSGROVE, JEMIMA MUSGROVE,
ACHSAH MUSGROVE (granddaughter), MARY MILLER + MARGARET MUSGROVE.

JG#2/130 + 131: Mr. THOMAS WOODFIELD administrator of JOSHUA HALL late of Anne
Arundel Co. deceased. 23 January 1809. Sureties: THOMAS BICKNELL + STEPHEN
BEARD (of STEPHEN). Fifths of the remaining balance to: HARRIET HALL, THOMAS
HALL, WILLIAM HALL, JOSHUA HALL + HENRY HALL.

JG#2/131: Mr. SAMUEL PEARCE administrator of JAMES BOWSE late of Anne Arundel
Co. deceased. 23 January 1809. Sureties: None indicated. Fifths of the remaining balance to: CAESAR BOWSE, JOHN BOWSE, EDWARD BOWSE, CATHARINE BOWSE +
the heirs of ESTHER BOWSE.

JG#2/131 + 132: Mr. ZACHARIAH JACOB executor of DORSEY JACOB late of Anne
Arundel Co. deceased. 27 January 1809. Sureties: RICHARD JACOB Jr. + CHARLES
WATERS. Legacy + funds to "compleat his studies" to ZACHARIAH JACOB; thirds
of the remaining balance to: ANN MACCUBBIN, HARRIET JACOB + ACHSAH JACOB.

JG#2/132 + 133: Mr. HENRY PURDY administrator of ELIZABETH GWINN late of Anne
Arundel Co. deceased. 31 January 1809. Sureties: LEWIS DUVALL + JOHN NICHOL-
SON. Eighths of the remaining balance to: ESTHER GWINN (now PHELPS), ELIZA-
BETH PEARCE, MARY PURDY, SUSANNAH MEDCALF, SARAH GWINN (now DRAIN), ANN GWINN,
HENRY GWINN + JOSEPH GWINN.

JG#2/133: Mrs. ANN MERRIKEN MACCUBBIN admistratrix de bonis non with will annexed of JOHN HENRY MACCUBBIN late of Anne Arundel Co. deceased. 25 March 1809.
Sureties: ZACHARIAH JACOB + STEPHEN HANCOCK. ANN MERRIKEN MACCUBBIN, widow's
third; remainder of the balance to JOHN HENRY MACCUBBIN.

JG#2/133 + 134: Mrs. DEBORAH LUSBY administratrix de bonis non of MARY LUSBY
late of Anne Arundel Co. deceased. 7 April 1809. Sureties: ROBERT WELCH (of
BENJAMIN) + HENRY LUSBY. Sevenths of the remaining balance to: DEBORAH LUSBY,
the heirs of JAMES MAYO, the heirs of EDWARD LUSBY, the heirs of SAMUEL LUSBY,
the widow of JAMES LUSBY, HENRY LUSBY + WILLIAM LUSBY.

JG#2/134 + 135: Mr. JOHN BOONE executor of JOHN BOONE (of NICHOLAS) late of
Anne Arundel Co. deceased. 11 April 1809. Sureties: ZACHARIAH JACOB + JOHN
ASHBAW. Legacies of varying value to: widow ELEANOR BOONE, JOHN BOONE, ANNE
JONES + CHARLOTTE BOONE.

JG#2/135: Mrs. ELEANOR DENT administratrix of JOHN DENT late of Anne Arundel
Co. deceased. 12 April 1809. Sureties: JOHN CHEW THOMAS + EDWARD ROBERTS.

ELEANOR DENT, widow's third; fifths of the remaining balance to: ERASMUS DENT, JOHN DENT, WALTER DENT, RICHARD DENT + ELIZABETH MARIA DENT.

JG#2/136: Mrs. ELIZABETH CRAWFORD administratrix of NATHANIEL CRAWFORD late of Anne Arundel Co. deceased. 17 April 1809. Sureties: LARKIN SHIPLEY + JOHN FI-GANSER. ELIZABETH CRAWFORD, widow's third; thirds of the remainder to JULIAN CRAWFORD, SOPHIA CRAWFORD + SARAH CRAWFORD.

JG#2/136: Mr. BASIL BROWN administrator of RICHARD MARRIOTT late of Anne Arundel Co. deceased. 9 June 1809. Sureties: JOHN WELCH + WILLIAM HAMMOND. JANE MARRIOTT, widow's third; fifths of the remainder to: WILLIAM MARRIOTT, RICHARD MARRIOTT, MARY MARRIOTT, REZIN MARRIOTT + ANNE MARRIOTT.

JG#2/137: Mrs. MARY ORME WOODWARD (of Anne Arundel Co.) + Mr. THOMAS HODGES (of Prince George's Co.) administrators of HENRY WOODWARD late of Anne Arundel Co. deceased. 20 June 1809. Sureties: BENJAMIN GAITHER + RICHARD WATERS. MARY ORME WOODWARD, widow's third; fifths of the remainder to children: WILLIAM WOODWARD, MARGARET WOODWARD, HARRIET WOODWARD, THOMAS WOODWARD + MARY ANN WOOD-WARD.

JG#2/137 + 138: Mrs. ANN MASH administratrix of JOSEPH MASH late of Anne Arundel Co. deceased. 9 August 1809. Sureties: BRYAN WILLIAMS + BASIL WILLIAMS. Thirds of the remainder to: widow ANN MASH + daughters PATIENCE + ANN MASH.

JG#2/138: Mr. EDWARD PUMPHREY administrator with will annexed of ZACHARIAH PUMPHREY late of Anne Arundel Co. deceased. 16 August 1809. Sureties: EDWARD PUMPHREY + RICHARD FISH. Widow ELIZABETH PUMPHREY, half of balance; grandson CHARLES BOONE, a horse + personalty; EDWARD PUMPHREY, remaining half.

JG#2/138 + 139: Mrs. SARAH TUCKER (now RICHARDS) administratrix of JOHN TUCKER late of Anne Arundel Co. deceased. 3 November 1809. Sureties: DANIEL WELLS + JAMES LOWE. SARAH TUCKER (now WELLS!), widow's third; halves of the remainder to: REBECCA FAIRBANK TUCKER + MARY ANNE LOWE TUCKER.

JG#2/139: Miss HELLEN TOOTELL administratrix of JAMES TOOTELL late of Anne Arundel Co. deceased. 10 November 1809. Sureties: JOHN MUIR + HENRY CHILDS. Fifths of the remainder of the balance to: ELIZABETH PLATER, HELLEN TOOTELL, ANN TOOTELL, MARY CHILDS + ROSANNA TOOTELL.

JG#2/139 + 140: Mr. SAMUEL DUVALL administrator with will annexed of EPHRAIM DUVALL late of Anne Arundel Co. deceased. 15 February 1810. Sureties: ZACHA-RIAH DUVALL + MAREEN B. DUVALL. EPHRAIM DUVALL + SAMUEL DUVALL, major benefic-iaries; SALLY DUVALL + JEMIMA DUVALL.

JG#2/140: Mr. THOMAS WOODFIELD executor of LANCELOT GREEN late of Anne Arundel Co. deceased. 21 March 1810. Sureties: JOHN WATKINS + JAMES JACOBS. Thirds of the remaining balance to: MARIA GREEN, SARAH GREEN + BENJAMIN GREEN.

JG#2/140 + 141: Mr. RICHARD BROWN executor of OBADIAH BROWN late of Anne Arundel Co. deceased. 11 May 1811. Sureties: CHARLES D. HODGES + JAMES P. WOOD. Halves of the remaining balance to RICHARD BROWN + RACHEL DEALE; a small legacy to ALTHEA BROWN.

JG#2/141: Mr. WILLIAM MACCUBBIN executor of RICHARD COLLINS late of Anne Arundel Co. deceased. 1 May 1810. Sureties: ABEL CHENEY + JOSIAS COLLINS. Fifths of the remaining balance to: PATIENCE COLLINS, CHARITY MACCUBBIN, RUTH COLLINS, RACHEL COLLINS + ANNE COLLINS.

JG#2/142: Mr. WILLIAM CROMWELL administrator of JOHN CROMWELL late of Anne Arundel Co. deceased. 24 March 1810. Sureties: JOHN JARVIS + THOMAS CROMWELL. Legatees: WILLIAM CROMWELL, JOSEPH CROMWELL, NANCY CROMWELL, SARAH CROMWELL, MICHAEL CROMWELL, RACHEL CROMWELL, LEVI CROMWELL, JOSHUA CROMWELL + THOMAS CROMWELL.

JG#2/142: Mrs. ANN JENNIFER + Mr. JOSEPH JENNIFER administrators of HENRIETTA MAYO late of Anne Arundel Co. deceased. 1 June 1810. Sureties: WILLIAM ALEXANDER + WILLIAM JOHNSON. Legatees: ANN JENNIFER, SARAH WILLIAMSON, HENRIETTA NORRIS, MARGARET LEE + the heirs of JAMES MAYO: WILLIAM MAYO, HANNAH MAYO + JOHN MAYO.

JG#2/143: Mrs. ESTHER BUCKMAN administrator of DAVID BUCKMAN late of Anne Arundel Co. deceased. 3 June 1810. Sureties: JOHN BUCKMAN + EDMUND BUCKMAN. ESTHER BUCKMAN, widow's third; tenths of the remaining balance to: HANNAH LINTON, RACHEL KNOWLES, JOHN BUCKMAN, DAVID BUCKMAN, EDMUND BUCKMAN, DEBORAH BUCKMAN, OLIVER BUCKMAN, BENJAMIN BUCKMAN, ESTHER BUCKMAN + ANN BUCKMAN.

JG#2/143 + 144: Messrs JOSEPH SANDS + JOHN BARBER administrators de bonis non with will annexed of RICHARD RAWLINGS late of Anne Arundel Co. deceased. 2 August 1810. Sureties: SAMUEL MAYNARD + GIDEON WHITE. Fourths of the remaining balance to ANN RAWLINGS, SUSANNA RAWLINGS (now BARBER), SALLY RAWLINGS (now SANDS) + JOHN MERCER STEVENS MACCUBBIN.

JG#2/144 + 145: Mrs. RACHEL WARFIELD + LANCELOT WARFIELD executors of LANCELOT WARFIELD late of Anne Arundel Co. deceased. 15 August 1810. Sureties: BASIL BROWN + STEVENS GAMBRILL. RACHEL WARFIELD, widow's third; varying bequests to: CHARLES WARFIELD, LEMUEL WARFIELD, SARAH WARFIELD, JOHN WARFIELD, ALLEN WARFIELD, RACHEL WARFIELD + LANCELOT WARFIELD.

JG#2/145: Messrs JAMES ANDERSON + EDWARD ANDERSON executors of WILLIAM ANDERSON late of Anne Arundel Co. deceased. 4 September 1810. Sureties: JAMES H. MARRIOTT + EPHRAIM MARRIOTT. Fourths of the remaining balance to: WILLIAM ANDERSON, SAMUEL ANDERSON, JAMES ANDERSON + EDWARD ANDERSON.

JG#2/145: Mr. JAMES N. WEEMS executor of JAMES DISNEY late of Anne Arundel Co. deceased. 6 September 1810. Sureties: ABSALOM RIDGELY + WILLIAM WILKINS. MARY DISNEY, widow's third; remainder of the balance to JAMES N. WEEMS.

JG#2/146: Mr. GEORGE ADAMS administrator of ANN VESSELS late of Anne Arundel Co. deceased. 10 September 1810. Sureties: ROBERT WELCH + GREENBURY SARK. Halves of the remainder to: LOUISA VESSELS + SARAH VESSELS.

JG#2/146 + 147: Mrs. SARAH GAITHER administratrix of ZACHARIAH GAITHER late of Anne Arundel Co. deceased. 9 October 1810. Sureties: JAMES WARFIELD + HENRY HOWARD (of JOHN). SARAH GAITHER, widow's third; other legatees: RACHEL GAITHER, LUCY GAITHER, JOHN GAITHER, JAMES GAITHER, EDWARD GAITHER, GREENBURY GAITHER + EVAN GAITHER.

JG#2/147: Mr. AARON HAWKINS administrator of SAMUEL HAWKINS late of Anne Arundel Co. deceased. 21 November 1810. Sureties: OLIVER CROMWELL + JOSEPH HAWKINS. Son SAMUEL HAWKINS whole of the balance.

JG#2/147 + 148: Mr. JOHN MOXLEY executor of THOMAS MOXLEY late of Anne Arundel

Co. deceased. 12 December 1810. Sureties: JOSEPH JEAN + RICHARD TURNER.
AMELIA MOXLEY, widow's third; legacies to: THOMAS MOXLEY, ANGELINA MOXLEY +
BASIL MOXLEY; eighths of the remainder to: FRANCES MOXLEY, CHARLES MOXLEY,
CAROLINE MOXLEY, NEHEMIAH MOXLEY, MARY MOXLEY, JOHN MOXLEY, LLOYD MOXLEY +
ANGELINA MOXLEY.

JG#2/148: Mrs. SUSANNAH OWENS administratrix of CHARLES OWENS late of Anne
Arundel Co. deceased. 22 January 1811. Sureties: THOMAS OWENS + BENJAMIN
OWENS. SUSANNA OWENS, widow's third; daughter ELIZABETH OWENS remainder of
the balance.

JG#2/148 + 149: Mrs. ELIZABETH WYVILL administratrix of MARMADUKE WYVILL
late of Anne Arundel Co. deceased. 6 February 1811. Sureties: WALTER WY-
VILL + HENRY CHILDS. ELIZABETH WYVILL, widow's third; daughter HARRIET WY-
VILL whole of the remainder of the balance.

JG#2/149: Mr. WILLIAM ATTWELL administrator de bonis non with will annexed
of DANIEL ATTWELL. 26 March 1811. Sureties: JACOB FRANKLIN Jr. + JOHN
JOHNS. MARY ATTWELL, widow's third; legatees also included: WILLIAM ATTWELL,
ROBERT ATTWELL's daughter CATHERINE, the representatives of BENJAMIN ATTWELL,
ELIZABETH PAISLEY, the representatives of JOSEPH ATTWELL, the grandchildren
of MARY LAVEY + the representatives of SAMUEL ATTWELL.

JG#2/150: Mrs. ANN FOREMAN (now PHIPPS) administratrix with will annexed of
JOSEPH FOREMAN late of Anne Arundel Co. deceased. 1 March 1811. Sureties:
ZACHARIAH RISTON + GEORGE ROBINSON. ANN FOREMAN, widow's third; varying
awards to: SAMUEL FOREMAN, JOSEPH FOREMAN + MARY FOREMAN.

JG#2/150 + 151: Mrs. ANN ASHBAW executrix of JOHN ASHBAW late of Anne Arun-
del Co. deceased. 26 March 1811. Sureties: BRYAN WILLIAMS + BENJAMIN THOM-
AS. ANN ASHBAW, widow's third; halves of the remainder to FRANCIS ASHBAW +
JOHN ASHBAW.

JG#2/151: Mrs. ELIZABETH DORSEY (now LINTHICUM) executrix of JOHN DORSEY
late of Anne Arundel Co. deceased. 9 April 1811. Sureties: GEORGE DORSEY
+ JOHN STRINGER. ELIZABETH DORSEY (now LINTHICUM), widow's third; remainder
to: ANN DORSEY, RICHARD DORSEY, SAMUEL _ DORSEY, ELIZABETH _ DORSEY + JOHN
DORSEY.

JG#2/151: Mr. HORATIO HUDSON executor of RUTH YOUNG late of Anne Arundel
Co. deceased. 16 April 1811. Sureties: JOHN WHITE (of OTHO) + SAMUEL RICH-
MOND Jr. Fourths of the remainder to: RACHEL JONES, ORPHA YOUNG, CHARLOTTE
YOUNG + grandchildren RICHARD + MICHA DEAN.

JG#2/152 + 153: Mr. ABEL HILL administrator of SUSANNA HILL late of Anne
Arundel Co. deceased. 18 April 1811. Sureties: RICHARD HUTTON + CHARLES
DRURY. Thirds of the remainder to: ABEL HILL, JOSEPH HILL + MORGAN HILL.

JG#2/153: Mr. HENRY JOHNSON administrator of BENJAMIN YEALDHALL late of Anne
Arundel Co. deceased. 22 April 1811. Sureties: WILLIAM SEWALL + JOHN SULLI-
VAN. Thirds of the remaining balance to: SUSANNA YEALDHALL, AARON YEALDHALL
+ HARRIET YEALDHALL.

JG#2/153 + 154: Mr. ELIJAH YEALDHALL administrator of SAMUEL YEALDHALL late
of Anne Arundel Co. deceased. 23 April 1811. Sureties: JOHN WELLHAM + ABNER

LINTHICUM. FRANCES YEALDHALL, widow's third; sevenths of the remaining balance to: ELIZABETH YEALDHALL, the heirs of JOSHUA YEALDHALL, the heirs of HENRY YEALDHALL, the heirs of WILLIAM YEALDHALL, ELIJAH YEALDHALL, AQUILA YEALDHALL + FREDERICK YEALDHALL.

JG#2/154: Mrs. MARGARET HEWITT administratrix of THOMAS W. HEWITT late of Anne Arundel Co. deceased. 30 April 1811. Sureties: LEWIS DUVALL + JOHN MUNROE. MARGARET HEWITT, widow's third; sixths of the remainder to: WILLIAM HEWITT, EDMOND HEWITT, THOMAS HEWITT, JAMES HEWITT, MARY ANN JANE HEWITT + SARAH ELLEN HEWITT.

JG#2/155: Mrs. ARIANA SANDS administratrix of SAMUEL SANDS late of Anne Arundel Co. deceased. 7 May 1811. Sureties: LEWIS DUVALL + WILLIAM TUCK. ARIANA SANDS, widow's third; eighths of the remainder to: ELIZABETH SANDS, MARY ANN SANDS, SAMUEL SANDS, ANN MARIA SANDS, GEORGE SANDS, SOPHIA SANDS, SUSANNA SANDS + JANE SANDS.

JG#2/155 + 156: Mrs. ELIZABETH CADLE executrix of SAMUEL CADLE late of Anne Arundel Co. deceased. 10 May 1811. Sureties: ANDERSON WARFIELD + THOMAS BICKNELL. ELIZABETH CADLE, widow's third; fourths of the remainder to: THOMAS CADLE, ELEANOR CADLE, WILLIAM CADLE + PRISCILLA CADLE.

JG#2/156: Mr. JUNINGHAM DRURY administrator with the will annexed of ZEBEDEE WOOD late of Anne Arundel Co. deceased. 30 May 1811. Sureties: None indicated. ANN WOOD, widow's third; thirds of the remainder to: HOPEWELL WOOD, CASSANDRA STONE + the heirs of ANN SCOTT.

JG#2/156 + 157: Mrs. DELILAH SANDS (now w/o ISAAC HOLLAND) administratrix of JOHN SANDS late of Anne Arundel Co. deceased. 1 July 1811. Sureties: ISAAC HOLLAND + JOHN RIGBY. DELILAH SANDS, widow's third; fifths of the balance to: ANN HOLLAND, ELIZA SANDS, WASHINGTON SANDS, JANE SANDS + THOMAS SANDS.

JG#1/157: Mr. JOHN WHITE administrator de bonis non of JOHN LEE late of Anne Arundel Co. deceased. 11 July 1811. Sureties: JACOB H. SLEEMAKER + ANDREW SLICER. Halves of the remainder to: JOSEPH LEE + JOHN WHITE in right of wife [unnamed], who is the daughter of the deceased.

JG#2/157 + 158: Mr. NEHEMIAH BIRKHEAD executor of NEHEMIAH BIRKHEAD Sr. late of Anne Arundel Co. deceased. 5 August 1811. Sureties: JACOB PATTERSON + SAMUEL BIRKHEAD. SARAH BIRKHEAD, widow's third; fourths of the remainder to: MARY BREWER, ELIZABETH BIRKHEAD, SARAH BIRKHEAD + NEHEMIAH BIRKHEAD.

JG#2/158: Mrs. ANN JACOB executrix of RICHARD JACOB late of Anne Arundel Co. deceased. 27 August 1811. Sureties: JOSHUA JOHNSON + CHRISTOPHER JOHNSON. ANN JACOB, widow's third; remainder of the balance to DORSEY JACOB.

JG#2/159: Mr. NICHOLAS SWORMSTADT administrator of EDWARD DAY late of Anne Arundel Co. deceased. 18 September 1811. Sureties: ROBERT WELCH + ZACHARIAH CROMWELL. REBECCA DAY, widow's third; halves of the remainder to: WILLIAM DAY + ISRAEL DAY.

JG#2/159: Mrs. SARAH LAWRENCE + Mr. LARKIN DORSEY administrators of LEVIN LAWRENCE late of Anne Arundel Co. deceased. 14 November 1811. Sureties: RICHARD DORSEY + ROBERT DORSEY. Sevenths of the remainder to: CALEB LAW-

RENCE, REBECCA LAWRENCE, JOHN LAWRENCE, LARKIN LAWRENCE, HAMMOND LAWRENCE, CAROLINE LAWRENCE + SALLY ANN LAWRENCE.

JG#2/160: Miss ELIZABETH DORSEY executrix of LUCY DORSEY late of Anne Arundel Co. deceased. 16 November 1811. Sureties: RICHARD DORSEY + THOMAS B. DORSEY. Sixths of the remaining balance to: ELIZABETH DORSEY, SALLY SPURRIER, RACHEL DORSEY, BETSEY DORSEY, POLLY DORSEY + JULIANA DORSEY.

JG#2/160 + 161: Mr. EDWARD COLLINSON administrator of CHARITY FRANKLIN late of Anne Arundel Co. deceased. 20 November 1811. Sureties: None indicated. Ninths of the remaining balance to: ELSEY HARPER, JOHN COLLINSON, EDWARD COLLINSON, WILLIAM COLLINSON, SARAH GOTT, BENJAMIN COLLINSON, MARY OWENS, SUSAN FRANKLIN + ARTRIDGE FRANKLIN.

JG#2/161: Mrs. ANN STEWART administratrix with will annexed of DAVID STEWART late of Anne Arundel Co. deceased. 26 November 1811. Sureties: CHARLES PUMPHREY + COCKEY PUMPHREY. ANN STEWART, widow's third; fifths of the remainder to: RACHEL STEWART, MARY STEWART, ANN STEWART, SUSANNA STEWART + DAVID STEWART.

JG#2/162: Mr. LYDE GRIFFITH executor of AMELIA WARFIELD late of Anne Arundel Co. deceased. 27 November 1811. Sureties: JOSHUA WARFIELD + HENRY WAYMAN. Legatees: daughters of JOSHUA WARFIELD: HARRIET DORSEY, RACHEL D. WARFIELD, MARGARET _ WARFIELD, AMELIA WARFIELD, MARY WARFIELD, ANNE WARFIELD + SARAH WARFIELD; daughters of CHARLES WARFIELD: RACHEL WARFIELD, SARAH WARFIELD, AMELIA WARFIELD, KITTY WARFIELD + ELEANOR WARFIELD; daughters of ANN WAYMAN: MARY CROW, RACHEL HOOD, ANN DORSEY, SARAH HOOD, AMELIA GRIFFITH + MILCAH WAYMAN.

JG#2/162 + 163: Mrs. MARY LEATHERWOOD administrator of THOMAS LEATHERWOOD late of Anne Arundel Co. deceased. 29 November 1811. Sureties: JOHN SHIPLEY Sr. + JOHN PORTER. MARY LEATHERWOOD, widow's third; fifths of the remainder to: ELIZABETH SHIPLEY, ANN LEATHERWOOD, SAMUEL LEATHERWOOD, PRISCILLA LEATHERWOOD + MARY LEATHERWOOD.

JG#3/1: Mr. FRANCIS HANCOCK administrator of STEPHEN HANCOCK late of Anne Arundel Co. deceased. 16 January 1812. Sureties: BRYAN WILLIAMS + ZACHARIAH CROMWELL. ANNE HANCOCK, widow's third; sixths of the remaining balance to: FRANCIS HANCOCK; the children of ANN BOONE: STEPHEN BOONE, ROBERT BOONE + MARY ANNE THOMAS (?); ANN WILLIAMS (d/o SALLY WILLIAMS); RHOADY STEWART; STEPHEN HANCOCK + ABSALOM HANCOCK.

JG#3/2: Mr. FRANCIS HANCOCK administrator of ANN HANCOCK late of Anne Arundel Co. deceased. 16 January 1812. Halves to the deceased's daughters: HENRIETTA CROMWELL + ANN CROMWELL.

JG#3/2 + 3: Mr. THOMAS POLTON executor of MARY POLTON late of Anne Arundel Co. deceased. 11 Maryach 1812. Sureties: JOHN MOXLEY + PHILIP BERRY. Legacies of varying amounts to: THOMAS POLTON, ELIZABETH POLTON, grandson JAMES CARROLL, grandson CHARLES POLTON, MARY POLTON, GIDEON GRAY, CHARLES CARROLL, CHARLES P. POLTON, NANCY ANTIST + the heirs of ELEANOR LITCHFIELD.

JG#3/3 + 4: Mr. JOSEPH GAMBRILL administrator of BENJAMIN GAMBRILL late of Anne Arundel Co. deceased. 19 March 1812. Sureties: MOSES LAWRENCE + RICHARD

FISH. Fourths of the remaining balance to: NANCY GAMBRILL, STEPHEN GAMBRILL, PEGGY GAMBRILL + RUTH GAMBRILL [who is probably the widow of the deceased's son, JOHN GAMBRILL].

JG#3/4: Mr. JOHN GOLDER administrator of ARCHIBALD GOLDER late of Anne Arundel Co. deceased. 2 April 1812. Sureties: SARAH GOLDER + JOHN JOHNSON. SARAH GOLDER, widow's third; fifths of the remainder to: JOHN GOLDER, HENRIETTA GOLDER, ARCHIBALD GOLDER, ROBERT GOLDER + GEORGE GOLDER.

JG#3/5: Mr. HENRY HAMMOND executor of THOMAS STINCHCOMB late of Anne Arundel Co. deceased. 7 April 1812. Sureties: THOMAS STINCHCOMB + NATHANIEL STINCHCOMB. SARAH STINCHCOMB, widow's third; sevenths of the remainder to: ANN KELLEY (?), THOMAS STINCHCOMB, HENRIETTA HAMMOND, HAMUTEL (?) BRIGHT, NATHAN STINCHCOMB, REBECCA PENNINGTON + WILLIAM STINCHCOMB.

JG#3/6: Mr. JOHN WATKINS administrator of ELIZABETH WATKINS late of Anne Arundel Co. deceased. Sureties: STEPHEN BEARD + CHARLES WATSON. Fourths of the remaining balance to: JOHN HALL, HESTER HALL, MARTHA HALL + HENRY HALL.

JG#3/6: Mr. CHARLES WORTHINGTON DORSEY administrator of THOMAS B. DORSEY (of CALEB). 21 April 1812. Sureties: CALEB DORSEY (of CALEB) + THOMAS B. DORSEY. SARAH DORSEY, widow's third; remainder of the balance to the deceased's son, CALEB DORSEY.

JG#3/6: Mrs. ELIZABETH WHITE + Mr. JOSEPH ATKINSON administrators of JOHN WHITE late of Anne Arundel Co. deceased. 10 June 1812. Sureties: JOSHUA YOUNG + JOSHUA EARP. ELIZABETH WHITE, widow's third; sevenths of the remainder to: JONATHAN WHITE, JOHN WHITE, JOSEPH WHITE, MARY ANN WHITE, MARGARET WHITE, GEORGE WHITE + ROBERT WHITE.

JG#3/7: Mr. JACOB FRANKLIN Jr. executor of MARY ATWELL late of Anne Arundel Co. deceased. 11 June 1812. Sureties: JOHN JOHNS + THOMAS FRANKLIN. Halves of the balance to ELIZABETH ZIGLER (niece) + MARY PHIPPS.

JG#3/7: Mr. ZACHARIAH DUVALL executor of ANN AILSWORTH late of Anne Arundel Co. deceased. 29 June 1812. Sureties: JAMES MACCUBBIN + RICHARD B. WATERS. Legatees include: MARY ANN MERRIKEN (dau); GRAFTON DUVALL (mention of ELIE DUVALL + ZACHARIAH MERRIKEN); MARGARET DUVALL: the children of MARY MERRIKEN: MARY MACCUBBIN, ELIZA MERRIKEN, RICHARD MERRIKEN, ZACHARIAH MERRIKEN + MARGARET MERRIKEN; + the children of HENRY DUVALL: GRAFTON DUVALL + ELIE DUVALL.

JG#3/8: Mr. ZACHARIAH DUVALL administrator of JONATHAN SELBY late of Anne Arundel Co. deceased. 1 July 1812. Sureties: LEWIS DUVALL + HENRY DUVALL. Thirds of the remaining balance to: JONATHAN SELBY, ROBERT SELBY + SUSANNAH SELBY.

JG#3/8: Mrs. SARAH JARVIS administratrix with will annexed of JOHN JARVIS late of Anne Arundel Co. deceased. 11 August 1812. Sureties: HENRY JOYCE + WILLIAM CROMWELL. SARAH JARVIS, widow's third; remainder of the balance to daughter SARAH JARVIS.

JG#3/9: Mrs. ELIZABETH WATERS administratrix of RICHARD WATERS late of Anne Arundel Co. deceased. 13 October 1812. Sureties: FRANCIS BELMEARE + JOHN EVEN (EBEN?) THOMAS. ELIZABETH WATERS, widow's third; sevenths of the remainder to: ELEANOR WOODFIELD, ZEBULON WATERS, ASA WATERS, ANN WATERS, ELIZABETH

WATERS, MARY ANN WATERS + RACHEL WATERS.

JG#3/9: Mrs. ELEANOR DAVIS administratrix of THOMAS DAVIS late of Anne Arundel Co. deceased. 13 October 1812. Sureties: THOMAS DAVIS + WILLIAM M. DAVIS. ELEANOR DAVIS, widow's third; sevenths of the balance to: SARAH MASON, ELIZABETH JONES, ELEANOR DAVIS, RUTHY DAVIS, THOMAS DAVIS, ORPHA DAVIS + WILLIAM M. DAVIS.

JG#3/10: Mr. ROBERT WARFIELD executor of LEVIN WARFIELD late of Anne Arundel Co. deceased. 24 November 1812. Sureties: BEALE WARFIELD + EDWARD WARFIELD. Sixths of the remaining balance to: EDWARD WARFIELD, ACHSAH BROWNING, ANN ETCHISON, RACHEL ETCHISON, MARY WARFIELD + SARAH WARFIELD.

JG#3/11: Mr. RICHARD CRANDALL administrator of THOMAS CRANDALL late of Anne Arundel Co. deceased. 9 December 1812. Sureties: JOHN WELCH + RICHARD FLEMING. Fifths of the remainder to: RICHARD CRANDALL, ANN RANDALL, WILOMENIA REYNOLDS, JANE MILLS + HENRY CRANDALL.

JG#3/11: Mrs. MARY YEALDHALL administratrix of JOSEPH YEALDHALL late of Anne Arundel Co. deceased. 14 January 1813. Sureties: GEORGE SANK + NIEL SANK. MARY YEALDHALL, widow's third; remainder of the balance to the deceased's son and daughters: HARRIET YEALDHALL, JOHN YEALDHALL + LOUISA YEALDHALL.

JG#3/12: Mr. EBENEZER THOMAS administrator with will annexed of DANIEL HOLLAWAY. 20 January 1813. Sureties: ELIJAH GRAY + BENJAMIN THOMAS. SARAH HOLLAWAY, widow's third; thirds of the remainder to NICHOLAS HOLLAWAY, RUTH TRON(?) + REBECCA TRON(?); legacy to the heirs of RUTH HANCOCK.

JG#3/12 + 13: Mr. JAMES TINGELL + Mr. JOHN FRANKLIN executors of JOHN FRANKLIN late of Anne Arundel Co. deceased. 13 July 1813. Sureties: BENJAMIN ALLEIN + CEPHAS WARD. ELIZABETH FRANKLIN, widow's third; thirds of the remainder to: SAMUEL FRANKLIN, ELIZABETH FRANKLIN + JOHN FRANKLIN.

JG#3/13: Messrs ROBERT JACOB + DANIEL P. JACOB administrators of SAMUEL JACOB late of Anne Arundel Co. deceased. 12 January 1814. Sureties: ROBERT DAVIS + JOHN WELCH (of BENJAMIN). Fourths of the net balance to: ROBERT JACOB, DANIEL P. JACOB, ARNOLD JACOB + SARAH JACOB (Mrs. _____ DAVIS).

JG#3/13: Mr. CALEB CRANE administrator of SAMUEL CRANE late of Anne Arundel Co. deceased. 26 February 1814. Sureties: NATHANIEL HANCOCK + PHILIP A. WATERS. Halves of the balance to: CALEB CRANE + JOHN CRANE.

JG#3/14: Mr. THOMAS HARRIS Jr. executor of JOHN GWINN Esq. late of Anne Arundel Co. deceased. 12 April 1814. Sureties: THOMAS HARRIS Sr. (Charles Co.) + JOSEPH HARRIS (St. Mary's Co.). Thirds of the net balance to: widow ELIZABETH GWINN, son JOHN GWINN + daughter ELIZABETH GWINN.

JG#3/14: Mrs. SARAH HUNTER (now SMITH) + JOHN HUNTER administrators of JAMES HUNTER late of Anne Arundel Co. deceased. 20 April 1814. Sureties: JOHN B. WEEMS + HENRY JOHNSON. SARAH HUNTER (now SMITH), widow's third; sevenths of the remainder to: JOHN HUNTER, MARY MILLER, ELEANOR MILLER, ELIZABETH ATKINSON, JAMES HUNTER, HENRY HUNTER + THOMAS HUNTER.

JG#3/15: Mrs. ANN WELLHAM administratrix of JOHN WELLHAM late of Anne Arundel Co. deceased. 26 April 1814. Sureties: WILLIAM WELLHAM + MORDECAI KELLY.

ANN WELLHAM, widow's third; sixths of the remainder to: WILLIAM WELLHAM, MARY
WELLHAM, WALLACE WELLHAM, JOHN WELLHAM, WILLIAM WELLHAM + NELSON WELLHAM.

JG#3/15: Dr. JOHN THOMAS SHAAFF executor of BENNETT LAKE (?) late of Anne
Arundel Co. deceased. 3 May 1814. Sureties: ARTHUR SHAAFF + BENJAMIN HARRI-
SON. Halves of the net balance to: NICHOLAS DARNALL + HENRY DARNALL.

JG#3/16: Dr. WILSON WATERS administrator of ARCHIBALD CHISHOLM late of Anne
Arundel Co. deceased. 11 May 1814. Sureties: ELIZABETH CHISHOLM + PHILIP W.
THERNEY. ELIZABETH CHISHOLM, widow's third; sixths of the remainder to: MARY
GIBBS, ELIZA COYLE, CHARLOTTE CHISHOLM, ELEANOR FITZHUGH, CATHARINE CHISHOLM
+ EMILY CHISHOLM.

JG#3/16: Mr. SOLOMON CLARIDGE administrator de bonis non with will annexed
of JAMES FLEHARTY. 15 July 1814. Sureties: HENRY HAMMOND + HENRY DUNBAR.
ELIZABETH CLARIDGE, widow's third; sevenths of the remainder to: ELIZABETH
JOINER, MARGARET HAYES, HOPKINS FLEHARTY, SUSANNA FLEHARTY, FREEBORN FLEHARTY,
MATTHEW FLEHARTY + RICHARD FLEHARTY.

JG#3/17: Messrs HORATIO RIDOUT + HENRY DUVALL executors of HELEN WEEDON late
of Anne Arundel Co. deceased. 9 August 1814. Sureties: SAMUEL RIDOUT + ZACH-
ARIAH DUVALL. Thirds of the remainder to: ELI WEEDON, CLOUDSBERRY WEEDON +
SAMUEL WEEDON.

JG#3/17: Mr. WILLIAM MERRIKIN administrator of CHARLES MERRIKIN late of Anne
Arundel Co. deceased. 11 January 1814. Sureties: ABEL CHENEY + THOMAS CHENEY.
Fifths of the net balance to WILLIAM MERRIKIN, JOSHUA MERRIKIN, JAMES MERRIKEN,
JOHN MERRIKEN + ELIZABETH MERRIKEN.

JG#3/18: Messrs LLOYD HAMMOND + DANIEL WARFIELD executors of SARAH MERI-
WETHER late of Anne Arundel Co. deceased. 23 March 1815. Sureties: NICHOLAS
MERIWETHER + GEORGE DORSEY. Legatees: MARY MERIWETHER, ELIZABETH MERIWETHER,
ELEANOR MERIWETHER + LOUISA MERIWETHER.

JG#3/18: Mr. JONATHAN BLOWERS administrator with will annexed of NICHOLAS
RAY late of Anne Arundel Co. deceased. 4 April 1815. Sureties: BRICE J.
GASSAWAY + JOSEPH RAY. ANN RAY (now BLOWERS), widow's third; fifths of the
remainder to JAMES RAY, WILLIAM ALFRED RAY, GEORGE WASHINGTON RAY, ASA RAY +
MARTHA ANN RAY.

JG#3/19: Mr. JACOB JONES administrator of JAMES KIRBY late of Anne Arundel
Co. deceased. 5 April 1815. Sureties: CHARLES FOX + THOMAS BUCKMAN. Sevenths
of the net balance to: JAMES KIRBY, JOHN KIRBY, WILLIAM KIRBY, NATHAN KIRBY,
ROBERT KIRBY, JACOB JONES (m. SARAH KIRBY) + the children of SILVANUS WARFIELD.

JG#3/19: Mr. THOMAS LANE administrator of HARRISON LANE late of Anne Arundel
Co. deceased. 10 June 1815. Sureties: RICHARD LANE + WILLIAM CHILDS. Fifths
of the remainder to: THOMAS LANE, JOSEPH LANE, WILEMINIA LANE, ELIZABETH LANE
+ RICHARD LANE.

JG#3/19: Mr. VACHEL BURGESS administrator of BENEDICT DORSEY late of Anne
Arundel Co. deceased. 12 June 1815. Sureties: GASSAWAY WATKINS + JOHN SPRIGG
BELT. Thirds of the remainder to: THOMAS DORSEY, ELIZABETH DORSEY + WASHING-
TON DORSEY.

JG#3/20: Mr. JOHN DUVALL administrator of JOHN RAWLINGS late of Anne Arundel
Co. deceased. 19 July 1815. Sureties: STEPHEN BEARD Sr. + WILLIAM DUVALL.
Eighths of the remainder to: MARY RAWLINGS (mother of the deceased), the chil-
dren of AARON RAWLINGS, STEPHEN BEARD (m. SUSANNA RAWLINGS), WILLIAM ATWELL
(m. ELIZABETH RAWLINGS), MOSES RAWLINGS, the children of MARY S___LEY + JOHN
DUVALL (m. REBECCA RAWLINGS).

JG#3/20: Mrs. SARAH FISH (now GAMBRILL) administratrix of RICHARD FISH late
of Anne Arundel Co. deceased. 26 October 1815. Sureties: JOSEPH GAMBRILL +
JOSHUA PUMPHREY. Halves of the net balance to: SARAH FISH (now GAMBRILL) +
HARRIET TUCKER.

JG#3/21: Mr. EDWARD BALDWIN executor of JAMES BALDWIN late of Anne Arundel
Co. deceased. 20 July 1815. Sureties: HENRY MAYNARDIER + BASIL BROWN. Ma-
jor heirs: ELLENDER BALDWIN + LIDIA SEWELL; equal shares of the remainder to:
ELIZABETH BRYAN, LYDIA BRYAN, SARAH BRYAN + JOHN BRYAN (grandson).

JG#3/22: Mrs. DINAH CHENEY (now BASFORD) administratrix of ABRAHAM CHENEY
late of Anne Arundel Co. deceased. 8 August 1815. Sureties: WILLIAM HOPKINS
+ DAVID SIMMONS. DINAH CHENEY (now BASFORD), widow's third; sevenths of the
remaining balance to: JOSEPH CHENEY, MARY CHENEY, BENJAMIN CHENEY, ABRAHAM
CHENEY, GASSAWAY CHENEY, SAMUEL CHENEY + ELIZABETH CHENEY.

JG#3/23: Mrs. ANN WELLHAM administratrix of WILLIAM WELLHAM late of Anne
Arundel Co. deceased. 8 August 1815. Sureties: WILLIAM WELLHAM + JOHN G.
CROMWELL. Sixths of the net balance to: ANN WELLHAM, WILLIAM WELLHAM, MARY
YEALDHALL, WALLACE WELLHAM, JOHN WELLHAM + NELSON WELLHAM.

JG#3/23: Mrs. SARAH BOONE (now JAMES) administratrix of JOHN BOONE late of
Anne Arundel Co. deceased. 1 September 1815. Sureties: EBENEZER THOMAS +
ROBERT GRIFFITH. SARAH BOONE (now JAMES), widow's third; sevenths of the re-
mainder to: BURLEY BOONE, ELIZA BOONE, HENRY BOONE, SARAH BOONE, MARGARET
BOONE, ANN BOONE + CHARLES BOONE.

JG#3/24: Mrs. SARAH JOYCE executrix of HENRY JOYCE late of Anne Arundel Co.
deceased. 7 September 1815. Sureties: JOHN _____ + DANIEL HALE. Fourths
of the remainder to: widow SARAH JOYCE, JOHN JOYCE, JOSHUA JOYCE + HENRY
JOYCE.

JG#3/25: Mr. GREENBURY LARK administrator of STEPHEN LARK late of Anne Arun-
del Co. deceased. 30 September 1815. Sureties: ROBERT WELCH + GEORGE ADAMS.
Half of the balance to: GREENBURY LARK; fifths of the remainder to: JANE
ROBINSON, THOMAS ROCKHOLD, CHARLES ROCKHOLD, ELIZABETH SWAIN + RICHARD ROBIN-
SON. [SARAH, widow of the deceased, is also deceased as of this date.]

JG#3/25 + 26: Mr. HENRY FOREMAN executor of NATHANIEL HANCOCK late of Anne
Arundel Co. deceased. 24 October 1815. Sureties: _____ FOREMAN + ELIJAH
GRAY. ELLENDER HANCOCK (now FOREMAN), widow's third; fifths + legacies of
varying value to: JOHN HANCOCK, ELIJAH HANCOCK, LANDY HANCOCK, ELIZABETH
HANCOCK + MARY HANCOCK.

JG#3/27: Mr. SAMUEL C. WATKINS executor of JAMES SIFTON late of Anne Arundel
Co. deceased. 28 October 1815. Sureties: _____ _____ + _____ S. HARWOOD.

Sixths of the remainder to: ELIZABETH SIFTON, THOMAS SIFTON, RICHARD SIFTON, CHARLES SIFTON, SAMUEL SIFTON + WILLIAM SIFTON.

JG#3/27 + 28: Mr. JOHN GARDINER executor of RICHARD GARDINER late of Anne Arundel Co. deceased. 2 November 1815. Sureties: HENRY DUVALL + HENRY HAM-MOND. Sixths of the remaining balance to: widow ANN GARDINER, JOHN GARDINER, CHARLES GARDINER, RICHARD GARDINER, JOSHUA MERRIKIN GARDINER + HENRY GARDINER.

JG#3/28: Mr. JOHN NORMAN administrator of RICHARD NORMAN late of Anne Arundel Co. deceased. 11 November 1815. Sureties: FRANCIS WELCH + FREDERICK GOOTEE. Thirds of the remaining balance to: SARAH NORMAN (now PARROTT), JANE NORMAN + NICHOLAS NORMAN.

JG#3/29: Mr. JOHN ATWELL executor of FRANCIS SUMBERLAND late of Anne Arundel Co. deceased. 6 November 1815. Sureties: HENRY DUNBAR + RICHARD SHEPHERD. Legacy to MARY MARSHALL; MARY SUMBERLAND, widow's third; halves of the remainder to: SARAH SUMBERLAND + REBECCA SUMBERLAND.

JG#3/29: Messrs JOSEPH WILLIAMS + THOMAS WILLIAMS administrators of JOSEPH WILLIAMS. 11 November 1815. Sureties: JAMES SANDERS + JOHN STOCKETT. Sixths of the net balance to: JOHN BALL (grandson), THOMAS WILLIAMS, JOSEPH WILLIAMS, SARAH KNIGHTON, ANN BIRD + MARY LEDNUM.

JG#3/30: Mr. THOMAS NORRIS executor of MARY HARRISON late of Anne Arundel Co. deceased. 14 November 1815. Sureties: BENJAMIN WINTERSON + HENRY CRANDALL. Fourths of the net balance to: THOMAS NORRIS, SARAH NORRIS, MARY DENNY (widow of THOMAS D. DENNY) + ELEANOR SANDS (w/o JOHN SANDS).

JG#3/30: Mr. WILLIAM WILLSON administrator of ANN WILLSON late of Anne Arundel Co. deceased. 13 December 1815. Sureties: ELISHA BROWN + WILLIAM BROWN. Sixths of the net balance to: WILLIAM WILLSON, SUSANNA WILLSON, ALETHEA WILL-SON, HENRY WILLSON, FIELDER WILLSON + OLIVER WILLSON.

JG#3/31: Mr. THOMAS HARRIS administrator of JOHN GWINN late of Anne Arundel Co. deceased. 9 February 1816. Sureties: THOMAS HARRIS Sr. (Charles Co.) + JOSEPH HARRIS (St. Mary's Co.). ELIZABETH GWINN, widow's third; son JOHN GWINN + daughter ELIZABETH GWINN (now STODDERT).

JG#3/31: Mr. HENRY C. DRURY administrator of JERNINGHAM DRURY late of Anne Arundel Co. deceased. 20 February 1816. Sureties: THOMAS SELLMAN + JOSEPH C. DRURY. Sevenths of the remainder to: MARGARET DRURY (mother), HENRY C. DRURY, CHARLES DRURY, SAMUEL DRURY, JOSEPH C. DRURY, MARY SIMMONS + ELIZABETH WELCH.

JG#3/32: Mr. THOMAS STALLINGS administrator of JOHN POOLE late of Anne Arundel Co. deceased. 2 April 1816. Sureties: LEONARY GARY + ALEXANDER MITCHELL. Halves of the net balance to: VERLINDA POOLE, widow; THOMAS STALLINGS.

JG#3/32: Mr. WILLIAM URQUHART administrator of BENJAMIN DEFORD late of Anne Arundel Co. deceased. 8 April 1816. Sureties: GASSAWAY WATKINS + HENRY C. DRURY. ANN DEFORD, widow's third; thirds of the remainder to: MARIA DEFORD (w/o WILLIAM URQUHART), BENJAMIN DEFORD + CHARLOTTE DEFORD.

JG#3/33: Mrs. MARGARET PUMPHREY administratrix of COCKEY PUMPHREY late of Anne Arundel Co. deceased. 15 April 1816. Sureties: JOHN CROMWELL + JACOB

WILLIAMS. MARGARET PUMPHREY, widow's third; fifths of the net balance to: RACHEL PUMPHREY, CORDELIA PUMPHREY, RHOADY PUMPHREY, ZACHIAS PUMPHREY + WILLIAM PUMPHREY.

JG#3/34: Mrs. ELIZABETH ROBINSON + Mr. CHARLES ROBINSON administrators of THOMAS ROBINSON late of Anne Arundel Co. deceased. 22 April 1816. Sureties: ABNER LINTHICUM + ZACHARIAH DUVALL. ELIZABETH ROBINSON, widow's third; fifths of the remainder to: BENJAMIN ROBINSON, ANN ROBINSON (now LINTHICUM), JAMES ROBINSON, CHARLES ROBINSON + THOMAS ROBINSON.

JG#3/34: Mr. THOMAS HARRIS administrator of JOHN GWINN Esq. late of Anne Arundel Co. deceased. 30 April 1816. No sureties indicated. Thirds of the net balance to: ELIZABETH GWINN, widow; son JOHN GWINN; daughter ELIZABETH GWINN (now STODDERT).

JG#3/35: Mr. JOHN WELCH executor of CHARLES WELCH late of Anne Arundel Co. deceased. 13 May 1816. Sureties: SAMUEL WELCH + SINGLETON WELCH. SARAH WELCH, widow's third; residue to: JOHN WARREN WELCH, HENRY JAMES WELCH, ANN WELCH, REASON WELCH, WALTER WELCH, HANNAH HOLLAND + JOHN WELCH.

JG#3/36: Mr. JOHN HILTON administrator with will annexed of ELISHA HALL late of Anne Arundel Co. deceased. 1 June 1816. Sureties: JOHN CROSS + GEORGE WATTS. Thirds of the net balance to: HENRY HALL, ELIZA HALL + JANE HALL.

JG#3/36: Mrs. HANNAH OWINGS administratrix of JESSE OWINGS late of Anne Arundel Co. deceased. 11 June 1816. Sureties: HENRY C. GAITHER (Montgomery Co.) + EPHRAIM GAITHER (also Montgomery Co.). HANNAH OWINGS, widow's third; thirds of the remainder to: THOMAS OWINGS, ELIZABETH HOOD OWINGS + JOHN HOOD OWINGS.

JG#3/37: Mr. GEORGE WATTS administrator of PHILIP H. WATTS late of Anne Arundel Co. deceased. 24 June 1816. Sureties: ROBERT WELCH + GREENBURY LARK. Widow SARAH WATTS; remainder to children: REBECCA WATTS, PHILIP KEY WATTS + ELIZA WATTS.

JG#3/37: Mr. EDWARD BLUNT administrator of JAMES MCQUILLAIN late of Anne Arundel Co. deceased. 23 June 1816. Sureties: FIELDER B. SMITH + JAMES LARIMORE. Thirds of the net balance to: widow ELIZABETH MCQUILLAIN, daughter ELIZA MCQUILLAIN + daughter MARY MCQUILLAIN.

JG#3/38: Mrs. ELIZABETH ALLEIN + Mr. THOMAS TONGUE Jr. executors of BENJAMIN ALLEIN late of Anne Arundel Co. deceased. 8 July 1816. Sureties: THOMAS TONGUE Sr. + JAMES OWENS. ELIZABETH ALLEIN, widow's third; residue of the balance to: MARY ANN ALLEIN, ELIZABETH ALLEIN, HARRIET ALLEIN, JOSEPH ALLEIN, JULIET ALLEIN, THOMAS ALLEIN, ANN ALLEIN, RACHEL ALLEIN + BENJAMIN ALLEIN.

JG#3/39: Dr. JOHN H. BROWN guardian to JULIANA BROWN et al. of Anne Arundel Co. 10 July 1816. Eighths of the net balance to: JOHN H. BROWN, ELIZABETH BROWN (now HAMMOND), HENRY H. BROWN, JULIANA BROWN, WILLIAM BROWN, REZIN BROWN, CLARISSA BROWN + PHILIP BROWN.

JG#3/39 + 40: Mrs. SARAH BROWN administratrix of JOHN R. BROWN late of Anne Arundel Co. deceased. 30 July 1816. Sureties: BRICE J. GASSAWAY + SAMUEL BROWN Jr. SARAH BROWN, widow's third; ninths of the remainder to: LOUISA BROWN, MARY ANN BROWN, HENRY G. BROWN, ELIZA BROWN, ACHSAH BROWN, ELIZABETH BROWN, SAMUEL BROWN, KITTY ANN BROWN + JOHN R. BROWN.

JG#3/40: Mrs. MARY ANN BOONE administratrix of JAMES BOONE late of Anne Arundel Co. deceased. 8 August 1816. Sureties: CHARLES PETTIBONE + NICHOLAS J. WATKINS. MARY ANN BOONE, widow's third; fourths of the remainder to: ANN E. BOONE, MARGARET S. BOONE, ELIZABETH BOONE + JOHN S. BOONE.

JG#3/41: Mr. JOHN IRELAND DORSEY administrator of VACHEL DORSEY late of Anne Arundel Co. deceased; the deceased son of NATHAN DORSEY. 13 August 1816. Sureties: SAMUEL HOWARD + JAMES I. DORSEY. Tenths of the net balance to: ELIZABETH DORSEY (now HALL), JOHN IRELAND DORSEY, JAMES IRELAND DORSEY, LOUISA DORSEY, ANDREW DORSEY, SAMUEL DORSEY, DANIEL HORATIO DORSEY, EZEKIEL DORSEY, SARAH ANN DORSEY + REBECCA DORSEY.

JG#3/42: Mr. WILLIAM RANDALL (of Baltimore Co.) administrator of PHILIP PEARCE late of Anne Arundel Co. deceased. 13 August 1816. Sureties: ABNER LINTHICUM + GEORGE WRIGHT. Eighths of the net balance to: LILLY DISNEY, POLLY RANDALL, SALLY PEARCE, RACHEL PEARCE, GEORGE PEARCE, WILLIAM PEARCE, the heirs of ABRAHAM PEARCE + JOHN PEARCE; five shillings to MATILDA PEARCE.

JG#3/43: Mr. JAMES TUCKER + Mr. WILLIAM O'HARA administrators with will annexed of WILLIAM DEALE late of Anne Arundel Co. deceased. 27 August 1816. Sureties: BENJAMIN WINTERSON + JOSEPH NORRIS. Fourths of the net balance to: MARTIN DEALE, ANN TUCKER, ELIZABETH DEALE + WILLIAM DEALE. The above balance reflects the subtraction of a legacy bequeathed to negroes WILLIAM + MARIA, who are to be manumitted on Christmas Day 1816.

JG#3/43: Mr. WILLIAM P. HARDISTY administrator of JAMES WHITTINGTON late of Anne Arundel Co. deceased. 27 August 1816. Sureties: JOHN WARD + SAMUEL PEACO. Thirds of the net balance to: widow MARY WHITTINGTON, ELIZABETH WHITTINGTON (w/o JOHN WARD) + ELEANOR WHITTINGTON (w/o WILLIAM P. HARDISTY).

JG#3/44: Mr. WILLIAM DUVALL administrator of FRANCIS TUCKER late of Anne Arundel Co. deceased. 30 August 1816. Sureties: GIDEON WHITE + SETH SWEETSER. Eighths of the net balance to: WILLIAM TUCKER, ABEL TUCKER, NANCY TUCKER, JAMES TUCKER, ENOCH TUCKER, ENOCH TUCKER, SAMUEL TUCKER, JOSEPH TUCKER + SELLY TUCKER.

JG#3/44: Mrs. ELIZABETH JOHNSON + Mr. DAVID ROBINSON administrators of JOSHUA JOHNSON late of Anne Arundel Co. deceased. 4 September 1816. Sureties: CHARLES ROBINSON + ZACHARIAH JOHNSON. ELIZABETH JOHNSON, widow's third; sevenths of the remainder to: BETTY JOHNSON (now ROBINSON), PATIENCE JOHNSON (now ROBINSON), AREA JOHNSON, RACHEL JOHNSON, CHRISTOPHER JOHNSON, JOSHUA JOHNSON + ELIZABETH JOHNSON.

JG#3/45: Mr. EDWARD CHAMBERS administrator of AMOS CHAMBERS late of Anne Arundel Co. deceased. 19 September 1816. Sureties: ELI MOLESWORTH + REZIN LOR____. ACHSAH CHAMBERS, widow's third; sevenths of the remainder to: EDWARD CHAMBERS, SENATHA CHAMBERS (now MOLESWORTH), AMOS CHAMBERS, AMELIA CHAMBERS (now MOLESWORTH), NANCY CHAMBERS (now SELLMAN), JOSHUA CHAMBERS + THOMAS CHAMBERS.

JG#3/45: Mr. BURLEY G. BOONE, guardian of the heirs of JOHN BOONE (of JOHN), of Anne Arundel Co. 19 October 1816. Eighths of the balance to: BURLEY G. BOONE, ELIZA BOONE, JOHN H. D. BOONE, SARAH BOONE, MARGARET BOONE, ANN BOONE, CHARLES BOONE + ELIZABETH BOONE.

JG#3/46: Mr. HOWARD ELLIOTT surviving administrator of LEANDER JOHNSON late of

Anne Arundel Co. deceased. 14 November 1816. Sureties: LLOYD JOHNSON + ZACHARIAH DUVALL. SARAH JOHNSON (now the w/o HOWARD ELLIOTT), widow's third; sixths of the remainder to: CHARLOTTE JOHNSON (now HALL), HORATIO JOHNSON, GRAFTON JOHNSON, HARRIET JOHNSON, MAHALA JOHNSON + GARRET JOHNSON.

JG#3/46: Mr. CHARLES WATERS administrator of NATHAN WILLIAMS late of Anne Arundel Co. deceased. 14 November 1816. Sureties: MATTHIAS HAMMOND + BARUCH FOWLER. Fifths of the net balance to: DELILAH WILLIAMS (now HALL), JESSE WILLIAMS, CHARLOTTE WILLIAMS (now CROMWELL), ALLISON WILLIAMS + ELIZABETH WILLIAMS.

JG#3/47: Mr. FERDINANDO TYDINGS administrator of JOHN TYDINGS late of Anne Arundel Co. deceased. 20 November 1816. Sureties: ROBERT WELCH (of BENJAMIN) + JOHN HUNTER. Tenths of the remainder to: FERDINANDO TYDINGS, SAMUEL TYDINGS, HORATIO TYDINGS, RICHARD TYDINGS, MARY ANN BRIGHT, SOPHIA SKIDMORE, CATHERINE TYDINGS, ELIZABETH PURDY, ANN TYDINGS + MARGARET WATKINS.

JG#3/47: Mrs. RISPAH HOWARD administratrix of BRICE HOWARD late of Anne Arundel Co. deceased. 26 November 1816. Sureties: FRANCIS MERCER + HORATIO HOBBS. RISPAH HOWARD, widow's third; eighths of the remainder to: ELEANOR LOUISA HOBBS, MARY ANN HOBBS, THOMAS HOWARD, BRICE HOWARD, WILLIAM HOWARD, SARAH HOWARD, GUSTAVUS HOWARD + ROBERT HOWARD.

JG#3/48: Mr. HENRY JONES administrator of WILLIAM TILLARD late of Anne Arundel Co. deceased. 19 December 1816. Sureties: THOMAS ELLIOTT + BENJAMIN ELLIOTT. Thirds of the net balance to: JOHN TILLARD, WILLIAM TILLARD + MARTHA TILLARD (now JONES).

JG#3/48: Mr. HENRY C. DRURY administrator of CHARLES DRURY (of WILLIAM) late of Anne Arundel Co. deceased. 20 December 1816. Sureties: GASSAWAY WATKINS + THOMAS ELLIOTT. MARGARET DRURY, widow's third; tenths of the remainder to: MARY DRURY (now BIRKHEAD), ELIZABETH DRURY (now GREEN), HARRIET DRURY, WILLIAM DRURY, THOMAS DRURY, SARAH DRURY, JOHN DRURY, ETHELDA DRURY, MARY DRURY + CHARLES DRURY.

JG#3/49: Mr. FRANCIS HANCOCK administrator of STEPHEN HANCOCK late of Anne Arundel Co. deceased. 28 December 1816. Sureties: ZACHARIAH CROMWELL + HENRY FOREMAN. Legatees: FRANCIS HANCOCK, the heirs of ANN THOMAS, RHODA HANCOCK (now STEWART), ABRAHAM HANCOCK + MARY ANN WILLIAMS (d/o SARAH WILLIAMS).

JG#3/49: Mr. RICHARD G. HUTTON administrator of ANN DEFORD late of Anne Arundel Co. deceased. 31 January 1817. Sureties: HENRY C. DRURY + SAMUEL DRURY. Halves of the balance to: BENJAMIN DEFORD + CHARLOTTE DEFORD.

JG#3/49: Mr. BENJAMIN WELCH executor of ROBERT WELCH (of JOHN?) late of Anne Arundel Co. deceased. 3 March 1817. Sureties: JOSEPH MCCENEY + ROBERT WELCH (of BENJAMIN). PRISCILLA WELCH, widow's third; sixths of the balance to: BENJAMIN WELCH, ROBERT WELCH, ELEANOR MERRIKIN (granddaughter), ROBERT WELCH (of ROBERT), ELIZABETH ADAMS + SUSANNA WELCH.

JG#3/50: Mr. CHARLES ROBINSON administrator of CHARLES BURTON late of Anne Arundel Co. deceased. 6 March 1817. Sureties: ZACHARIAH JOHNSON + LLOYD JOHNSON. Eighths of the net balance to: ANN JOHNSON, SARAH REYNOLD, ELIZABETH GRAY, NICHOLAS JOHNSON, BAKER JOHNSON, MARK JOHNSON, JOSEPH JOHNSON + ANN JOHNSON.

JG#3/50: Mr. THOMAS SELLMAN administrator of JOHN WILLSON COMPTON late of
Anne Arundel Co. deceased. 19 March 1817. Sureties: LEONARD SELLMAN + JOHN
IGLEHART. SUSANNA COMPTON, widow's third; fourths of the balance to: EVELINA
COMPTON, JULIA ANN COMPTON, WILLSON COMPTON + MARY COMPTON.

JG#3/51: GARRARD(?) DUVALL administrator with the will annexed of JESSE DU-
VALL late of Anne Arundel Co. deceased. 2 April 1817. Sureties: THOMAS MAC-
GILL + RICHARD PEARCE. Major heirs: BASIL DUVALL, MARGARET DUVALL, EDWARD DU-
VALL, MARY DUVALL + SAMUEL DUVALL; other legatees: WILLIAM DUVALL, MAREEN DU-
VALL, ELISHA DUVALL, ELIZABETH TALBOTT + LEONARD DUVALL.

JG#3/51: Mr. BENJAMIN RAYNER administrator of SAMUEL RAYNER late of Anne Arun-
del Co. deceased. 8 April 1817. Sureties: RICHARD CROMWELL + OLIVER CROMWELL.
Fourths of the net balance to: HARRIET MITCHELL, RIZDON RAYNER, RACHEL RAYNER +
NELSON RAYNER.

JG#3/53: Mrs. NANCY SWORMSTADT (now SEWELL) administratrix of NICHOLAS SWORM-
STADT late of Anne Arundel Co. deceased. 25 June 1817. Sureties: PHILIP HAM-
MOND + ANDREW HAMMOND. NANCY SWORMSTEADT (now SEWELL), widow's third; eighths
of the remainder to: MARY SWORMSTADT (now WILLAMAN?), SARAH SWORMSTADT (now
STANSBURY), LEVI SWORMSTADT, SAMUEL SWORMSTADT, LUTHER SWORMSTADT, SIDNEY SWORM-
STADT, MATILDA SWORMSTADT + LORENZO SWORMSTADT.

JG#3/54: Mr. WEST BURGESS administrator of SAMUEL WEST BURGESS late of Anne
Arundel Co. deceased. 30 June 1817. Sureties: GEORGE FOX + DAVID FUNDER-
BOURGH. Legatees: ELIZABETH WARFIELD BURGESS, RICHARD BURGESS + MARGARET ANN
BURGESS.

JG#3/54: Mr. CHARLES ROBINSON administrator of ONEAL JOHNSON late of Anne Arun-
del Co. deceased. 17 July 1817. Sureties: DAVID ROBINSON + ZACHARIAH JOHNSON.
ANN JOHNSON (now w/o WILLIAM SMITH), widow's third; remainder of the balance to:
ARCHIBALD JOHNSON.

JG#3/55: Mrs. MARY YEALDHALL (now HAWKINS) administratrix of AQUILA YEALD-
HALL late of Anne Arundel Co. deceased. 19 April 1817. Sureties: JOHN G.
CROMWELL + WILLIAM WELLHAM. MARY YEALDHALL (now HAWKINS), widow's third;
fourths of the net balance to: ANN ELIZA YEALDHALL, ELIJAH YEALDHALL, HENRI-
ETTA YEALDHALL + _____ YEALDHALL.

JG#3/55: Mr. MORDECAI STEWART surviving executor of NATHANIEL ALWELL late of
Anne Arundel Co. deceased. 27 August 1817. Sureties: FRANCIS HANCOCK + ROBERT
MARSHALL. ANN ALWELL, widow's third; fourths of the remainder to: ELIZA AL-
WELL, RHODA ALWELL, ANN ALWELL + WESLEY ALWELL.

JG#3/56: Mr. PHILIP DARNALL administrator of ELIZABETH DARNALL late of Anne
Arundel Co. deceased. 3 September 1817. Sureties: REZIN ESTEP + RICHARD G.
HUTTON. Thirds of the remaining balance to: the heirs of FRANCIS DARNALL, who
are five in number and unnamed; the heirs of HENRY DARNALL, who are four in
number and unnamed; + PHILIP DARNALL.

JG#3/56: Mrs. SARAH GOODWIN administratrix de bonis non of RICHARD GOODWIN
late of Anne Arundel Co. deceased. 8 September 1817. Sureties: NICHOLAS
BREWER + JOHN BREWER. SARAH GOODWIN, widow's third; the remainder to RICHARD
RAWLINGS GOODWIN.

JG#3/56: Mr. CHARLES ROBINSON administrator of JOHN BURTON late of Anne

Anne Arundel Co. deceased. 12 September 1817. Sureties: LLOYD JOHNSON + DAVID ROBINSON. Eighths of the remaining balance to: ANN BURTON (now BROWN), SARAH BURTON (now JOHNSON), JOHN BURTON, MARY BURTON, PATSY BURTON, LOUISA BURTON, WILLIAM BURTON + EDMOND BURTON.

JG#3/57: Mr. NICHOLAS WORTHINGTON (of THOMAS) executor of MARY CRAYCROFT late of Anne Arundel Co. deceased. 17 September 1817. Sureties: GEORGE CRAYCROFT + WILLIAM WELSEY. Sixths of the remaining balance to: GERARD CRAY-CROFT (plus a large legacy), ANN CRAYCROFT (plus a large legacy), BENJAMIN CRAYCROFT, the heirs of ELIZABETH DUVALL, MARGARET WEEMS + JOHN THOMPSON.

JG#3/58: Mr. ABNER LINTHICUM administrator of JOHN MARKEL late of Anne Arun-del Co. deceased. 19 September 1817. Sureties: SAMUEL YEALDHALL + THOMAS BENSON. ANN MARKEL, widow's third; the remainder of the balance to STEPHEN MARKEL.

JG#3/58: Mr. GERARD A.(?) SNOWDEN + Mr. RICHARD SNOWDEN administrators of JOHN SNOWDEN late of Anne Arundel Co. deceased. 24 September 1817. Sureties: RICHARD RIDGELY + JOHN B. WEEMS. RACHEL SNOWDEN, widow's third; sevenths of the remainder to: RICHARD P. SNOWDEN, GERARD A. (or H.) SNOWDEN, ANN MARIA SNOWDEN (w/o JOSEPH R. HOPKINS), JOHN T. SNOWDEN, MARGARET H. SNOWDEN, REZIN A.(?) SNOWDEN + RACHEL SNOWDEN.

JG#3/59: Mrs. MARY HOLLIDAY administratrix of JOHN HOLLIDAY late of Anne Arundel Co. deceased. 16 October 1817. Sureties: JOSEPH N. STOCKETT + THOMAS HOLLIDAY, MARY HOLLIDAY, widow's third; fourths of the remainder to: THOMAS HOLLIDAY, RICHARD G. HOLLIDAY, JOHN HOLLIDAY + NICHOLAS HOLLIDAY.

JG#3/59: Mr. SAMUEL DRURY Sr. administrator de bonis non with the will an-nexed of PLUMMER IJAMS late of Anne Arundel Co. deceased. 23 October 1817. Sureties: LEONARD GARY + WILLIAM SMITH. Thirds of the remaining balance to: the heirs of PLUMMER IJAMS (of PLUMMER), who are five in number and unnamed; WILLIAM DRURY Sr. (m. ELIZABETH IJAMS); + SAMUEL DRURY Sr. (m. ANN IJAMS).

JG#3/60: Mr. BENJAMIN WELLS Jr. surviving executor of BENJAMIN WELLS Sr. late of Anne Arundel Co. deceased. 29 October 1817. Sureties: BENJAMIN WIN-TERSON + THOMAS ATWELL. Thirds of the remainder to: widow ELIZABETH WELLS, BENJAMIN WELLS Jr. + ONERAH (?) WELLS (w/o BENJAMIN ATWELL).

JG#3/60: Mr. HORATIO RIDOUT administrator with will annexed of MARY WEEMS late of Anne Arundel Co. deceased. 4 November 1817. Sureties: SAMUEL RIDOUT + JOHN RIDOUT. Thirds of the remaining balance to: ANN RIDOUT, WILLIAM WEEMS + MARY D. WEEMS "in her own right and as the surviving legatee of MAR-GARET H. WEEMS deceased."

JG#3/61: Mrs. ELEANOR CHILDS administratrix of JOSEPH CHILDS late of Anne Arundel Co. deceased. 25 November 1817. Sureties: HENRY CHILDS + JERNING-HAM DRURY. Sixths of the balance to the deceased's children: JONATHAN CHILDS, NATHAN S. CHILDS, JULIANA CHILDS, WILLIAM CHILDS, MARY CHILDS + HENRY LLOYD CHILDS.

JG#3/62: Mr. JOHN NICHOLSON Jr. executor of JOHN NICHOLSON Sr. late of Anne Arundel Co. deceased. 7 January 1818. Sureties: JOHN STOCKETT + SOLOMON GROVES. MARY NICHOLSON, widow's third; fourths of the remaining balance to: JOHN NICHOLSON, NICHOLAS NICHOLSON, JOSEPH NICHOLSON + JAMES NICHOLSON.

JG#3/63: Mr. JOSEPH NEWTON BREWER administrator with will annexed of SARAH
BIRKHEAD late of Anne Arundel Co. deceased. 21 January 1818. Sureties: SAM-
UEL BIRKHEAD + DAVID RIDGELY. Legacies of varying value to: NEHEMIAH BIRKHEAD
III, MARY BREWER, SARAH ELEANOR DOWELL, ELIZABETH DOWELL, SARAH RICHARDSON
BIRKHEAD, NEHEMIAH RICHARDSON BIRKHEAD + SARAH ANN BREWER.

JG#3/64: Mr. JOSEPH NEWTON BREWER executor of SARAH R. BIRKHEAD late of
Anne Arundel Co. deceased. 21 January 1818. Sureties: WILLIAM BREWER +
JOHN BREWER. Legacies of varying value to: REBECCA BREWER (d/o JOSEPH N.
BREWER), JOHN + JOSEPH BREWER (of JOSEPH N.), MARY JANE + ELIZABETH BREWER
(of JOSEPH N.), SARAH ANN BREWER (of JOSEPH N.), NEHEMIAH RICHARDSON BIRKHEAD
(of NEHEMIAH III), MARY BIRKHEAD (w/o NEHEMIAH BIRKHEAD III), MARY BREWER +
REBECCA BREWER.

JG#3/65: Mrs. MARY ARMIGER (now HUTTON) + Mr. RICHARD G. HUTTON administra-
tors with will annexed of JOHN ARMIGER late of Anne Arundel Co. deceased. 31
January 1818. Sureties: HENRY C. DRURY + PHILIP DARNALL. MARY ARMIGER,
widow's third; tenths of the remaining balance to: SAMUEL ARMIGER, BENJAMIN
ARMIGER, THOMAS ARMIGER, WILLIAM ARMIGER, RICHARD ARMIGER, MARY ARMIGER (now
CARR), SARAH ANN ARMIGER, SUSANNAH ARMIGER, JOHN FRANCIS ARMIGER + RACHEL
ARMIGER.

JG#3/66: Mr. JAMES HOOD (of JOHN) administrator with the will annexed of
JOHN HOOD late of Anne Arundel Co. deceased. 13 February 1818; Sureties:
WILLIAM SHIPLEY, RICHARD DORSEY + THOMAS HOOD Sr. Major legatee: JOHN MERRI-
WEATHER (of ELIZABETH MERRIWEATHER); sixths of the remainder to: JAMES HOOD
(of JOHN), BENJAMIN HOOD, THOMAS HOOD, SARAH WORTHINGTON, ELIZABETH MERRI-
WEATHER + HANNAH OWINGS.

JG#3/66: Mrs. ARTRIDGE KNIGHTON + Mr. WILLIAM O'HARA administrators of SAM-
UEL KNIGHTON late of Anne Arundel Co. deceased. 28 January 1818. Sureties:
JOSEPH GWINN + ROBERT THOMAS. ARTRIDGE KNIGHTON, widow's third; sevenths of
the remainder to: SAMUEL KNIGHTON, NICHOLAS KNIGHTON, JOHN KNIGHTON, RICHARD
KNIGHTON, THOMAS KNIGHTON, SARAH KNIGHTON + JANE KNIGHTON.

JG#3/67: Mr. THOMAS SELLMAN executor of ELIZABETH SELBY late of Anne Arundel Co. deceased. 31 March 1818. Sureties: JOHN CROSS + JAMES IGLEHART.
More or less equal shares to: CHARLES PETTIBONE, JEMIMA CROSS, ELIZABETH
SELBY, HARRIET SELBY, MARIA SELBY + JOHN SELBY. [Mention is made of a legacy
devised to CHARLES PETTIBONE who, apparently, is deceased.]

JG#3/67: Mr. THOMAS FRANKLIN administrator de bonis non of FERDINANDO BATTEE
late of Anne Arundel Co. deceased. 3 April 1818. Sureties: JAMES DEALE +
BENJAMIN FRANKLIN. Half of the balance to ELIZABETH BATTEE; fourths of the
remainder to: SAMUEL FRANKLIN, ANN FRANKLIN, BENJAMIN FRANKLIN + THOMAS
FRANKLIN.

JG#3/68: JAMES MACCUBBIN Esq. administrator of FREDERICK MACCUBBIN late of
Anne Arundel Co. deceased. 7 April 1818. Sureties: GEORGE MACCUBBIN + NICHO-
LAS BREWER. MARY MACCUBBIN, widow's third; fourths of the remainder to: JU-
LIAN E. MACCUBBIN, ELEANOR M. MACCUBBIN, CAROLINE L. MACCUBBIN + MARTHA R.
MACCUBBIN.

JG#3/69: Messrs STEPHEN BEARD Jr. + JOHN BEARD executors of STEPHEN BEARD
Sr. late of Anne Arundel Co. deceased. 8 Mary 1818. Sureties: JOSHUA LIN-
THICUM + THOMAS DAVIS. SUSANNA BEARD, widow's third; sevenths of the bal-

ance to: STEPHEN BEARD (also slaves), JOHN BEARD (also slaves), SUSANNA BEARD (now HULMS?), ELIZABETH BEARD (now LINTHICUM), MARY BEARD (now DAVIS), REBECCA BEARD (now LUSBY) + JOHN STOCKETT.

JG#3/69: Mr. FRANCIS HANCOCK administrator de bonis non of HEZEKIAH ROBIN-SON late of Anne Arundel Co. deceased. 5 May 1818. Sureties: MORDECAI STEW-ART + BENJAMIN THOMAS. ELEANOR ROBINSON, widow's third; remainder of the balance to RHOADY ROBINSON (now CHARD).

JG#3/69: Mr. STEPHEN BEARD (of STEPHEN) administrator of JOHN STOCKETT late of Anne Arundel Co. deceased. 15 May 1818. Sureties: CHARLES WATSON + JOHN BEARD. Fifths of the remaining balance to: STEPHEN BEARD, JOHN BEARD, ELIZA-BETH LINTHICUM, MARY DAVIS, REBECCA LUSBY.

JG#3/70: Mr. JOHN BLACK administrator of CHRISTOPHER BLACK late of Anne Arun-del Co. deceased. 2 June 1818. Sureties: JOSHUA BLACK + WILLIAM BLACK Sr. ELIZABETH BLACK, widow's third; eighths of the remainder to the deceased's chil-dren: JOSHUA BLACK, WILLIAM BLACK, JOHN BLACK, CHRISTOPHER BLACK, REBECCA BLACK, JAMES BLACK, ELIZABETH BLACK + ELI A. BLACK.

JG#3/71: Mr. GEORGE SHAW surviving administrator of JOHN V. WEYLIE late of Anne Arundel Co. deceased. 6 June 1818. Sureties: JOHN SHAW + JAMES SHAW. MARTHA J. WEYLIE, widow's third; halves of the remainder to: JAMES ANDERSON, who m. the deceased's sister, ELEANOR WEYLIE; + ANN WEYLIE, deceased's sister.

JG#3/71: Mrs. HANNAH HOPKINS administratrix of SAMUEL HOPKINS late of Anne Arundel Co. deceased. 10 June 1818. Sureties: JOHN COWMAN + SAMUEL S. HOP-KINS. HANNAH HOPKINS, widow's third; elevenths of the remainder to: JOSEPH J. HOPKINS, JOHN HOPKINS, ELIZA HOPKINS, SARAH ? HOPKINS, HANNAH HOPKINS, SAMUEL HOPKINS, MAHLON HOPKINS, PHILIP HOPKINS, MARGARET HOPKINS, GERRARD HOPKINS + MARY HOPKINS.

JG#3/72: Mr. SAMUEL PARROTT executor of JOHN PARROTT late of Anne Arundel Co. deceased. 10 June 1818. Sureties: JOHN HOLLIDAY Sr.(?) + EDWARD HOLLAND. Fifths of the remainder to: JOHN PARROTT, GEORGE PARROTT, RICHARD PARROTT, ABRAHAM PARROTT + MARY PARROTT.

JG#3/72: Messrs JOHN MILLER + PETER MILLER executors of MARGARET SHEPPARD late of Anne Arundel Co. deceased. 19 June 1818. Sureties: JAMES HUNTER + GEORGE SCHWARD(?). Legacies: JOHN SHEPPARD + MARGARET SCHWARD(?); halves of the remainder to: MARY SHEPPARD + ELIZABETH SHEPPARD.

JG#3/73: Messrs JAMES TUCKER + WILLIAM O'HARA administrators with will an-nexed of WILLIAM DEALE late of Anne Arundel Co. deceased. 11 July 1818. Sureties: BENJAMIN WINTERSON + JOSEPH NORRIS. Legacy to negroes WILLIAM + MARIA, who are to be freed on Christmas Day, 1816; legacies of varying value to: MARTIN DEALE, ANN TUCKER, ELIZABETH DEALE + WILLIAM DEALE.

JG#3/74: Mr. HENRY HODGES administrator of DAVID ROWLES late of Anne Arundel Co. deceased. 27 July 1818. Sureties: JOHN G. CROMWELL + FRANCIS LAWRENCE. TEMPERANCE ROWLES, widow's third; thirds of the remainder to: ELIZABETH ROWLES, REBECCA ROWLES + NEHEMIAH ROWLES.

JG#3/74: Mrs. ELIZABETH SUNDERLAND administratrix of JESSE SUNDERLAND late of Anne Arundel Co. deceased. 15 August 1818. Sureties: LEONARD GARY +

WILLIAM SMITH. ELIZABETH SUNDERLAND, widow's third; remainder of the balance to MARIA ANN FRANCES SUNDERLAND.

JG#3/75: Mr. FRANCIS HANCOCK administrator de bonis non of ANN ALWELL late of Anne Arundel Co. deceased. 23 August 1818. Sureties: BENJAMIN THOMAS + MORDECAI STEWART. Fourths of the remainder to: ELIZA ALWELL, RHODA ALWELL, ANN ALWELL + WESLEY ALWELL.

JG#3/75: Mrs. HESTER CRANDALL administratrix with will annexed of THOMAS CRAN-DALL late of Anne Arundel Co. deceased. 23 August 1818. Sureties: GASSAWAY WATKINS + JOHN T. ROBINSON. HESTER CRANDALL, widow's third; remainder of the balance to: ELIZABETH CAROLINE CRANDALL.

JG#3/76: Mr. WALTER SELLMAN executor of JOHN SELLMAN late of Anne Arundel Co. deceased. 26 August 1818. Sureties: THOMAS MULLINEAUX + JOHN BECROFT. Token legacies to: BENJAMIN HORNER, JENNY POOLE, PEGGY BREWER + NANCY SHIP-LEY; widow BETSY SELLMAN, whole of the remainder of the balance.

JG#3/76: Mrs. SARAH DITTY (now DAVIS) administratrix de bonis non with will annexed of ROGER DITTY late of Anne Arundel Co. deceased. 31 August 1818. Sureties: DANIEL P. JACOB + ROBERT WELCH (of BENJAMIN). SARAH DITTY (now DA-VIS), widow's third; fourths of the remainder to: GEORGE P. DITTY, JOHN DITTY, SAMUEL DITTY + THOMAS R. DITTY.

JG#3/77: Mr. THOMAS WATERS (of PLUMMER) + Mrs. BENJAMIN CARR Sr.(?) adminis-trators of JOHN BEALL late of Anne Arundel Co. deceased. 1 September 1818. Sureties: THOMAS WATERS Sr. + RICHARD CARR. ELEARNOR BEALL, widow's third; remainder of the balance to: MARY BEALL + MARGARET D. BEALL.

JG#3/77: Messrs RICHARD CROMWELL + THOMAS CROMWELL administrators of OLIVER CROMWELL late of Anne Arundel Co. deceased. 22 September 1818. Sureties: CHARLES PUMPHREY + EDWARD PUMPHREY. Thirds of the remainder to: RICHARD CROM-WELL, THOMAS CROMWELL + RACHEL CROMWELL, daughter of the deceased.

JG#3/78: Mr. JAMES H. MARRIOTT executor of JOSHUA MARRIOTT late of Anne Arun-del Co. deceased. 25 September 1818. Sureties: ANDERSON WARFIELD + EDWARD E.(?) ANDERSON. Legacies to: the heirs of THOMAS MARRIOTT (six in number and unnamed), the heirs of JOSHUA MARRIOTT + JOSHUA MARRIOTT; fourths of the re-mainder to: JAMES H. MARRIOTT, HOMEWOOD MARRIOTT, ANN THOMSON + RACHEL IJAMS.

JG#3/78: Mr. LEONARD GARY administrator of JAMES PRICE late of Anne Arundel Co. deceased. 3 October 1818. Sureties: ALEXANDER MITCHELL + MORGAN SULLI-VAN. ANN PRICE, widow's third; fourths of the remainder to: BENJAMIN PRICE, LUCINDA PRICE, ANN PRICE + JAMES GASSAWAY PRICE.

JG#3/79: Mr. ABNER LINTHICUM administrator of SARAH JARVIS late of Anne Arun-del Co. deceased. 8 October 1818. Sureties: RICHARD LINTHICUM + RALPH HAW-KINS. Fourths of the balance to: ELIZABETH MERRIKIN, NANCY LINTHICUM, SARAH JARVIS + JOHN MERRIKIN. [Reference is made to final accounts of 5 October 1812 + 12 October 1815.]

JG#3/79: Mr. JOSEPH A. WALLACE administrator of HENRY MCCOY late of Anne Arundel Co. deceased. 21 October 1818. Sureties: JOHN S. BELT + ARCHIBALD DORSEY. DORCAS MCCOY, widow's third; fifths of the remainder to: ISAAC S.(?) MCCOY, REBECCA M. WALLACE, SARAH M. MCCOY, AMOS H. MCCOY + ALEXANDER MCCOY.

JG#3/80: Mrs. MARY HENWOOD administratrix of ROBERT HENWOOD late of Anne Arundel Co. deceased. 27 October 1818. Sureties: CHARLES ROBINSON + DAVID ROBINSON. MARY HENWOOD, widow's third; halves of the balance to the deceased's daughters: NANCY HENWOOD + MARY HENWOOD.

JG#3/80: Mr. PHILEMON WARFIELD administrator of BEALL WARFIELD late of Anne Arundel Co. deceased. 3 November 1818. Sureties: GEORGE DORSEY + HENRY WELLING. Thirds of the remaining balance to: CATHERINE WARFIELD, GEORGE W. WARFIELD + WILLIAM R. WARFIELD.

JG#3/81: Mr. JOSEPH NORRIS administrator of ELIZABETH WELLS late of Anne Arundel Co. deceased. 23 November 1818. Sureties: JAMES TUCKER + SILAS JOHNSON. Halves of the remainder to: ANN TRAVERSE (now NORRIS) + REBECCA TRAVERSE (now JOHNSON).

JG#3/81: Mr. JACOB WILLIAMS + Mr. FRANCIS HANCOCK administrators de bonis non of FRANCIS CROMWELL late of Anne Arundel Co. deceased. Date not recorded. Sureties: JOHN CROMWELL + ELIJAH WEEMS. Thirds of the balance to: SARAH JOHNSON, ELIZABETH JONES + MARY CROMWELL.

JG#3/81: Mr. NICHOLAS WATKINS (of THOMAS) administrator of JOHN WATKINS late of Anne Arundel Co. deceased; the deceased was s/o STEPHEN WATKINS. 6 January 1819. Sureties: JOSEPH HOWARD + STEPHEN BEARD Jr. Fourths of the balance to: WILLIAM WATKINS, ELEANOR WATKINS, RACHEL SPRIGG WATKINS + ELIZABETH WATKINS.

JG#3/82: Mrs. ELIZABETH LOWMAN executrix of WILLIAM LOWMAN late of Anne Arundel Co. deceased. 27 January 1819. Sureties: GEORGE WATTS + SAMUEL GARDINER. Nominal legacy to: ANN HANCE; halves of the remainder of the balance to: widow ELIZABETH LOWMAN + ELIZABETH DAWSON.

JG#3/82: Mr. THOMAS COALE administrator of ELIZABETH SMITH late of Anne Arundel Co. deceased. 28 January 1819. Sureties: BENJAMIN WARFIELD + RICHARD PHELPS. Sixths of the remainder to: JOSEPH COALE, MARGERY CECIL, MARY BERRY, THOMAS COALE, JOHN COALE + the heirs of SARAH LOWE (three in number, unnamed).

JG#3/83: Mr. WILLIAM SMITH administrator of RICHARD SMITH late of Anne Arundel Co. deceased. 4 March 1819. Sureties: RICHARD G. HUTTON + RICHARD SMITH. SARAH SMITH, widow's third; fourths of the remainder to: RICHARD SMITH, AZARIAH SMITH, WILLIAM SMITH + SARAH SMITH (now SHECKELLS).

JG#3/83: Mr. THOMAS NORRIS (of THOMAS) administrator with will annexed of MATILDA DENNY. 13 April 1819. Sureties: SARAH NORRIS + BENJAMIN WINTERSON. Halves of the remainder to: THOMAS B. DENNY + ELLEN DENNY.

JG#3/84: Messrs BASIL BURGESS + THOMAS BURGESS administrators of MICHAEL BURGESS late of Anne Arundel Co. deceased. 20 April 1819. Sureties: BASIL BURGESS + PEREGRINE BURGESS. SARAH BURGESS, widow's third; elevenths of the remainder to: RODERICK BURGESS, BASIL BURGESS, MARY BURGESS (now CARR), THOMAS BURGESS, MICHAEL BURGESS, JOSEPH BURGESS, REBECCA BURGESS, ABSALOM BURGESS, JOSHUA BURGESS + WILLIAM BURGESS.

JG#3/85: Mr. ROBERT FRANKLIN administrator of MARTIN DEALE late of Anne Arundel Co. deceased. 26 May 1819. Sureties: EDWARD RANDALL + JOHN FORD. RACHEL DEALE, widow's third; thirds of the remainder to: WILLIAM DEALE, JAMES DEALE + MARTIN DEALE.

JG#3/85: Mr. WILLIAM G. RIDGELY administrator of HENRY RIDGELY late of Anne
Arundel Co. deceased. 29 May 1819. Sureties: RICHARD RIDGELY + RICHARD M.
CHASE. MATILDA RIDGELY widow's third; sixths of the remainder to: WILLIAM G.
RIDGELY, ANN C. RIDGELY, MATILDA L. RIDGELY, EMILY C. RIDGELY, HESTER T.
RIDGELY + SAMUEL CHASE RIDGELY.

JG#3/86: Mrs. MARGARET CALLAHAN administratrix of THOMAS CALLAHAN late of
Anne Arundel Co. deceased. 1 June 1819. Sureties: MARY CALLAHAN + WILLIAM
S. GREEN. Sixths of the remainder to: MARGARET CALLAHAN; MARY CALLAHAN; the
heirs of JOHN CALLAHAN: RICHARD HARWOOD for wife SARAH, SAMUEL MAYNARD for
wife ANN, JOHN RIDGELY for wife HARRIET, as well as ELIZABETH CALLAHAN, JAMES
CALLAHAN + MARIA CALLAHAN; the heirs of NICHOLAS HARWOOD (m. NANCY CALLAHAN):
LEWIS DUVALL for wife SARAH, WILLIAM S. GREEN for wife MARY, as well as ANN
HARWOOD + HENRY HARWOOD; the heirs of WILLIAM MUNROE: JONATHAN PINKNEY for
wife ELIZABETH, JOHN MUNROE, THOMAS MUNROE, WILLIAM MUNROE, HORATIO G. MUNROE
+ JOHN NELSON (of REBECCA, d/o WILLIAM MUNROE); + MAJOR MUNROE (son + heir of
ALEXANDER MUNROE).

JG#3/87: Mr. JACOB WILLIAMS executor of ANN MARSH late of Anne Arundel Co.
deceased. 2 July 1819. Sureties: ELIJAH WILLIAMS + EPHRAIM DUVALL. Halves
of the remainder to: PATIENCE MARSH + ANN MARSH.

JG#3/87: Mr. JOHN SMITH executor of MARGARET SMITH late of Anne Arundel Co.
deceased. 26 August 1819. Sureties: BENJAMIN GAITHER + OSBORN WILLIAMS.
Fifths of the remainder to: JANE IGLEHART, JOHN SMITH, ANTHONY SMITH, PHILIP
SMITH + ELIZABETH SMITH.

JG#3/87: Mr. CHARLES G. WARFIELD administrator of VACHEL WARFIELD late of
Anne Arundel Co. deceased. 8 September 1819. Sureties: OWEN ELDER + SAMUEL
E. HUSBAND. ELLENA WARFIELD, widow's third; sixths of the remainder to the
deceased's children: CHARLES G. WARFIELD, SARAH ELLIOTT, HENRIETTA MARRIOTT,
VACHEL H. WARFIELD, WILLIAM WARFIELD + ALLEN D. WARFIELD.

JG#3/88: Mr. EDWARD COLLINSON administrator de bonis non with the will annexed of WILLIAM FRANKLIN late of Anne Arundel Co. deceased. 23 September
1819. Sureties: GIDEON WHITE + JAMES LARIMORE. Sevenths of the remainder to:
ANN OWENS, SARAH FRANKLIN, MARY LEITCH, RACHEL DEALE, ISABELLA FRANKLIN, SU-
SANNA CONNER + ARTRIDGE WELLS.

JG#3/88: Mr. JOHN YOUNG administrator of ZACHARIAH RISTON late of Anne Arun-
del Co. deceased. 10 September 1819. Sureties: HENRY HAMMOND + BENJAMIN
NICHOLSON. Thirds of the remainder to: ANN RISTON (now GARDINER), REBECCA
RISTON (now REDMAN) + RACHEL RISTON (now TYDINGS).

JG#3/89: Miss? MARGARET CALLAHAN administratrix of THOMAS CALLAHAN late of
Anne Arundel Co. deceased. 20 October 1819. Sureties: MARY CALLAHAN +
WILLIAM S. GREEN. Repeats JG#3/86, except that the breakdown is into fifths,
and MAJOR MUNROE, son + heir of ALEXANDER MUNROE, is not listed here.

JG#3/90: Mrs. MARY WOOD administratrix of JOHN WOOD late of Anne Arundel Co.
deceased. 16 November 1819. Sureties: JOHN SCRIVENER + JOHN WHITTINGTON.
MARY WOOD, widow's third; halves of the remainder to: the heirs of JOHN WOOD
(number and names unspecified) + RICHARD WOOD, son of the deceased, as was
the JOHN WOOD, whose heirs are alluded to here.

JG#3/90: Mr. ABEL TUCKER administrator of WILLIAM TUCKER late of Anne Arundel Co. deceased. 17 December 1819. Sureties: ROBERT WELCH (of BENJAMIN) +

REZIN SPURRIER. Sixths of the balance to: MARY ANN TUCKER, RACHEL TUCKER, THOMAS TUCKER, NANCY TUCKER, JANE TUCKER + SARAH TUCKER.

JG#3/91: Mr. JOSEPH SANDS administrator of DANIEL FOWLER late of Anne Arundel Co. deceased. 18 November 1819. Sureties: RICHARD B. WATTS + _____ SLEMAKER (?). MARY FOWLER, widow's third; thirds of the remaining balance to: GEORGE FOWLER, the heirs of BENJAMIN FOWLER, and WILLIAM KING for the right of his (unnamed) wife.

JG#3/91: JAMES MACCUBBIN Esq administrator of MARTHA R MACCUBBIN late of Anne Arundel Co. deceased. 20 November 1819. Sureties: HORATIO RIDOUT + LEWIS NETH Jr. Fourths of the balance to: mother MARY MACCUBBIN, sister JULIAN E MACCUBBIN, sister ELEANOR M MACCUBBIN + CAROLINE L MACCUBBIN.

JG#3/92: Mr. THOMAS WATERS (of PLUMMER) administrator of HENRY DEAVER late of Anne Arundel Co. deceased. 24 November 1819. Sureties: BENJAMIN CARR Jr + SAMUEL GARTRELL. Fifths of the balance to: STEPHEN GARTRELL, the heirs of ELEANOR BEALL, SARAH WATERS (w/o THOMAS), LUCY CARR + MARGARET GARTRELL.

JG#3/92: Mr. THOMAS WORTHINGTON executor of AUGUSTIN SEWELL late of Anne Arundel Co. deceased. 26 January 1820. Sureties: AUGUSTIN GAMBRILL + THOMAS FURLONG. Legacy to JOHN M SEWELL; fifths of the remaining balance to: AUGUSTIN SEWELL, GEORGE SEWELL, JULIA WORTHINGTON, ELEANOR SEWELL + MARY BALDWIN.

JG#3/93: Mr. JOSEPH SANDS administrator of DANIEL FOWLER late of Anne Arundel Co. deceased. 11 February 1820. Sureties: RICHARD B. WATTS + JACOB H. SLEMAKER (?). Thirds to: GEORGE FOWLER, the heirs of BENJAMIN FOWLER + WILLIAM KING in right of his (unnamed) wife. [It appears that the status of widow MARY FOWLER changed between 18 November 1819 and this date.]

JG#3/93: Mr. DORSEY STEWART administrator with will annexed of EZEKIEL STEWART late of Anne Arundel Co. deceased. 1 March 1820. Sureties: EZEKIEL STEWART + EDWARD PUMPHREY. Sixths of the balance to: the heirs of MARK STEWART, the heirs of ELIZABETH STEWART, the heirs of RACHEL SANK, the heirs of REBECCA STEWART, the heirs of MARY YEALDHALL + daughter ANN STEWART.

JG#3/94: Mr. JOHN GRAY administrator of JOHN BOONE late of Anne Arundel Co. deceased. 19 April 1820. Sureties: ELIJAH GRAY + BENJAMIN THOMAS. Halves to: sister CHARLOTTE BOONE (now GRAY) + brother NICHOLAS BOONE.

JG#3/94: Mr. HENRY H BROWN surviving administrator of BASIL BROWN late of Anne Arundel Co. deceased. 24 May 1820. Sureties: ANDERSON WARFIELD + PHILIP HAMMOND Jr. HENRIETTA BROWN, widow's third; eighths of the remaining balance to: JOHN H BROWN, ELIZA BROWN (now HAMMOND), HENRY H BROWN, JULIANA BROWN (now GAMBRILL), WILLIAM H BROWN, REZIN H BROWN, CLARISSA BROWN + PHILIP H BROWN.

TH#1/1 + 2: Mr. OSBORN BELT Jr administrator of OSBORN BELT Sr late of Anne Arundel Co deceased. 18 July 1820. Sureties: JAMES BELT + SAMUEL BRADFORD. DOROTHY BELT, widow's third; twelfths of the remaining balance to: DARKUS BROWN (granddaughter), son JOSEPH BELT, daughter RACHEL LUCAS, daughter ELSEY ISAAC, son JAMES BELT, son OSBORN BELT, the heirs of BENJAMIN BELT, the heirs of RICHARD BELT, the heirs of BASIL BELT, son JOHN BELT, daughter MARGARET BRADFORD + daughter ISABELLA SISCEL.

TH#1/2: Mr. NICHOLAS D. WARFIELD executor of BALA WARFIELD late of Anne Arundel Co. deceased. 12 August 1820. Sureties: SAMUEL HOPKINS + AZEL WARFIELD.

ACHSAH WARFIELD, widow's third; sixths of the remaining balance to: LUCRETIA
WARFIELD, MARY WARFIELD, SARAH WARFIELD, JULIA WARFIELD, RACHEL WARFIELD +
ACHSAH WARFIELD.

TH#1/3: Mr. SAMUEL DORSEY administrator of STEPHEN B DORSEY late of Anne Arundel Co deceased. 22 August 1820. Sureties: RODERICK DORSEY + RICHARD DORSEY.
HARRIET DORSEY (now BENTLEY), widow's third; daughter MARGARET DORSEY, residue.

TH#1/3: Major CHARLES ROBINSON administrator of JOHN JOHNSON late of Anne
Arundel Co deceased. 5 September 1820. Sureties: LLOYD JOHNSON + ZACHARIAH
JOHNSON. ARA JOHNSON, widow's third; equal shares of the remainder to daugh-
ter CECEALIA CHASE and son GREENBURY JOHNSON.

TH#1/4 + 8: Mr. WALTER PUMPHREY Jr executor of WALTER PUMPHREY Sr late of Anne
Arundel Co deceased. 20 September 1820. Sureties: THOMAS BICKNELL + JOHN GRAY.
Fifths of the balance to: DELILAH PUMPHREY (now HODGE), WALTER PUMPHREY, ELIZA-
BETH JOHNSON, CHARLES PUMPHREY + CATHARINE PUMPHREY. [On page 8 DELILAH PUMPH-
REY is corrected to read ADELIA (PUMPHREY) HODGE.]

TH#1/4: Mr. JOHN I (or J) DORSEY executor of ELIZABETH IRELAND late of Anne
Arundel Co deceased. 26 September 1820. Sureties: JOHN H GRIFFITH + JAMES I
(or J) DORSEY. Ninths of the balance to: JOHN I (J?) DORSEY, JAMES I (J?)
DORSEY, LOUISA DORSEY, ANDREW DORSEY, SAMUEL DORSEY, DANIEL H DORSEY, EZEKIEL
DORSEY, SARAH A DORSEY + REBECCA DORSEY.

TH#1/5: Mr. SAMUEL TROTT administrator of MARGARET SIMMONS late of Anne Arundel
Co. deceased. 7 November 1820. Sureties: PATRICK H O'RIELLY + WILLIAM T HAR-
DESTY. Halves to: GILBERT SIMMONS + JEREMIAH SIMMONS.

TH#1/5: Mr. ISAAC WRIGHT executor of GEORGE WRIGHT late of Anne Arundel Co deceased. 19 November 1820. Sureties: ABNER LINTHICUM + RICHARD LINTHICUM.
Halves of the balance to: widow ANN WRIGHT + ISAAC WRIGHT.

TH#1/6: Mr. LLOYD JOHNSON administrator of HORATIO JOHNSON late of Anne Arun-
del Co deceased. 2 December 1820. Sureties: SAMUEL GARDNER + BENJAMIN R NUHON.
Fourths of the balance to: GRAFTON JOHNSON, HARRIET JOHNSON, MAHALA JOHNSON +
JERRARD JOHNSON.

TH#1/7: Mr. JAMES MACKUBIN administrator of CAROLINE L MACKUBBIN late of Anne
Arundel Co deceased. 7 January 1821. Sureties: THOMAS H DORSEY + HENRY DUVALL.
Thirds to: mother MARY MACKUBIN, sister JULIAN E MACKUBIN + sister ELEANOR M
MACKUBIN.

TH#1/7: Mr. HENRY WILLIAMS administrator of WILLIAM JAMES late of Anne Arundel
Co deceased. 4 February 1821. Sureties: JACOB WILLIAMS + BENJAMIN THOMAS.
Slaves and cash to JOHN BONNER + HENRY WILLIAMS.

TH#1/9: Mrs. MARGARET LEE surviving executor of EDWARD LEE late of Anne Arundel
Co. deceased. 13 February 1821. Sureties: SAMUEL C WATKINS + ROBERT WELCH (of
BENJAMIN). MARGARET LEE, widow's third; thirds of the remainder to: ELIZABETH
LEE, HENRIETTA LEE + JOSEPH LEE, children of the deceased.

TH#1/10: Mr. THOMAS FRANKLIN executor of JACOB FRANKLIN late of Anne Arundel
Co deceased. 20 February 1821. Sureties: BENJAMIN FRANKLIN + SAMUEL FRANKLIN.
Fifths of the balance to: daughter ANN FRANKLIN, the heirs of daughter MARY
DEALE, son BENJAMIN FRANKLIN, son SAMUEL FRANKLIN + son THOMAS FRANKLIN.

TH#1/11: Mr. HOWARD ELLIOTT administrator of JACOB ELLIOTT late of Anne Arun-
del Co deceased. 21 February 1821. Sureties: HENRY DUVALL + GEORGE WATTS.
SARAH ELLIOTT (now MANNING), widow's third; eighths of the remaining balance to:
RICHARD ELLIOTT, HOWARD ELLIOTT, AMELIA ELLIOTT, SARAH ELLIOTT, JACOB ELLIOTT,
AQUILLA ELLIOTT, MARGERY ELLIOTT + ANN ELLIOTT.

TH#1/11: Mr. GEORGE WARFIELD administrator of ELI WARFIELD late of Anne Arundel Co deceased. 14 August 1821. [Distribution is not then presented; see
below.]

TH#1/12: Dr. RICHARD DUCKETT administrator de bonis non with the will annexed
of MARGARET HALL late of Anne Arundel Co deceased. 28 February 1821. Sureties:
THOMAS W HALL + JOSEPH HALL. Tenths to: sister MARTHA HOWARD, sister ANN WAT-
KINS, sister ELIZABETH WATKINS, sister MARY STEWART, niece MARGARET STEWART,
niece ELIZA DUCKETT, niece ELEANOR HOWARD, niece MARTHA HOWARD, niece MARGERY
HOWARD + niece CATHARINE HOWARD.

TH#1/13: Mr. FRANCIS HANCOCK administrator of CHARLES BOONE late of Anne Arun-
del Co deceased. 26 March 1821. Sureties: BENJAMIN THOMAS + HENRY WILLIAMS.
Sixths of the balance to: BURLEY G. BOONE, ELIZA BOONE (now THOMAS), JOHN H D
BOONE, MARGARET BOONE, ANN BOONE + SARAH BOONE.

TH#1/14: Mr. CHARLES ROBINSON administrator of ZACHARIAH GRAY late of Anne
Arundel Co deceased. 16 March 1821. Sureties: CHARLES STEWART + BARUCH FOW-
LER. ELIZABETH GRAY, widow's third; remainder to son JOHN GRAY.

TH#1/14: Mr. WILLIAM P HARDISTY administrator of MARY WHITTINGHAM late of Anne
Arundel Co deceased. 17 March 1821. Sureties: SAMUEL PEARCE + JOHN WORTHING-
TON. Halves to: ELIZABETH WHITTINGHAM (now WARD) + ELEANOR WHITTINGHAM (now
HARDESTY).

TH#1/15: Mr. JOSEPH NORRIS administrator of THOMAS NORRIS late of Anne Arundel
Co deceased. 23 March 1821. Sureties: RICHARD MARE + THOMAS ATWELL. HENRI-
ETTA NORRIS, widow's third; eighths of the remaining balance to: JOHN M NORRIS,
JOSEPH NORRIS, SAMUEL NORRIS, THOMAS NORRIS, SARAH NORRIS, ELEANOR NORRIS,
EDWARD NORRIS + MARY NORRIS.

TH#1/15: Mr. GEORGE WASHINGTON MILLER administrator of ZACHARIAH JACOB late
of Anne Arundel Co deceased. 10 April 1821. Sureties: GEORGE M SELLMAN +
SAMUEL MINSKY. Fourths of the balance to: ANN M MINSKY, HENRIETTA MILLER,
niece SARAH ANDERSON + nephew DORSEY JACOB.

TH#1/16: Mr. PHILEMON DARNALL administrator of ELIZABETH DARNALL late of Anne
Arundel Co deceased. 18 April 1821. Sureties: REZIN ESTEP + RICHARD G HUTTON.
Thirds to: HENRY DARNALL, PHILEMON DARNALL + the heirs of FRANCIS DARNALL.

TH#1/16: Mr. BRICE J WORTHINGTON administrator of ELIZABETH WORTHINGTON late
of Anne Arundel Co deceased. 8 Mary 1821. Sureties: THOMAS WORTHINGTON (of
NICHOLAS) + HENRY MANADIER. Sixths of the balance to: THOMAS WORTHINGTON,
CHARLES WORTHINGTON, the heirs of CATHARINE JOHNSON, BRICE J WORTHINGTON, ACH-
SAH GOLDSBOROUGH + WILLIAM GOLDSBOROUGH.

TH#1/17: Mrs. ELIZABETH SMALLWOOD executrix of JESSE SMALLWOOD late of Anne
Arundel Co deceased. 5 June 1821. Sureties: BASIL WARFIELD + SAMUEL CECIL.
ELIZABETH SMALLWOOD, widow's third; sixths of the balance to: daughter ELIZA-
BETH SMALLWOOD, daughter REBECCA SMALLWOOD, son PHILIP SMALLWOOD, daughter
ANN SMALLWOOD, daughter CATHARINE SMALLWOOD + daughter EVALINA SMALLWOOD.

TH#1/18: Mrs. ACHSAH SIMMONS (now HARDESTY) administratrix of EZEKIEL SIM-
MONS late of Anne Arundel Co deceased. 16 June 1821. Sureties: JOHN SIMMONS
+ JOSEPH MORTON. ACHSAH SIMMONS (now HARDESTY), widow's third; remainder to
son WILLIAM H SIMMONS.

TH#1/18: Mr. BENJAMIN THOMAS administrator of EBENEZER THOMAS late of Anne
Arundel Co deceased. 10 August 1821. No sureties indicated. ANN C THOMAS
(now FOREMAN), widow, a fourth; equal shares of the remainder to: daughter
MATHILDA THOMAS, son HENRY C THOMAS + daughter SARAH A THOMAS.

TH#1/19: NANCY SEWELL administratrix of MATILDA SWARMSTADT late of Anne Arun-
del Co deceased. 13 August 1821. Sureties: PHILIP HAMMOND Jr + ALLEN WARFIELD.
Eighths of the balance to: NANCY SEWELL, LUCY SWARMSTADT, SAMUEL SWARMSTADT.
MARY SWARMSTADT, SARAH SWARMSTADT, LUTHER SWARMSTADT, SIDNEY SWARMSTADT.+ LOR-
ENZA SWARMSTADT.

TH#1/19 + 20: Mr. GEORGE WARFIELD administrator of ELI WARFIELD late of Anne
Arundel Co deceased. 14 August 1821. Surety: CALEB MOCKBEE. FRANCES WAR-
FIELD, widow's third; sevenths of the remainder to: GEORGE WARFIELD, ELI G
WARFIELD, SETH WARFIELD, REUBEN WARFIELD, RUFUS WARFIELD, LOUISA WARFIELD +
ELEANOR WARFIELD.

TH#1/20: Mr. LLOYD JOHNSON administrator of HORATIO JOHNSON late of Anne Arun-
del Co deceased. 26 August 1821. Sureties: SAMUEL GARDINER + BENJAMIN NICHOL-
SON. Fourths of the balance to: GRAFTON JOHNSON, JARRET JOHNSON, MAHALA JOHN-
SON + HARRIET JOHNSON.

TH#1/21: Dr. ANDERSON WARFIELD administrator with the will annexed of ELIZA-
BETH WORTHINGTON late of Anne Arundel Co deceased. 11 September 1821. Sure-
ty: EDWARD E. ANDERSON. Two-fifths of the balance to: the heirs of BASIL SIMP-
SON; remaining fifths to: JOHN T WORTHINGTON, JOHN WORTHINGTON + B____ J____
B____ WORTHINGTON. [On folio 24 (but dated 20 August 1821), the name B J B
Worthington is given as T____ B____ WORTHINGTON.]

TH#1/21: Messrs ELIJAH REDMAN + ROBERT HEATH administrators de bonis non of
SARAH MACKUBIN late of Anne Arundel Co deceased. 27 October 1821. Sureties:
DAVID RIDGELY + JOHN ARNOLD. Fourths of the balance to: RACHEL HEATH, KINSEY
TYDINGS, RALPH JOHNSON + THOMAS JOHNSON.

TH#1/22: Mrs. ELEANOR CHILDS administratrix of HENRY L CHILDS late of Anne
Arundel Co deceased. 13 November 1821. Sureties: ROBERT CARR + GIDEON WHITE.
Fifths to: mother ELEANOR CHILDS, brother NATHAN CHILDS, sister JULIANA CHILDS,
sister MARY CHILDS + brother WILLIAM CHILDS. [Immediately followed by an entry
that the distribution is to be thirds to: mother ELEANOR CHILDS, sister MARY
CHILDS + brother WILLIAM CHILDS.]

TH#1/23: SARAH WARD administratrix de bonis non of MARY WARD late of Anne
Arundel Co deceased. 27 November 1821. Sureties: JOSEPH G. HARRISON + JOHN
SCRIVENER. Fourths of the balance to: YATE WARD, ELIZABETH WARD, WILLIAM WARD
+ SARAH E WARD.

TH#1/23: Mr. SAMUEL TROTT administrator of MARGARET SIMMONS late of Anne Arundel Co deceased. 7 November 1821. Sureties: PATRICK H O'RIELY + WILLIAM T
HARDESTY. Equal division between: GILBERT SIMMONS + JEREMIAH SIMMONS.

TH#1/24: Mr. RICHARD KELLY one of the securities of the administration of

WILLIAM SAPPINGTON late of Anne Arundel Co deceased. 18 January 1822. No other sureties indicated. Fourths of the **balance** to: CAROLINE SAPPINGTON, MARGARET ELENDER, WILLIAM SAPPINGTON + REBECCA SAPPINGTON.

TH#1/25: Mr. JOHN SMITH executor of MARGARET SMITH late of Anne Arundel Co deceased. 31 January 1822. Sureties: BENJAMIN GAITHER + OSBORN WILLIAMS. Fifths of the balance to: ELIZA SMITH, ANTHONY SMITH, PHILIP P SMITH, JOHN SMITH + JANE SMITH.

TH#1/25 + 26: Messrs JACOB + HENRY BASSFORD administrators de bonis non of JOHN BASSFORD, with will annexed. 6 February 1822. Sureties: JAMES IGLEHART Jr, WILLIAM MCPARLIN, WILLIAM WARFIELD + NICHOLAS J. WALKINS(?). Sixths of the balance to: HENRY BASSFORD, JOHN BASSFORD, JACOB BASSFORD, THOMAS BASSFORD, ANN WHITTINGTON + SARAH CROSS.

TH#1/26: Mr. JOHN H. TILLARD administrator of WILLIAM S TILLARD late of Anne Arundel Co deceased. 12 February 1822. Sureties: LEONARD GARY + WILLIAM H HALL. Thirds of the balance to: sister MATILDA DRURY, sister SARAH TILLARD + brother JOHN H TILLARD.

TH#1/27: Mr. JAMES MACKUBIN executor of WILLIAM SUDLER late of Anne Arundel Co deceased. 23 February 1822. Sureties: THOMAS H. DORSEY + JOSEPH SANDS. CHARLOTTE SUDLER, widow's third; remainder to daughter JULIAN M. SUDLER.

TH#1/27: Mrs. MARY TUCKER administratrix of ABEL TUCKER late of Anne Arundel Co deceased. 27 February 1822. MARY TUCKER, widow's third; sixths of the remaining balance to: ELIZA TUCKER, JOHN TUCKER, CHARLOTTE TUCKER, MARY TUCKER, WILLIAM TUCKER + EDWARD TUCKER.

TH#1/28: Mr. JACOB WILLIAMS administrator de bonis non of BYRAN WILLIAMS late of Anne Arundel Co deceased. 13 March 1822. Sureties: ZACHARIAH CROM-WELL + EBENEZER THOMAS. Fifths of the balance to: ELIJAH WILLIAMS, JACOB WILLIAMS, RACHEL LEWIS, HENRY WILLIAMS + ELIZABETH WILLIAMS.

TH#1/29: Mrs. ELEANOR BIRCKHEAD administratrix of SAMUEL BIRCKHEAD late of Anne Arundel Co. deceased. 19 March 1822. Sureties: WALTER TYVILLE + HENRY CHILDS. ELEANOR BIRCKHEAD, widow's third; sixths of the balance to: CHRIS-TIANNA BIRCKHEAD, ELIZABETH BIRCKHEAD, SARAH BIRCKHEAD, MARY E BIRCKHEAD, JOHN J BIRCHKHEAD + SAMUEL J BIRCKHEAD.

TH#1/30: Mr. JACOB WILLIAMS one of the administrators de bonis non, with will annexed, of BRYAN WILLIAMS. 3 April 1822. Sureties: ZACHARIAH CROMWELL + EBENEZER THOMAS. Fifths of the balance to: ELIJAH WILLIAMS, JACOB WILLIAMS, RACHEL LEWIS, HENRY WILLIAMS + ELIZABETH WILLIAMS.

TH#1/31: First distribution of JONATHAN PINKNEY administrator of HORATIO G MUNROE late of Anne Arundel Co deceased. 10 November 1821. Sureties: WILLIAM H.MARRIOTT + Mr.(?) E____ PINKNEY. Fifths of the balance to: THOMAS MUNROE, JONATHAN PINKNEY, WILLIAM T MUNROE, J____ M____ NELSON + the heirs of JOHN MUNROE.

TH#1/32: Mrs. SARAH WOOD administratrix of WILLIAM WARD late of Anne Arundel Co deceased. 16 October 1821. Sureties: LEONARD GARY + JOSEPH G HARRISON. SARAH WARD (WOOD?), widow's third; fourths to YATE WARD, ELIZABETH WARD, WIL-LIAM WARD + SARAH E WARD.

TH#1/32 + 33: Mr. BENJAMIN STANSBURY administrator with the will annexed of

JOSEPH STANSBURY late of Anne Arundel Co deceased. 2 April 1822. STEPHEN
Boone + Charles Stewart sureties. Thirds of the balance to: BETY STANS-
BURY, KITTY STANSBURY + BENJAMIN STANSBURY.

TH#1: 33: Mr. JOSEPH TYDINGS administrator of SARAH KNIGHTON late of Anne
Arundel Co deceased. 22 January 1822. No sureties cited. Balance divided
between the deceased's mother, ARTRIDGE TYDINGS, and sister, JANE KNIGHTON.

TH#1/34 + 35: Mr. ELIJAH REDMAN executor of THOMAS REDMAN late of Anne Arundel Co deceased. 4 May 1822. Sureties: WILLIAM WARFIELD + JOHN ARNOLD.
Halves of the balance to: widow REBECCA REDMAN and father ELIJAH REDMAN.

TH#1/33 + 34: Mrs. MARGARET DISNEY administratrix of EDWARD DISNEY late of
Anne Arundel Co deceased. 31 May 1822. Sureties: NICHOLAS J WATKINS + WIL-
LIAM DISNEY. MARGARET DISNEY, widow's third; remainder divided equally be-
tween JOHN DISNEY + EDWARD DISNEY.

TH#1/34 + 35: Mr. RICHARD LINTHICUM administrator of MARY BREWER late of Anne
Arundel Co. deceased. 7 May 1822. Sureties: ABNER LINTHICUM + JOHN R. THOMAS.
Thirds of the balance to: ELIZA YEALDHALL, WILLIAM BREWER + JOHN YEALDHALL.

TH#1/35: Mr. EDWARD GAITHER executor of MARY GAITHER late of Anne Arundel
Co deceased. 4 June 1822. No sureties cited. Sevenths of the balance to:
brother JOHN R GAITHER, sister AGNESS GAITHER, sister NANCY GAITHER, brother
SAMUEL GAITHER, the heirs of VACHEL (RACHEL?) GAITHER, the heirs of ZACHA-
RIAH GAITHER + the heirs of SUSANNA WATERS.

TH#1/36: Mr. NATHAN CHILDS administrator of JONATHAN CHILDS late of Anne
Arundel Co deceased. 12 June 1822. Sureties: J____ G_____ HARRISON +
JOHN SCRIVENER. Fourths of the balance to: NATHAN CHILDS, WILLIAM CHILDS,
JULIANNA CHILDS + MARY E CHILDS.

TH#1/36 + 37: Mr. JAMES IGLEHARD administrator de bonis non of JOHN CROSS
late of Anne Arundel Co deceased. 10 July 1822. Sureties: JOSEPH EVANS +
WILLIAM WARFIELD. JEMIMA CROSS (now WIGGINS), widow's third; thirds of the
remainder to: daughter ELIZABETH CROSS, daughter MARY ANN CROSS + daughter
REBECCA CROSS.

TH#1/37: ELIZABETH ROBINSON administratrix of CHARLES PETTIBONE late of Anne
Arundel Co deceased. 18 July 1822. Sureties: HENRY DUVALL + ANDREW SLICER.
Thirds of the balance to: EDWARD WILLIAMS, PHILIP PETTIBONE (brother) +
JOHN PETTIBONE (brother).

TH#1/38: Mr. CHARLES WARFIELD administrator of JOHN BARNES late of Anne
Arundel Co. deceased. 15 July 1822. Sureties: HUMPHREY DORSEY + GEORGE WAR-
FIELD. ELIZABETH BARNES, widow's third; ninths of the remainder to: THOMAS
BARNES, JOHN D BARNES, BENJAMIN BARNES, JAMES A BARNES, RHODA BARNES, RUFUS
BARNES, HARRY BARNES, MARCELA BARNES + JOSHUA YOUNG (in right of wife).

TH#1/39: ELIZABETH ROBINSON administratrix of CHARLES PETTIBONE late of Anne
Arundel Co deceased. 18 July 1822. Sureties: HENRY DUVALL + ANDREW SLICER.
Fifths of the balance to: ELIZABETH SELBY, JERRIMIAH SELBY, MARIAH SELBY, JOHN
S SELBY + HARRIET SELBY.

TH#1/39: Mr. SAMUEL WOOD executor of REBECCA WOOD late of Anne Arundel Co deceased. 27 July 1822. Sureties: JERRINGHAM DRURY + SAMUEL PEASE(?). Halves of the remaining balance to: MATILDA BURGESS + JOHN WOOD.

TH#1/40: Mrs. ANN PHIPPS + JACOB WHITWRIGHT administrators of NATHANIEL PHIPPS late of Anne Arundel Co deceased. 7 August 1822. Sureties: RICHARD MACE + JO-SEPH NORRIS. ANN PHIPPS, widow's third; fifths of the remainder to: THOMAS PHIPPS, RANDOLPH PHIPPS, MARY ANN PHIPPS, JOHN WILSON PHIPPS + NICHOLAS PHIPPS.

TH#1/40: CAREL(?) W EDELEN administratrix of THOMAS EDELEN late of Anne Arundel Co deceased. 19 April 1822. Sureties: JOHN RANDALL + JOHN CHANDLER. Thirds of the balance to: CAREL(?) W EDELEN, THOMAS H EDELEN + EDWARD EDELEN.

TH#1/41: Mrs. ANN DORSEY executrix of RICHARD DORSEY late of Anne Arundel Co. deceased. 11 June 1821. Sureties: FRANCIS T(?) CLEMENTS + LEWIS DUVALL. Fifths of the balance to: widow ANN DORSEY, children CALEB DORSEY, ANN DORSEY, EDWARD DORSEY + MARY DORSEY.

TH#1/41: Mr. THOMAS BENSON administrator of BASIL SMITH late of Anne Arundel Co deceased. 22 October 1822. Sureties: SAMUEL YEALDHALL + RICHARD BENSON. Fourths of the balance to: ELIZABETH BENSON, BASIL S BENSON, ANN S BENSON + JOSEPH S BENSON.

TH#1/42 + 43: Distribution of the estate of WILLIAM P RIDGELY according to his will. (No executor or administrator, date, or sureties cited.) Heirs: WILLIAM WARFIELD, KITTY WARFIELD + GEORGE WARFIELD (children of BEAL + AMELIA WARFIELD); brother PHILEMON DORSEY RIDGELY's children: MILO RIDGELY, WILLIAM RIDGELY, SAMUEL RIDGELY, CYNTHIA RIDGELY, LUCY RIDGELY, LLOYD RIDGELY, FANNY RIDGELY + MILTON RIDGELY; the children of JOSHUA GRIFFITH by his wife BETSY (testator's sister): REMUS GRIFFITH, WILLIAM R GRIFFITH, LYDIA CROW + RUTH CUMMINGS; the children of GEORGE DORSEY + RACHEL his wife: RACHEL DORSEY, PHILEMON DORSEY, WILLIAM DORSEY, JULIA DORSEY, NACKY DORSEY, FANNY DORSEY, SALLY DORSEY, RACHEL DORSEY + BETSEY DORSEY; brother CHARLES G RIDGELY.

TH#1/44: Mrs. ELIZABETH LINTHICUM + Mr. THOMAS DAVIS administrators of JOSHUA LINTHICUM late of Anne Arundel Co deceased. 31 August 1822. Sureties: SAMUEL R LUSBY + JOHN BEARD. ELIZABETH LINTHICUM, widow's third; sevenths of the balance to: RICHARD B LINTHICUM, STEPHEN LINTHICUM, JOHN F. LINTHICUM, THOMAS F LINTHICUM SARAH A LINTHICUM, REBECCA LINTHICUM + MARY LINTHICUM.

TH#1/45: Mr. JONATHAN PINKNEY administrator of HORATIO MUNROE late of Anne Arundel Co deceased. 26 October 1822. Sureties: WILLIAM H MARRIOTT + WILLIAM E PINKNEY. Fifths of the balance to: THOMAS MUNROE, JONATHAN PINKNEY + wife, WILLIAM T MUNROE, JOHN M. NELSON + the heirs of JOHN MUNROE (unnamed).

TH#1/45 + 46: Mr. HUMPHREY DORSEY administrator of CHARLES B DORSEY late of Anne Arundel Co deceased. 30 October 1822. Sureties: RICHARD DORSEY + HENRY WAYMAN. JULIANA DORSEY, widow's third; fifths of the balance to: brother RICHARD DORSEY, brother HUMPHREY DORSEY, sister MARGARET GAITHER, niece MAR-GARET A DORSEY + nephew JOHN DORSEY.

TH#1/46: Mrs. SUSANNAH LINSTED administratrix with will annexed of JOHN LIN-STED late of Anne Arundel Co deceased. 20 December 1822. Sureties: ELIJAH ROCKHOLD + JOHN GRAY. SUSANNAH LINSTED, widow's third; fourths of the remain-der to: GEORGE W LINSTED, WILLIAM LINSTED, daughter SUSANNAH LINSTED + daugh-ter CHARLOTTE ROCKHOLD.

TH#1/47: Mr. JACOB WILLIAMS one of the administrators with will annexed of
BRYAN WILLIAMS late of Anne Arundel Co deceased. 15 January 1823. Sureties:
ZACHARIAH CROMWELL + EBENEZER THOMAS. Two-thirds of the balance to: ELIJAH
WILLIAMS + JACOB WILLIAMS; the remaining third divided among ELIJAH WILLIAMS,
JACOB WILLIAMS, RACHEL LEWIS, HENRY WILLIAMS + ELIZABETH WILLIAMS.

TH#1/47: Mr. ELIAS SHIPLEY one of the executors of WILLIAM SHIPLEY late of
Anne Arundel Co deceased. 25 March 1823. Sureties: THOMAS HOOD + WILLIAM
SHIPLEY (of ROBERT). Legatees: SUSAN GOLDSBOROUGH, DENTON GEOHAGAN (in right
of wife), ELIAS SHIPLEY, WILLIAM SHIPLEY, WILLIAM SELLMAN (in right of wife),
THOMAS SHIPLEY, JOSHUA(?) SHIPLEY, DENTON SHIPLEY, THOMAS J WARFIELD (in
right of wife), HENRY GOLDSBOROUGH (in right of wife), UPTON D. WELCH (in
right of wife) + ROBERT SHIPLEY.

TH#1/49: Mr. THEOPHILUS NORMAN administrator of THOMAS NORMAN late of Anne
Arundel Co deceased. 14 April 1823. Sureties: JAMES TONGUE + JOHN HURST.
MARGARET NORMAN, widow's third; fifths of the remaining balance to: son THEO-
PHILUS NORMAN, son WILLIAM NORMAN, son SAMUEL NORMAN, son SOLOMON NORMAN +
daughter RACHEL WEEMS.

TH#1/49: Mr. JOSHUA HAWKINS administrator of WILLIAM WILLHAM late of Anne
Arundel Co deceased. 19 April 1823. Sureties: SAMUEL HAWKINS + JOHN WILL-
HAM. MARY WILLHAM, widow's third; balance to son HEZEKIAH WILLHAM.

TH#1/50: Mr. GEORGE HARMAN + Mrs. MARY HARMAN administrators of JOHN HARMAN
late of Anne Arundel Co deceased. 26 April 1823. Sureties: PETER HARMAN +
WILLIAM DISNEY. MARY HARMAN, widow's third; thirds of the remainder to: CARO-
LINE E HARMAN (daughter), JULIAN HARMAN (daughter) + JOHN M HARMAN.

TH#1/50 + 51: Mr. RICHARD WARFIELD one of the administrators of AZEL WAR-
FIELD late of Anne Arundel Co deceased. 23 May 1823. No sureties indicated.
ELIZABETH WARFIELD, widow's third; twelfths of the remaining balance to:
RICHARD WARFIELD, AZEL WARFIELD, ELIZABETH WARFIELD, WILLIAM W WARFIELD, MARY
WARFIELD, MATILDA WARFIELD, HENRY WARFIELD, ELIZA WARFIELD, SARAH WARFIELD,
ANN WARFIELD, GEORGE WARFIELD + CHARLES WARFIELD.

TH#1/51: Mr. SAMUEL DEALE administrator of JOSEPH DEALE late of Anne Arundel
Co deceased. 12 May 1823. No sureties indicated. Sixths of the balance to:
JAMES DEALE, JOHN HARRISON, NATHAN DEALE, WILLIAM DEALE, JOSEPH COWLEY + SAM-
UEL DEALE.

TH#1/52: Mr. RICHARD WEEMS executor of MARY DISNEY late of Anne Arundel Co
deceased. 31 May 1823. No sureties indicated. Fourths of the balance to:
RICHARD WEEMS, the heirs of JOHN WEEMS, the heirs of JAMES WEEMS + the heirs
of SARAH H. GANTTS.

TH#1/52: Third distribution of JONATHAN PINKNEY administrator of HORATIO G
MUNROE. 10 July 1823. Sureties: WILLIAM H MARRIOTT + WILLIAM E PINKNEY.
Fifths of the balance to: THOMAS MUNORE, JONATHAN PINKNEY, WILLIAM S(J?) MUN-
ROE, JOHN M NELSON + the heirs of JOHN MUNROE.

TH#1/53: Mrs. ELIZABETH CLAGETT administratrix of WILLIAM CLAGETT late of
Anne Arundel Co deceased. 8 July 1823. Sureties: THOMAS BICKNELL + THOMAS
GIBBS. ELIZABETH CLAGETT, widow's third; sevenths of the balance to: EDMUND
CLAGETT, JOHN U(N?) CLAGETT, THOMAS CLAGETT, SAMUEL A CLAGETT, RICHARD H. CLAG-

ETT, MARY E CLAGETT + WILLIAM CLAGETT.

TH#1/53: Fourth distribution of Mr. JONATHAN PINKNEY administrator of HORA-
TION G. MUNROE late of Anne Arundel Co. deceased. 11 August 1823. Sureties:
WILLIAM H. MARRIOTT + WILLIAM E PINKNEY. Fifths to: THOMAS MUNROE, JONATHAN
PINKNEY, WILLIAM T MUNROE, JOHN M NELSON + the heirs of JOHN MUNROE.

TH#1/54: Mrs.ELIZABETH CRAGGS administratrix of GEORGE CRAGGS late of Anne
Arundel Co deceased. 21 August 1823. No sureties indicated. Thirds to:
ELIZABETH CRAGGS (widow), JOSEPH H. CRAGGS + MARY A CRAGGS, children of the
deceased.

TH#1/54: Mrs. JANE GAITHER administratrix of JOHN V(?) GAITHER late of Anne
Arundel Co deceased. 20 August 1823. Sureties: JAMES ALLISON + PHILIP CLAY-
TON. JANE GAITHER, widow's third; remainder to daughter ELIZABETH A GAITHER.

TH#1/55: Mr. JOHN IGLEHART administrator of GEORGE C SELLMAN late of Anne
Arundel Co deceased. 19 July 1823. Sureties: JAMES IGLEHART Jr + RICHARD
J COWMAN. Thirds of the balance to siblings: JOHN S SELLMAN, MARY A D SELL-
MAN + JANETTA C SELLMAN.

TH#1/55: Mr. NICHOLAS SANK administrator of EDWARD GRANGER late of Anne Arundel Co deceased. 9 September 1823. No sureties indicated. Sevenths of the
balance to: the heirs of JAMES GRANGER, the heirs of WILLIAM GRANGER, SARAH
ROWERS (BOWERS?), CHARLOTTE MEDFORD, the heirs of ANN WRIGHT, the heirs of
EDWARD GRANGER + CLEMENT GRANGER.

TH#1/56: Mr. JOHN SAPPINGTON administrator of JOHN SAPPINGTON late of Anne
Arundel Co deceased. 5 August 1823. No sureties indicated. Sevenths of the
balance to JOHN SAPPINGTON, ANN SAPPINGTON, CALEB SAPPINGTON, REBECCA SAPPING-
TON, MARTHA SAPPINGTON, ELIZABETH SAPPINGTON + CAROLINE SAPPINGTON.

TH#1/56: Mr. RICHARD ESTEP executor of THOMAS LATTIN late of Anne Arundel Co
deceased. 25 October 1823. Sureties: RICHARD ESTEP + T____ A____ HALL.
MARY LATTIN, widow's third; remainder to PLUMMER LATTIN.

TH#1/57: Mr. ROBERT FRANKLIN administrator of NICHOLAS NORMAN late of Anne
Arundel Co deceased. 2 December 1823. Sureties: WILLIAM NORMAN + ROBERT NOR-
MAN. Sixths of the balance to: the heirs of WILLIAM NORMAN (brother), the
heirs of BENJAMIN NORMAN (brother), the heirs of THOMAS NORMAN (brother), the
heirs of PRISCILLA OWENS (sister), the heirs of MARGARET CHALK (sister), and
the heirs of ELIZABETH GOTT (sister).

TH#1/57 + 58: Mr. EMANUEL DADDS administrator of BENJAMIN PIERCE late of Anne
Arundel Co deceased. 20 December 1823. Sureties: GIDEON WHITE + JAMES IGLE-
HART. Eighths of the balance to: MARY PIERCE (mother), the heirs of WILLIAM
PIERCE (brother), JOSEPH PIERCE (brother), SARAH PURDY (sister), MARY DADDS
(sister), DELILAH WHITE (sister), RICHARD PIERCE (brother) + RACHEL COLMWOOD
(sister).

TH#1/58: Mr. RICHARD WARFIELD one of the administrators of AZEL WARFIELD late
of Anne Arundel Co deceased. 13 January 1824. No sureties indicated. "Twel-
fths" (but 13 persons listed) to: ELIZABETH WARFIELD, RICHARD WARFIELD, AZEL
WARFIELD, ELIZABETH WARFIELD, WILLIAM W WARFIELD, MARY WARFIELD, MATILDA WAR-
FIELD, HENRY WARFIELD, ELIZA WARFIELD, SARAH WARFIELD, ANN WARFIELD, GEORGE WAR-
FIELD + CHARLES WARFIELD.

TH#1/59: Fifth distribution of Mr. JONATHAN PINKNEY administrator of HORATIO G MUNROE. 13 February 1824. Sureties: WILLIAM H. MARRIOTT + WILLIAM E PINKNEY. Fifths of the balance: THOMAS MUNROE, JONATHAN PINKNEY, WILLIAM T MUNROE, JOHN M.NELSON + the heirs of JOHN MUNROE.

TH#1/59 + 60: Messrs. JOHN HARMAN + ANDREW HARMAN executors of ANDREW HARMAN late of Anne Arundel Co deceased. 27 January 1824. Sureties: RODERICK DORSEY + ENOCH SHIPLEY. EVA HARMAN, widow's third; fourths of the remaining balance to: KITTY HARMAN, ELIZABETH MEEK, ANN SHIPLEY + CAROLINE HARMAN.

TH#1/60 + 61: Mrs. ELIZA PRITCHARD administratrix of WILLIAM PRITCHARD late of Anne Arundel Co deceased. 25 May 1824. Sureties: JONATHAN HUTTON + RICHARD S HUTTON. ELIZA PRITCHARD, widow's third; fourths of the remainder to: daughter MARGARET PRITCHARD, daughter ANN PRITCHARD, son ARTHUR PRITCHARD + daughter ISABELLA PRITCHARD.

TH#1/61: Mr. RICHARD GARDINER administrator of ANN GARDINER late of Anne Arundel Co deceased. 5 June 1824. Sureties: RICHARD MOSS + STEPHEN BOONE. Thirds of the balance to: JOHN GARDINER, CHARLES GARDINER + RICHARD GARDINER.

TH#1/61 + 62: Mr. PHILEMON WARFIELD surviving executor of VACHEL WARFIELD late of Anne Arundel Co deceased. 22 June 1824. Sureties: THOMAS BATSON + BASIL BURGESS. Sixths of the balance to: son ALLEN WARFIELD, son PHILEMON WARFIELD, son LLOYD WARFIELD, son JOSHUA WARFIELD, son GREENBURY WARFIELD + LOT LINTHICUM in right of his wife CATHARINE.

TH#1/62 + 63: Mr. WILLIAM GRAVES administrator of JOSHUA GRAY late of Anne Arundel Co deceased. 5 June 1824. Sureties: MOSES LAWRENCE + GABRIEL VERNON. MARY GRAY, widow's third; fourths of the remainder to: GEORGE GRAY, JOSHUA GRAY, JOSEPH GRAY + JOHN GRAY.

TH#1/63: Mr. LEWIS DUVALL administrator de bonis non of NICHOLAS HARWOOD late of Anne Arundel Co deceased. 8 May 1824. Sureties: HOWARD DUVALL + FIELDER CROSS. Sixths of the balance to: NICHOLAS HARWOOD, JAMES HARWOOD, HENRY S HARWOOD, ANN HARWOOD, LEWIS DUVALL in right of wife (unnamed) + WILLIAM SHEREEN in right of wife (unnamed).

TH#1/64: Mr. REZIN ESTEP administrator de bonis non of JOHN SUNDERLAND late of Anne Arundel Co deceased. 23 April 1824. Sureties: ZACHARIAH SUNDERLAND + JOSEPH MCCENERY. Fourths to: WILLIAM G JONES in right of wife ELIZABETH + MARIA SUNDERLAND; eighths of the remaining balance to: ELIZA SUNDERLAND, MARY SUNDERLAND, JOHN SUNDERLAND + RICHARD SUNDERLAND.

TH#1/64 + 65: Mr. ZACHARIAH JOHNSON administrator of CHARLES ROBINSON late of Anne Arundel Co deceased. 3 July 1824. Sureties: RICHARD GRAY + CHARLES PUMPHREY. PATIENCE ROBINSON, widow's third; fourths of the remainder to: LEWIS ROBINSON, DAVID ROBINSON, ISABELLA ROBINSON + WILLIAM ROBINSON.

TH#1/66 + 67: Mr. JOHN WARFIELD administrator of HARRIET DORSEY late of Anne Arundel Co deceased. 20 April 1824. Sureties: NICHOLAS WATKINS + WILLIAM P WATKINS. Sevenths of the balance to: RALPH J DORSEY, JOSHUA A DORSEY, MARIA MCCOY, RICHARD DORSEY, BENJAMIN H DORSEY, MARY A J DORSEY + RINALDO W DORSEY.

TH#1/66: Mr. NICHOLAS MILLER administrator of NEHEMIAH MILLER late of Anne Arundel Co deceased. 3 July 1824. Sureties: JAMES O'ROURKE + JAMES MILLER.

Eighths of the balance to children: ELIZABETH MARRIOTT, KITTY HARRISON, NICHO-
LAS MILLER, MARY DISNEY, ENOCH MILLER, DENTON MILLER, CALEB MILLER + LOUISA
MILLER.

TH#1/66 + 67: Messrs ELIJAH REDMAN + ROBERT HEATH administrators de bonis non
of SARAH MACCUBBIN late of Anne Arundel Co deceased. 22 April 1824. Sureties:
DAVID RIDGELY + JOHN ARNOLD. Fourths of the balance to: ROBERT HEATH, RALPH
JOHNSON, MARY JOHNSON + REBECCA JOHNSON.

TH#1/67: Mr. JOSEPH HOBBS executor of THOMAS HOBBS late of Anne Arundel Co
deceased. 31 July 1824. Sureties: HENRY WHALLEN + CALEB HOBBS. Ninths of
the balance to: GERARD HOBBS (brother), CALEB HOBBS (brother), JOSEPH HOBBS
(brother), the heirs of ELIZABETH PEDDICORD, AMELIA PEDDICORD, the heirs of
NANCY BAKER, SARAH HOOD, HANNAH SHEETS + CORDELIA BARNES.

TH#1/68: Mr. JACOB BARRY administrator of JAMES BARRY late of Anne Arundel Co
deceased. 10 August 1824. Sureties: WILLIAM DISNEY + ELISHA BARRY. Thirds of
the balance to: JACOB BARRY, SARAH DISNEY + RACHEL BARRY.

TH#1/68: Mrs. ELIZABETH CROSS administratrix of JEREMIAH CROSS late of Anne
Arundel Co deceased. 8 January 1823. No sureties indicated. ELIZABETH CROSS,
widow's third; eighths of the balance to: JOSEPH CROSS, DENNIS CROSS, STEPHEN
CROSS, ABETHA CROSS, ELIZABETH CROSS, ISAIAH CROSS, EMMA CROSS + LYDIA CROSS.

TH#1/69: Mr. JOHN HALL administrator of EZEKIEL STEWART late of Anne Arundel
Co deceased. 20 October 1824. Sureties: CHARLES PUMPHREY + CHARLES FRIZEL.
Sixths of the balance to children: GASSAWAY STEWART, CHARLOTTE STEWART, MARY
STEWART, SUSAN STEWART, CHARLES STEWART + ELEANOR STEWART.

TH#1/69 + 70: Mrs. SARAH WARFIELD administratrix of AMOS WARFIELD late of
Anne Arundel Co deceased, 20 October 1824. Sureties: JOHN H WARFIELD + WARREN
WELSH. SARAH WARFIELD, widow's third; fourths of the remainder to children:
MARY WARFIELD, LYDIA WARFIELD, CATHARINE WARFIELD + SETH W WARFIELD.

TH#1/70: Mr. HENRY CHILDS administrator of JOHN GRIFFIS late of Anne Arundel
Co deceased. 21 October 1824. Fifths of the balance to children: JOHN GRIFFIS,
ANN CRANDEL, ELIZABETH GRIFFIS, JOSEPH GRIFFIS + WILLIAM GRIFFIS.

TH#1/70 + 71: Mr. JOSEPH HODGES executor of JOSEPH HODGES late of Anne Arundel
Co deceased. 30 October 1824. No sureties indicated. REBECCA HODGES, widow's
third; fifths of the balance to: JOSEPH HODGES, RHODA CHAIRS, HENRY HODGES,
the heirs of ELIZABETH ASHPAN + MARTHA ANN HODGES. The entire item is immediately
repeated, dated 20 November 1824.

TH#1/71 + 72: Sixth distribution of Mr. JONATHAN PINKNEY administrator of
HORATIC G MUNROE late of Anne Arundel Co deceased. 28 January 1825. Fifths
of the balance to: THOMAS MUNROE, JONATHAN PINKNEY, WILLIAM T MUNROE, JOHN M
NELSON + the heirs of JOHN MUNORE.

TH#1/72: Mr. JOHN HALL administrator of JOHN ASHPAN late of Anne Arundel Co
deceased. 7 February 1825. Sureties: BENJAMIN ROBINSON + ARCHIBALD MENSHAW.
Fourths of the balance to: CATHARINE ASHPAN, GEORGE ASHPAN, JOSEPH ASHPAN +
JOHN ASHPAN.

TH#1/72: Mr. JAMES SMITH administrator de bonis non of BENJAMIN RAINER late
of Anne Arundel Co deceased. 14 February 1825. Sureties: CHARLES FRIZEL +
WILLIAM PUMPHREY. ANN RAINER, widow's third; remainder to BENJAMIN RAINER, son.

TH#1/73: Mrs. ANN FROST executrix of JAMES FROST late of Anne Arundel Co deceased. 2 April 1825. No sureties indicated. ANN FROST, widow's third; fifths of the remainder to: MARY FROST, ANN FROST, WILLIAM FROST, HARRIET FROST + JAMES FROST.

TH#1/73: Mr. THOMAS COOK executor of JOHN COOK late of Anne Arundel Co deceased. 18 April 1825. No sureties indicated. ANN COOK, widow's third; thirds of the remainder to children: ELISHA COOK, LARKIN COOK + ANN S COOK.

TH#1/74: Mr. JOHN S. SELBY administrator of ELIZABETH CROSS late of Anne Arundel Co deceased. 9 June 1825. Sureties: HARRIET SELBY + JAMES IGLEHART. Thirds to the deceased's sisters: MARY ANN CROSS, REBECCA CROSS + HARRIET W WIGGINS.

TH#1/74: Mr. NICHOLAS WORTHINGTON (of THOMAS) administrator of LUTHER H WARFIELD late of Anne Arundel Co deceased. 18 June 1825. No sureties indicated. Sixths of the remaining balance to: ANN WORTHINGTON (mother), ELIZABETH A. WARFIELD, JAMES H WARFIELD, GEORGE H WARFIELD, LABON WARFIELD + CHARLES M WARFIELD.

TH#1/75: Mrs. SARAH KING administrator of SAMUEL KING late of Anne Arundel Co deceased. 18 June 1825. No sureties indicated. SARAH KING, widow's third; sixths of the remainder to: LETHA KING, THOMAS KING, SARAH KING, WILLIAM H. KING, HENRY H KING + ANN M KING.

TH#1/75: Mr. JOHN HALL administrator of JOHN ASHPAN late of Anne Arundel Co deceased. 16 July 1825. No sureties indicated. Fourths of the remaining balance to: CATHERINE ASHPAN, GEORGE ASHPAN, JOSEPH ASHPAN + JOHN ASHPAN.

TH#1/76: Mr. JOHN WARFIELD administrator of RALPH DORSEY late of Anne Arundel Co deceased. 16 August 1825. No sureties indicated. Sevenths of the remainder to: MARIA M DORSEY, JOHN H DORSEY, RINALDO W DORSEY, MARY A J DORSEY, RALPH J DORSEY, RICHARD G DORSEY + BENJAMIN H DORSEY.

TH#1/76: Mrs. SARAH A WATERS administratrix of JONATHAN WATERS late of Anne Arundel Co deceased. 20 August 1825. No sureties indicated. SARAH A WATERS, widow's third; fourths of the remainder to: THOMAS G. WATERS, JULIANNA WATERS, NICHOLAS R WATERS + JAMES L WATERS.

TH#1/77: Mr. JOHN ADDISON administrator of GEORGE O BEVENS late of Anne Arundel Co deceased. 9 August 1825. No sureties indicated. Thirds of the remaining balance to: LAURA BEVENS, JOHN T. BEVENS + MARY R BEVENS.

TH#1/77: Mrs. MARY HOPKINS (now IGLEHART) administratrix of SAMUEL HOPKINS late of Anne Arundel Co deceased. 24 August 1825. No sureties indicated. MARY HOPKINS, widow's third; sixths of the remainder to: SARAH HOPKINS, CATHERINE HOPKINS, JONATHAN HOPKINS, DAVID HOPKINS, ELIZA HOPKINS + SAMUEL HOPKINS.

TH#1/77: Mr. SAMUEL L SWARMSTADT one of the administrators of BENJAMIN STANSBURY late of Anne Arundel Co deceased. 17 September 1825. No sureties indicated. SARAH BRADFORD, widow's third; fourths of the remainder to: GEORGE STANSBURY, RUTHA ANN STANSBURY, ELIZABETH STANSBURY + ISABELLA STANSBURY.

TH#1/78: Mrs. HESTER PHELPS administratrix of ZACHARIAH PHELPS late of Anne Arundel Co deceased. 19 September 1825. No sureties indicated. HESTER PHELPS, widow's third; fourths of the remainder to: WALTER P PHELPS, SARAH PHELPS, ZACHARIAH PHELPS + JOSEPH H PHELPS.

TH#1/78: FRANCES MOXLEY (now MOORE) administrator de bonis non with will annexed of AMELIA MOXLEY late of Anne Arundel Co deceased. 1 October 1825. No sureties indicated. Sevenths of the remainder to: BASIL MOXLEY, LLOYD MOXLEY, ANGELINA MOXLEY, THOMAS MOXLEY, CAROLINE PENN, MARY CAMPER + FRANCES MOORE.

TH#1/79: Mrs. FRANCES MOXLEY (now MOORE) administratrix of JOHN MOXLEY late of Anne Arundel Co deceased. 1 October 1825. No sureties indicated. FRANCES MOXLEY (now MOORE), widow's third; sixths of the remainder to: CHARLES MOXLEY, LLOYD MOXLEY, EVELINE MOXLEY, CECILIA MOXLEY, JEREUSA MOXLEY + LUTHER MOXLEY.

TH#1/79: Mr. SAMUEL LEWIS administrator of SARAH SWAIN late of Anne Arundel Co deceased. 8 October 1825. No sureties indicated. Thirds of the remainder to: mother ELIZABETH SMITH, HORATIO SMITH + JEMIMA SMITH.

TH#1/79 + 80: Mrs. ELEANOR THOMPSON administratrix of JOHN THOMPSON late of Anne Arundel Co.deceased. 15 October 1825. No sureties indicated. ELEANOR THOMPSON, widow's third; sevenths of the remainder to: ALICIA THOMPSON, MARY A THOMPSON, SARAH E THOMPSON, CHARLES THOMPSON, HENRY J THOMPSON, MARGARETT THOMPSON + EMILY B THOMPSON.

TH#1/80: Mr. RICHARD PHELPS administrator of FREDERICK YEALDHALL late of Anne Arundel Co deceased. 19 October 1825. Halves of the balance to: ELIZABETH YEALDHALL + MARY YEALDHALL.

TH#1/81: Mr. FRANCIS BIRD executor of JOSEPH PEAKE late of Anne Arundel Co deceased. 5 November 1825. No sureties indicated. Halves of the balance to: WILLIAM PEAKE + ELIZA PEAKE.

TH#1/81: Mr. THOMAS TONGUE executor of THOMAS TONGUE late of Anne Arundel Co deceased. 10 November 1825. No sureties indicated. Thirds of the balance to: ANN COLLINSON, HARRIET WATERS + ELIZABETH ALLEIN.

TH#1/81: Mrs. SARAH DORSEY administratrix of JOHN DORSEY late of Anne Arundel Co deceased. 15 November 1825. No sureties indicated. SARAH DORSEY, widow's third; eighths of the balance to children: HAMMOND DORSEY, BAKER DORSEY, LARKIN SHEREDINE DORSEY, RICHARD DORSEY, MARY DORSEY, REBECCA DORSEY + ELIZABETH DORSEY.

TH#1/82: Mrs. ARAMINTA WOOTTEN administratrix of RICHARD WOOTTEN late of Anne Arundel Co deceased. 8 December 1825. No sureties indicated. ARAMINTA WOOTTEN, widow's third; fifths of the remainder to: WILLA MARIA WOOTTEN, ELIZABETH JANE WOOTTEN, WILLIAM THOMAS WOOTTEN, ARAH ANN WOOTTEN + RICHARD ARTHUR WOOTTEN.

TH#1/82: Mr. ELIJAH YEALDHALL executor of FRANCIS YEALDHALL late of Anne Arundel Co deceased. 9 December 1825. No sureties indicated. Halves of the balance to: ELIJAH YEALDHALL + FREDERICK YEALDHALL.

TH#1/82 + 83: Mr. NELSON PHELPS one of the administrators of EZEKIEL PHELPS late of Anne Arundel Co deceased. 10 December 1825. No sureties indicated. MARGARET PHELPS, widow's third; fourths of the remainder to: WILSON PHELPS, WALTER PHELPS, MARY ANN SCOTT + MIDDLETON PHELPS.

TH#1/83: Mr. JOHN A WHITTINGTON administrator of JACOB PATTERSON late of Anne Arundel Co deceased. 13 December 1825. No sureties indicated. Fifths of the balance to: NICA DOWELL, SARAH WHITTINGTON, ELIZABETH WARD, PRISCILLA DOWELL + MARY PATTERSON, all daughters of the deceased.

TH#1/83: Mr. RICHARD GARDINER administrator of CHARLES GARDINER late of Anne
Arundel Co deceased. 7 January 1826. No sureties indicated. Halves of the
balance to: JOHN GARDINER + RICHARD GARDINER.

TH#1/84: Mr. THOMAS IGLEHART administrator of JAMES SANDERS late of Anne Arundel Co deceased. 28 January 1826. Sureties: SAMUEL IGLEHART + JAMES IGLEHART.
Fifths of the balance to: ELEANOR SANDERS, ELIZABETH SANDERS, HENREITTA SANDERS,
SARAH L SANDERS + JULIA SANDERS. This item, with same distributees, repeated
on folios 85 + 86.

TH#1/84 + 85: Mr. THOMAS IGLEHART administrator of ROBERT SANDERS late of
Anne Arundel Co deceased. 28 January 1826. Sureties: JOHN IGLEHART + THOMAS
WELCH. Fifths of the balance to: ELEANOR SANDERS, ELIZABETH SANDERS, HENRIETTA
SANDERS, SARAH L SANDERS + JULIA SANDERS. Item repeated on folios 85 + 86;
sureties changed there to SAMUEL E DUVALL + JAMES IGLEHART.

TH#1/86: Mrs. SARAH BATTEE executrix of RICHARD BATTEE late of Anne Arundel
Co deceased. 24 February 1826. No sureties indicated. SARAH BATTEE, widow's
third; halves of the remainder to ANN BATTEE + MATILDA BATTEE.

TH#1/86: Mrs. SARAH ARNOLD administratrix of ROBERT ARNOLD late of Anne Arundel Co deceased. 11 March 1826. Sureties: RICHARD WELLS + JOHN BEARD. SARAH
ARNOLD, widow's third; balance of the remainder to: RICHARD ARNOLD.

TH#1/87: Mr. SAMUEL GOVER administrator of JULIAN WILSON late of Anne Arundel
Co deceased. 15 March 1826. Sureties: PATRICK H O'RILEY + GASSAWAY PINDLE.
Halves of the balance to: MARY WILSON + JOHN WILSON.

TH#1/87: Mr. NICHOLAS WORTHINGTON (of THOMAS) + BRICE J G WORTHINGTON administrators of THOMAS WORTHINGTON late of Anne Arundel Co deceased. 18 March 1826.
No sureties indicated. Sixths of the balance to: NICHOLAS WORTHINGTON  BRICE
J G WORTHINGTON, CHARLES G WORTHINGTON, ANN WORTHINGTON, JOHN G WORTHINGTON +
the heirs of THOMAS WORTHINGTON.

TH#1/88: Mr. JOSEPH N BREWER one of the administrators of JOHN B ROBINSON late
of Anne Arundel Co deceased. 18 June 1822. Sureties: SAMUEL HARRISON + JAMES
LARIMORE. Sixths of the balance to: THORNTON F ROBINSON, WESTLY ROBINSON,
SARAH ANN ROBINSON, MORDECAI S ROBINSON, JAMES ROBINSON + GEORGE W. ROBINSON.

TH#1/89: Mrs. ANN DORSEY executrix of RICHARD DORSEY (of CALEB) late of Anne
Arundel Co deceased. 3 April 1826. Sureties: FRANCIS T. CLEMENTS + LEWIS DU-
VALL. Fifths of the balance to: widow ANN DORSEY, CALEB DORSEY, ANN DORSEY,
EDWARD DORSEY + MARY SELLMAN.

TH#1/89 + 90: Mr. JOHN P DAVIS administrator de bonis non of ROBERT JACOB late
of Anne Arundel Co deceased. 25 April 1826. No sureties indicated. ANN JACOB,
widow's third; ninths of the balance to: SARAH HODGES, MARY ANN JACOB, SUSANNA
JACOB, CAROLINE JACOB, MATILDA JACOB, ELIZABETH JACOB, EDWARD JACOB, JULIAN
JACOB + BENJAMIN JACOB.

TH#1/90: Mr. JOHN S SELLMAN administrator of MARY A D SELLMAN late of Anne
Arundel Co deceased. 13 May 1826. Sureties: THOMAS H DORSEY + JOHN IGLEHART.
Halves of the balance to: JOHN S SELLMAN + JANNETTA C SELLMAN.

TH#1/90: Mr. HENRY THOMPSON executor of ELIZABETH THOMPSON late of Anne Arundel
Co deceased. 20 June 1826. No sureties indicated. Halves of the balance to:
MATILDA A THOMPSON + ALICIA A THOMPSON.

TH#1/90 + 91: Mr. NATHAN CHILDS executor of ELENOR CHILDS late of Anne Arundel Co deceased. 6 June 1826. Sureties: RICHARD BREWER + JOHN T WILSON. Fourths of the balance to: NATHAN CHILDS, JULIAN BROWN, WILLIAM P CHILDS + MARY E CARR.

TH#1/91: Mr. LEONARD IGLEHART administrator de bonis non of WILLIAM WATSON late of Anne Arundel Co deceased. 12 June 1826. Sureties: STEPHEN BEARD + JAMES IGLEHART. Fifths of the balance to: the heirs of RICHARD DORSEY (of CALEB), the heirs of CHARLES WATSON, the heirs of MARY WATSON, RICHARD WATSON + the heirs of _____ HAMMOND.

TH#1/92: Mr. REZIN ESTEP administrator of NATHAN WELLS late of Anne Arundel Co deceased. 14 July 1826. Sureties: THOMAS D DORSEY + WILLIAM H MARRIOTT. _____ WELLS, widow's third; fifths of the balance to: SARAH TELLOTT, GEORGE WELLS, MATILDA WELLS, FLOYD WELLS + JAMES WELLS.

TH#1/92: Mr. JOHN BEARD administrator of ROBERT THOMAS late of Anne Arundel Co deceased. 29 September 1826. Sureties: STEPHEN BEARD + JOHN W. BEARD. ANN THOMAS, widow's third; eighths of the balance to: MARY THOMAS, JULIA THOMAS, JOHN THOMAS, MARGARET THOMAS, SUSAN THOMAS, MARIA THOMAS, ROBERT THOMAS + CAROLINE THOMAS.

TH#1/93: Mr. NICHOLAS WORTHINGTON (of THOMAS) + Mr. BRICE J G WORTHINGTON administrators of THOMAS WORTHINGTON late of Anne Arundel Co deceased. 18 March 1826. Sureties: REZIN MOSELY + ZACHARIAH POLTON. Sixths of the balance to: NICHOLAS WORTHINGTON (of THOMAS), BRICE J G WORTHINGTON, CHARLES G WORTHINGTON, ANN WORTHINGTON, JOHN G WORTHINGTON + the heirs of THOMAS WORTHINGTON.

TH#1/93: Mr. HENRY WELLING executor of WILLIAM RIDGELY late of Anne Arundel Co deceased. 16 October 1826. Sureties: WILLIAM WELLING + BASIL BURGESS. Sixths of the balance to: HENRY WELLING, CHARLES G. RIDGELY, PHILEMON D RIDGELY, RACHEL DORSEY, the heirs of JOSHUA GRIFFITH + the heirs of B____ WARFIELD.

TH#1/94: Mr. JOHN SELLMAN administrator of WILLIAM FISHER late of Anne Arundel Co deceased. 4 November 1826. No sureties indicated. HENRIETTA FISHER (now RODGERS), widow's third; fifths of the remainder to: JOHN H FISHER, WILLIAM FISHER, MARY A FISHER, HEZEKIAH FISHER + SUSANNAH FISHER.

TH#1/94: JONYE(?) HOPKINS administrator of SARAH HOPKINS late of Anne Arundel Co deceased. 9 December 1826. Sureties: ISRAEL DAVIDSON + WILLIAM HOPKINS. Eighths of the balance to: WILLIAM HOPKINS, SAMUEL HOPKINS, the heirs of JOSEPH HOPKINS, the heirs of PHILIP HOPKINS, JONYE(?) HOPKINS, ELIZABETH HOPKINS, MARGARET HOPKINS + SARAH HOPKINS.

TH#1/95: Mr. JEREMIAH BERRY administrator of SARAH KING late of Anne Arundel Co deceased. 23 December 1826. Sureties: VACHEL BROWN + JOHN CARROLL. Thirds of the balance to: WILLIAM H KING, HENRY H KING + ANN M KING.

TH#1/95: Mr. HENRY HAMMOND one of the administrators of ELIJAH PENNINGTON late of Anne Arundel Co deceased. 12 January 1827. Sureties: JOHN DAY + PHILIP PETTIBONE. Thirds of the balance to: WILLIAM PENNINGTON, REBECCA PENNINGTON + MARY PENNINGTON.

TH#1/96: Mr. DANIEL MAHONY administrator of ROBERT MAHONY late of Anne Arundel

Co deceased. 29 January 1827. Sureties: ANDREW SLICER + WALTER CROSS. Fifths of the balance to: DANIEL MAHONY, ROBERT MAHONY, JAMES MAHONY, HENRY MAHONY + BARNETT MAHONY.

TH#1/97: Mr. JOHN WELLS + Mr. ABSALOM BEALMEAR administrators of SUSAN WELLS late of Anne Arundel Co deceased. 14 February 1827. Sureties: JACOB WATERS + RICHARD WILLIAMS. Ninths of the balance to: WILLIAM WELLS, FREDERICK WELLS, ANN MUNROE, the heirs of DANIEL WELLS, JOHN WELLS, MARY CARTER, SARAH HYDE, RICHARD WELLS + ELIZABETH WATERS.

TH#1/98: Mr. JOHN WELLS + Mr. ABSALOM BEALMEAR administrators de bonis non with the will annexed of DANIEL WELLS. 14 February 1827. Sureties: JACOB WATERS + RICHARD WILLIAMS. Ninths of the balance to: children of WILLIAM WELLS, FREDERICK WELLS, ANN MUNROE, the children of DANIEL WELLS, JOHN WELLS, MARY CARTER, the children of SARAH HYDE, RICHARD WELLS + ELIZABETH WATERS.

TH#1/99: Mr. JOHN WOOD administrator of THOMAS PARROTT late of Anne Arundel Co deceased. 13 February 1827. No sureties indicated. MARY PARROTT, widow's third; sixths of the remaining balance to: THOMAS PARROTT, KNIGHTON PARROTT, JOHN PARROTT, the heirs of WALTER CARR, JOHN STALLINGS in right of his (unnamed) wife + the children of JOHN A RIELY.

TH#1/99: Mr. BENJAMIN WINTERSON administrator of JOHN TUCKER late of Anne Arundel Co. deceased. 20 February 1827. Sureties: WILLIAM O'HARA + BENNETT HURST. Fourths of the balance to: JAMES TUCKER, WILLIAM O'HARA in right of (unnamed) wife, the heirs of THOMAS TUCKER + BENJAMIN WINTERSON.

TH#1/100: Mr. REZIN ESTEP administrator with will annexed of LEONARD ARMIGER late of Anne Arundel Co deceased. 23 March 1827. No sureties indicated. Fifths of the balance to: ANN ARMIGER, JOHN ARMIGER, RACHEL GREENWELL, MARY ANN ARMIGER + _____ ARMIGER.

TH#1/100: Mr. GRAFTON MUNROE administrator of JAMES MUNROE late of Anne Arundel Co deceased. 3 Mary 1827. Sureties: JONATHAN MUNROE + GIDEON WHITE. Eighths of the balance to: ANN MUNROE, MARY MUNORE, ELIZABETH MUNROE, JONATHAN MUNROE, GRAFTON MUNROE, THOMAS MUNROE, CHARLES MUNROE + REBECCA MUNROE. Additional distribution (27 March 1827), f. 101.

TH#1/101: Mr. JOHN WELHAM administrator of NELSON WELHAM late of Anne Arundel Co deceased. 3 April 1827. No sureties indicated. Fourths of the balance to: JOHN WELHAM, WALLACE WELHAM, MARY WELHAM + HEZEKIAH WELHAM.

TH#1/102: Mrs. MARY HOWARD administratrix with will annexed of JOSEPH HOWARD late of Anne Arundel Co deceased. 17 April 1827. No sureties indicated. Thirds of the balance to: MARY HOWARD, widow; AZEL WATERS in right of his (unnamed) wife + the heirs of CORNELIUS HOWARD.

TH#1/102: Mr. HENRY HOBBS executor of HENRY C HOBBS late of Anne Arundel Co deceased. 17 April 1827. Sureties: JASPER PEDDICORD + WILLIAM O'HARA. Halves of the balance to: ELIZABETH HOBBS + ACHSAH HOBBS.

TH#1/103: Mr. WILLIAM OWENS one of the administrators of THOMAS OWENS late of Anne Arundel Co. deceased. 28 April 1827. Sureties: JOHN WELCH, JOSEPH OWENS, NICHOLAS OWENS (of JAMES) + JAMES OWENS. Tenths of the balance to: WILLIAM OWENS, BENJAMIN OWENS, ISAAC OWENS, JOSEPH OWENS, the heirs of NICHOLAS OWENS,

PRISCILLA WELCH, the heirs of MARGARET LAWREY, the heirs of CHARLES OWENS, the heirs of ELIZABETH OWENS + the heirs of ANN CHILDS.

TH#1/103: Mrs. MARY SELBY administratrix of JONATHAN SELBY late of Anne Arundel Co deceased. 12 Mary 1827. Sureties: RICHARD TYDINGS + JOHN TYDINGS. MARY SELBY, widow's third; remainder to: SUSAN SELBY + SARAH SELBY.

TH#1/104: First Distribution of THOMAS J HALL administrator of JESSE LEITCH late of Anne Arundel Co deceased. 18 May 1827. No sureties indicated. Ninths of the balance to: the heirs of THOMAS LEITCH, the heirs of DRAYDEN FOWLER, the heirs of ELIZABETH TRUEMAN, WILLIAM LEITCH, ANN ELLIS, the heirs of JAMES LEITCH, the heirs of BENJAMIN LEITCH, the heirs of ELLENDER SMITH + the heirs of MARY BALL.

TH#1/104 + 105: Mr. JOHN HALL administrator of CHARITY STEWART late of Anne Arundel Co deceased. 5 June 1827. Sureties: JOSEPH HODGES + GEORGE W. LINSTED. Fourths of the balance to: GASSAWAY STEWART, SUSAN STEWART, ELEANOR STEWART + MARY STEWART.

TH#1/105 + 106: Mr. RICHARD HARWOOD (of THOMAS) + HENRY H HARWOOD administrators of BENJAMIN HARWOOD. 21 July 1827. No sureties indicated. THOMAS HARWOOD's heir: RICHARD HARWOOD, a seventh; JOHN HARWOOD's heirs: a sixth of a seventh to: THOMAS LYLES in right of his wife MARGARET, WALTER JAMES, CARD-WELL BREATHETT, JOHN HARWOOD, HENRY HARWOOD, ODLE TALBOTT; SAMUEL HARWOOD's heirs: half of a seventh to: ELIZABETH JAMES + MARY WARFIELD; WILLIAM HARWOOD's heirs: a ninth of a seventh to: ANN WATKINS, ELEANOR WATKINS, MARGARET WATKINS, JOHN SEFTON, MARIA HARWOOD, RICHARD STEWART, FREDERICK HARWOOD, RICHARD HAR-WOOD + JOHN THOMAS HARWOOD; MARY STOCKETT's heirs: a sixth of a seventh to: MARY ALEXANDER, HELLEN MCGILL, RODERICK WARFIELD, TUREENE W WATKINS, RICHARD G STOCKETT + JOSEPH N STOCKETT; NICHOLAS HARWOOD's heirs: half of a seventh to: WILLIAM S. GREEN in right of his wife MARY + LEWIS DUVALL; seventh to bro-ther RICHARD HARWOOD.

TH#1/107: Mr. FRANCIS HANCOCK surviving executor of ZACHARIAH CROMWELL late of Anne Arundel Co deceased. 18 July 1837. Sureties: JOHN CROMWELL + ELIJAH WILLIAMS. Third to ONEAL CROMWELL in right of his (unnamed) wife; fourths of the remainder to: ELIZABETH WHITELOCK, PATIENCE CROMWELL, MARGARET CROMWELL + HARRIET CROMWELL.

TH#1/108: Mr. NICHOLAS BREWER Jr administrator of JOHN N W STEWART late of Anne Arundel Co deceased. 1 September 1827. Sureties: NICHOLAS BREWER + WIL-LIAM BREWER. Fourths of the balance to: SAMUEL HARRISON, RICHARD H MERRIKEN, NICHOLAS BREWER Jr. + CHARLES STEWART.

TH#1/108 + 109: Mr. BASIL WARFIELD surviving administrator of PHILIP CECIL late of Anne Arundel Co deceased. 8 September 1827. Sureties: JONATHAN BLA-WERS + JESSE SMALLWOOD. Legatees: the heirs of ZEPHENIAH CECIL, the heirs of JOHN SMITH, the heirs of BENJAMIN BELT, the heirs of JESSE SMALLWOOD, the heirs of JOHN BELT, the heirs of SAMUEL CECIL, ZACHARIAH CECIL + BASIL WARFIELD.

TH#1/109: Mr. ASA ANDERSON administrator de bonis non with will annexed of JULIA GIBBS late of Anne Arundel Co deceased. 10 October 1827. Sureties: THOMAS J HALL + PHILIP PINDELL. Halves of the balance to: MARY GIBBS + CAS-SANDRA GIBBS.

TH#1/110: Mr. ALFRED SELLMAN administrator de bonis non of JONATHAN SELLMAN

18 October 1827. Sureties: JOSEPH N STOCKETT + DAVID M BROGDEN. ANN SELLMAN, widow's third; sixths of the balance to: ALFRED SELLMAN, JOSEPH N STOCKETT, RICHARD SELLMAN, THOMAS WELCH, DAVID M BROGDEN + JOHN H.SELLMAN.

TH#1/110: Mr. THOMAS J HALL one of the administrators of JOHN TILLARD late of Anne Arundel Co deceased. 4 December 1827. No sureties indicated. Thirds to: EMMELINE TILLARD, MARY E TILLARD + JANNETTA H TILLARD.

TH#1/111: Mrs. RACHEL RICHARDSON executrix of JOHN S RICHARDSON late of Anne Arundel Co deceased. 1 January 1828. Sureties: JOHN S RICHARDSON + JAMES DOOLEY. RACHEL RICHARDSON, widow's third; ninths of the balance to: JOHN RICHARDSON, WILLIAM RICHARDSON, MIRANDA RICHARDSON, ELIZABETH RICHARDSON, MARGARET RICHARDSON, MARTHA RICHARDSON, ELLIOTT RICHARDSON + DEBORAH RICHARDSON.

TH#1/111 + 112: Mr. JOHN HALL administrator of EZEKIEL STEWART late of Anne Arundel Co deceased. 8 January 1828. No sureties indicated. Fifths of the balance to: GASSAWAY STEWART, WILLIAM PUMPHREY, MARY STEWART, SUSAN STEWART,+ ELEANOR STEWART.

TH#1/112: Mr. ONEAL CROMWELL administrator of JOHN CROMWELL late of Anne Arundel Co deceased. 15 January 1828. No sureties indicated. Sevenths of the balance to: FRANCES MACCUBBIN, ELIZABETH PHILLIPS, MARGARET PUMPHREY, RUTH MACCUBBIN, RACHEL WILLIAMS, WILLIAM RIDGELY + ONEAL CROMWELL.

TH#1/113: Mr. ISRAEL DAVIDSON administrator of JOHN DAVIDSON late of Anne Arundel Co deceased. 15 January 1828. No sureties indicated. Thirds of the balance to: ISRAEL DAVIDSON, EZEKIEL DAVIDSON + HENRIETTA DAVIDSON.

TH#1/113: Mr. JEREMIAH BERRY administrator of SARAH KING late of Anne Arundel Co deceased. 15 January 1828. No sureties indicated. Thirds of the balance to: WILLIAM H KING, HENRY H KING + ANN M KING.

TH#1/113 + 114: Mr. NICHOLAS BREWER Jr. administrator of SARAH ROBINSON late of Anne Arundel Co deceased. 29 January 1828. Sureties: WILLIAM BREWER + NICHOLAS BREWER. Sixths of the balance to: JOHN W. ROBINSON, FLEMMING ROBINSON, STEWART ROBINSON, JAMES ROBINSON, GEORGE W ROBINSON + JAMES W PACA in right of his wife ANN.

TH#1/114: Mr. SAMUEL WATKINS administrator of REZIN WATKINS late of Anne Arundel Co deceased. 12 February 1828. No sureties indicated. Fifths of the balance to: SAMUEL WATKINS, WALTER WATKINS, JOHN HUNTER in right of his (unnamed) wife, SAMUEL TYDINGS in right of his (unnamed) wife + WILLIAM WATKINS.

TH#1/115: Mr. REZIN ESTEP administrator of FRANCES SUNDERLAND late of Anne Arundel Co deceased. 14 February 1828. Halves of the balance to: ZACHARIAH SUNDERLAND + the heirs of A_____ F_____ SUNDERLAND.

TH#1/115: Mrs. REBECCA SULLIVAN administratrix of JOHN SULLIVAN late of Anne Arundel Co deceased. 28 Marych 1828. No sureties indicated. REBECCA SULLIVAN, widow's third; fifths of the balance to: REZIN D BALDWIN in right of his (unnamed) wife; the heirs of LEMUEL H SULLIVAN, JOHN SULLIVAN, JULIAN SULLIVAN + WILLIAM SULLIVAN.

TH#1/116: Mr. ABNER LINTHICUM one of the administrators of HENRY A JOHNSON late of Anne Arundel Co deceased. 4 March 1828. Sureties: WILLIAM JOHNSON + EZEKIEL

-74-

F JOHNSON. ANN JOHNSON, widow's third; sixths of the balance to: ANN RIGBY, ELEANOR THOMPSON, MARY WHEELER, WILLIAM ARNOLD, ELIZA JOHNSON + THOMAS JOHNSON.

TH#1/116 + 117: Mr. SAMUEL SHEPHERD one of the administrators with the will annexed of JOHN SHEPHERD late of Anne Arundel Co deceased. 15 March 1828. No sureties indicated. MARY SHEPHERD, widow's third; sevenths of the balance to: ELIZA SHEPHERD, ELIZABETH SHEPHERD, MARY SHEPHERD, SUSANNA SHEPHERD, SAMUEL SHEPHERD, WILLIAM SHEPHERD + JOSEPH SHEPHERD.

TH #1/117: Mr. WILLIAM W. SEEDERS administrator of JOHN YEWELL late of Anne Arundel Co deceased. 18 March 1828. No sureties indicated. Sixths of the balance to: BASIL YEWELL, WILLIAM W SEEDERS, JAMES SEEDERS, JOHN YEWELL, SAMUEL OWENS + the heirs of HENRY YEWELL.

TH#1/118: Mr. GEORGE W. LINSTED administrator de bonis non with will annexed of JOHN LINSTED late of Anne Arundel Co deceased. 22 April 1828. Sureties: JOHN ROBINSON + SAMUEL BAUM. Fourths of the balance to: GEORGE W LINSTED, ELIJAH ROCKHOLD, WILLIAM LINSTED + JOHN FOWLER.

TH#1/118: Mr. HENRY WELLING executor of WILLIAM RIDGELY late of Anne Arundel Co. deceased. 23 April 1828. Sureties: WILLIAM WELLING + BASIL BURGESS. Sixths to: CHARLES G. RIDGELY, PHILEMON D RIDGELY, RACHEL DORSEY + SARAH WELLING; third of a sixth to: CATHARINE D WARFIELD, GEORGE W WARFIELD, WILLIAM R WARFIELD, REMUS GRIFFITH, LYDIA CRAN + RUTH H CUMMINS.

TH#1/119: Mr. JACOB W BIRD administrator of JOHN BIRD late of Anne Arundel Co deceased. 20 May 1828. Sureties: NATHANIEL CHEW + THOMAS BIRD. MARY BIRD, widow's third; sixths of the remaining balance to: JOHN BIRD, MARY BIRD, RICHARD BIRD, MARGARET BIRD, LEMUEL BIRD + FRANCIS BIRD.

TH #1/119 + 120: Mr. WILLIAM G JONES administrator of MARIA A F SUNDERLAND late of Anne Arundel Co deceased. 13 May 1828. No sureties indicated. Fourths of the balance to: WILLIAM G. JONES, BENJAMIN JONES, WILLIAM JONES + JOHN JONES.

TH#1/121: Mrs. MARY WELCH administratrix de bonis non of AARON WELCH late of Anne Arundel Co deceased. 13 September 1828. No sureties indicated. Sevenths of the balance to: AARON WELCH, HENRY WELCH, MARY WELCH (now JOHNSON), JOHN WELCH, CHARLES WELCH, BENJAMIN WELCH + JOSEPH WELCH.

TH#1/122: Mr. FRANCIS HANCOCK administrator of PATIENCE CROMWELL late of Anne Arundel Co deceased. 26 September 1828. No sureties indicated. Fourths of the balance to: SARAH CROMWELL, ELIZABETH WHITELOCK, MARGARET CROMWELL + HARRIOT CROMWELL.

TH#1/123: Mr. SAMUEL BRADFORD administrator of NATHAN BRADFORD late of Anne Arundel Co deceased. 21 October 1828. Sureties: GEORGE BRADFORD + HENRY HAMMOND. SARAH BRADFORD (now LUCAS), widow's third; the remaining balance to LEVY SWAMSTEAD.

TH#1/124 + 125: Dr. BENJAMIN OGLE executor of HENRY M OGLE late of Anne Arundel Co deceased. 10 October 1828. No sureties indicated. MARY CONNER, a third; thirds of the remainder to: MARY BEVANS, LAURA BEVANS + JOHN BEVANS.

TH#1/126: Mr. THOMAS BURLEIGH administrator with will annexed of ELEANOR BURLEIGH late of Anne Arundel Co deceased. 15 October 1828. Sureties: ELEANOR

BURLEIGH + VACHEL SEVERN. Thirds of the balance to: ANN BURLEIGH, ELEANOR BUR-
LEIGH + THOMAS BURLEIGH.

TH#1/127: Mr. JOHN R THOMAS administrator of ANN R HAMMOND late of Anne Arundel Co deceased. 9 December 1828. No sureties indicated. Halves of the balance to: REZIN HAMMOND + MARY HAMMOND.

TH#1/128: Mrs. FRANCES MOXLEY administratrix of JOHN MOXLEY late of Anne Arundel Co deceased. 22 October 1828. No sureties indicated. FRANCES MOXLEY,
widow's third; sixths of the balance to: CHARLES MOXLEY, LLOYD MOXLEY, LUTHER
MOXLEY, GERUSA(?) MOXLEY, EVELINE MOXLEY + CELICE MOXLEY.

TH#1/129: Mr. THOMAS ANDERSON administrator of JAMES SMITH late of Anne Arundel Co deceased. 6 November 1828. No sureties indicated. Sixths of the balance to: RACHEL A SMITH, OCTAVIA O SMITH, JAMES A SMITH, EDWARD O SMITH, THOMAS
O SMITH + GUSTAVUS A SMITH.

TH#1/130: Mrs. CATHERINE MANAKA administrator with will annexed of WILLIAM
MANAKA. 10 November 1828. No sureties indicated. CATHERINE MANAKA, widow's
third; fourths of the balance to: JOHN MANAKA, REUBEN MANAKA, JOSEPH MANAKA +
MARY MANAKA.

TH#1/131? Mr. REZIN ESTEP administrator de bonis non with will annexed of JO-
SEPH SMITH late of Anne Arundel Co deceased. 13 November 1828. No sureties in-
dicated. Thirteenths of the balance to: THOMAS SMITH, JOSEPH SMITH, WILLIAM
SMITH, SAMUEL SMITH, JAMES SMITH, MARY PARROTT, ELIZABETH BIRD, ANN STALLINGS,
FANNY GRIFFITH, RACHEL RINE, SARAH CRANDELL, CATHERINE WHITTINGTON + HENRIETTA
YOUNG.

TH#1/132: Mr. THOMAS S. ALEXANDER administrator of MARY H ALEXANDER late of
Anne Arundel Co deceased. 21 May 1828. Sureties: R____ G____ STOCKETT +
G____ L____ STOCKETT. Sixths of the balance to: THOMAS S ALEXANDR, MARY ALEX-
ANDER, WILLIAM ALEXANDER, ANN ALEXANDER, JOHN H ALEXANDER + JANE ALEXANDER.

TH#1/132: Mr. BARUCH FOWLER administrator of ANN M MINSKY late of Anne Arundel Co deceased. 3 June 1828. No sureties indicated. Fifths of the balance
to: JOHN H MACCUBBIN, HARRIET R MINSKY, JOHN S MINSKY, HANSON MINSKY + ROBERT
MINSKY.

TH#1/133: Mr. JOHN H BROWN administrator of HENRIETTA BROWN late of Anne Arundel Co deceased. 10 June 1828. No sureties indicated. Eighths of the balance
to: HENRY H BROWN, JOHN H BROWN, JAMES NEWBORN, GEORGE G GAMBRILL, THOMAS J
STOCKETT, REZIN BROWN, PHILIP BROWN + WILLIAM BROWN.

TH#1/134: Mr. BENJAMIN MCCENEY administrator of MARTHA MCCENEY Jr. late of
Anne Arundel Co deceased. 10 June 1828. No sureties indicated. Fifths of the
balance to: JOSEPH OWENS, BENJAMIN MCCENEY, JACOB MCCENEY, JOHN CLAYTON + ED-
WARD MCCENEY.

TH#1/136: Mr. THOMAS ANDERSON administrator of JAMES SMITH late of Anne Arundel Co deceased. 11 June 1828. No sureties indicated. Fifths of the balance
to: RACHEL A SMITH, OCTAVIA O SMITH, JAMES A SMITH, EDWARD O SMITH + JOHN T
SMITH.

TH#1/137: Mr. JOHN KNIGHTON + Mr. RICHARD WILLIAMS administrators of MARY LEAD-
INHAM late of Anne Arundel Co deceased. 17 June 1828. No sureties indicated.
Halves of the balance to: JOSEPH WILLIAMS + GASSAWAY KNIGHTON in right of his wife

TH#1/138: Mr. HEZEKIAH LINTHICUM administrator of ANROSE LINTHICUM late of
Anne Arundel Co deceased. 17 June 1828. No sureties indicated. Eighths of
the balance to: ZACHARIAH LINTHICUM, MARY A LINTHICUM, SARAH L LINTHICUM, MAT-
THIAS LINTHICUM, ADALINE LINTHICUM, WILLIAM A LINTHICUM, ELIZABETH LINTHICUM +
CHARLES LINTHICUM.

TH#1/138: Mr. THOMAS J HALL administrator of JESSE LEITCH late of Anne Arundel
Co deceased. 1 July 1828. No sureties indicated. Ninths of the balance to:
the heirs of THOMAS LEITCH, the heirs of DRAYDON FOWLER, the heirs of ELIZABETH
TRUEMAN, WILLIAM LEITCH, ANN ELLIS, the heirs of JAMES LEITCH, the heirs of
BENJAMIN LEITCH, the heirs of ELLENDER SMITH + the heirs of MARY BALL.

TH#1/138: Mr. BARUCH FOWLER administrator de bonis non of SAMUEL MINSKY late
of Anne Arundel Co deceased. 13 February 1828. No sureties indicated. ANN M
MINSKY, widow's third; fourths of the remaining balance to: HANSON MINSKY,
JOHN S MINSKY, HARRIET MINSKY + ROBERT MINSKY.

TH#1/139: Mr. BARUCH FOWLER administrator of ANN M MINSKY late of Anne Arundel
Co deceased. 13 February 1828. No sureties indicated. Fifths of the balance
to: JOHN H MACCUBBIN, HANSON MINSKY, JOHN S MINSKY, HARRIET MINSKY + ROBERT
MINSKY.

TH#1/140: Mr. REZIN ESTEP administrator of ELIZABETH CROSBY late of Anne Arundel Co deceased. 17 September 1828. Sureties: JOHN WEEKES + THOMAS HODGES.
Ninths of the balance to: BENJAMIN CARR, WALTER CARR, WILLIAM CARR, the heirs
of JACOB CARR, the heirs of JESSE DEW, THOMAS DAWKINS, the heirs of SAMUEL DEW,
the heirs of MARY CARR + the heirs of JOHN CARR.

TH#1/141: Mr. JAMES ANDERSON administrator of ANDREW ANDERSON late of Anne
Arundel Co deceased. 13 January 1829. No sureties indicated. ANN ANDERSON,
widow's third; sevenths of the balance to: JESSE ORME, JOSEPHUS BISHUP, CABEL
BARNEY, BENJAMIN PENN, FRANCES ANDERSON, JAMES ANDERSON + LEONARD ANDERSON.

TH#1/142: Mr. THOMAS BENSON executor of RICHARD BENSON late of Anne Arundel
Co deceased. 16 December 1828. No sureties indicated. Thirds of the balance
to: RICHARD BENSON, JOHN BENSON + SAMUEL BENSON.

TH#1/143: Mr. RICHARD SELLMAN administrator of ELIZABETH WATKINS late of Anne
Arundel Co deceased. 27 January 1829. Sureties: WILLIAM J HALL + JOSEPH N
STOCKETT. Halves of the balance to: THOMAS B HALL in right of his (unnamed)
wife + RICHARD SELLMAN in right of this (unnamed) wife.

TH#1/144: Mr. VACHEL R SHIPLEY administrator of RACHEL SHIPLEY late of Anne
Arundel Co deceased. 20 April 1829. Sureties: WARNER WELCH + SAMUEL RIDGELY.
Thirteenths of the balance to: STEPHEN DEVER, BASIL DEVER, RICHARD DEVER, SAM-
UEL DEVER, JOSEPH DEVER, HENRY DEVER, PHILIP DEVER, DEBORAH DEVER, SARAH SHIP-
LEY, MARGARET NIVIS, NANCY BROTHERS, SUSAN MACKELY + MARY MUSGROVE.

TH#1/145: Mr. JOHN BROOKS administrator of DANIEL MAHAND late of Anne Arundel
Co deceased. 21 April 1829. Sureties: JOHN SMITH + CHARLES SHORTER. NANCY
MAHAND, widow's third; sixths of the balance to: ANN BROOKS, NANCY MAHAND, SUSAN
DRAPER, CHARLES MAHAND, SARAH MAHAND + DANIEL MAHAND.

TH#1/146: Mr. WILLIAM KNIGHTON administrator of SUSANNA KNIGHTON late of Anne
Arundel Co deceased. 18 May 1829. Sureties: BENJAMIN CHANEY + JOSEPH WAYSON.
Thirds to: RICHARD KNIGHTON + WILLIAM KNIGHTON; sixths to: SUSANNA COLE + WES-
LEY COLE.

TH#1/146:  Mr. ROBERT H MCPHERSON administrator of THOMAS MCPHERSON late of
Anne Arundel Co deceased.  20 May 1829.  Sureties: JOSEPH ALLEN + ISAAC OWENS
(of BENJAMIN).  MARY MCPHERSON, widow's third; sixths of the remaining balance
to: THOMAS T MCPHERSON, ROBERT H MCPHERSON, ISAAC OWENS (of BENJAMIN), ROBERT
GARNER, MARGARET H MCPHERSON + WILLIAM H MCPHERSON.

TH#1/147:  Messrs THOMAS PUMPHREY + WILLIAM PUMPHREY executors of WILLIAM PUM-
PHREY late of Anne Arundel Co deceased.  15 June 1829.  Sureties: ABRAHAM C.
STEWART + JOSEPH HAWKINS.  Sevenths of the balance to: THOMAS PUMPHREY, WILLIAM
PUMPHREY, MARGARET BENSON, MARY BENSON, HARRIET BENSON, LLOYD RIDGELY + MARY
ANN JOHNSON.

TH#1/148:  Mr. ELIE MOLESWORTH administrator of JOSEPH MOLESWORTH late of Anne
Arundel Co deceased.  17 August 1829.  Sureties: CHARLES D WARFIELD + ADAM DE-
LANDER.  Sevenths of the balance to: GEORGE MOLESWORTH, ELIE MOLESWORTH, SAMUEL
MOLESWORTH, HARRIET MOLESWORTH, NANCY MOLESWORTH, JAMES MOLESWORTH + HENRIETTA
MOLEWWORTH.

TH#1/149:  Mr. MORTIMER DORSEY administrator of RICHARD DORSEY late of Anne
Arundel Co deceased.  17 August 1829.  Sureties: CALEB DORSEY + HUMPHREY DOR-
SEY.  ANNE DORSEY, widow's third; twelfths of the remaining balance to: MORTI-
MER DORSEY, ELIZA A NORRIS, CAROLINE WHEELER, JOHN DORSEY, RICHARD DORSEY, CALEB
DORSEY, LOUISA HOOD MARY DORSEY, ACHSAH DORSEY, HANSON DORSEY, SEPTIMUS DORSEY
+ HENRY DORSEY.

TH#1/150:  Mr. WILLIAM HASLIP administrator with will annexed of WILLIAM HASLIP
late of Anne Arundel Co deceased.  19 August 1829.  Sureties: JOHN MCCAULEY +
JOHN STRINGER.  Fourths of the balance to: GIDEON WHITE, JOHN WEAVER, ANN FELL
+ WILLIAM HASLIP.

TH#1/151:  Mr. ROBERT HEATH one of the administrators de bonis non of SARAH
MACCUBBIN late of Anne Arundel Co deceased.  18 September 1829.  Sureties:
DAVID RIDGELY + JOHN ARNOLD.  Thirds of the balance to: KENSEY TYDINGS in right
of his wife MARY, ROBERT HEATH in right of his wife NANCY + THOMAS JOHNSON in
right of his mother REBECCA JOHNSON.

TH#1/152:  Mr. JOHN A.WHITTINGTON administrator of JACOB PATTERSON late of Anne
Arundel Co deceased.  21 September 1829.  Sureties: WILLIAM URQUHART + HENRY
CHILDS.  Fifths to daughters: NICA DOWELL, SARAH WHITTINGTON, ELIZABETH WARD,
PRISCILLA DOWELL + MARY GRIFFITH.

TH#1/153:  Mrs. SARAH ANN RIDGELY administratrix of ARCHIBALD RIDGELY late of
Anne Arundel Co deceased.  23 September 1829.  Sureties: GASSAWAY WATKINS +
JOHN P(?) BELT.  SARAH ANN RIDGELY (now WHITE), widow's third; thirds of the remaining balance to: ARCHIBALD RIDGELY, W_____ C_____ RIDGELY + DANIEL BANDA(?)
in right of his wife EMELIA.

TH#1/153:  Mrs. ELIZABETH GRIFFITH administratrix of CHARLES GRIFFITH late of
Anne Arundel Co deceased.  22 September 1829.  Sureties: JOHN IJAMS + WILLIAM
HASLIP.  ELIZABETH GRIFFITH, widow's third; halves of the remaining balance to:
RICHARD GRIFFITH + CHARLES GRIFFITH.

TH#1/154:  Mrs. REBECCA SULLIVAN administrator of JOHN SULLIVAN late of Anne
Arundel Co deceased.  23 September 1829.  Sureties: BASIL SHEPHERD + JOHN SUL-
LIVAN.  REBECCA SULLIVAN, widow's third; fifths of the remaining balance to:
REZIN D BALDWIN in right of his (unnamed) wife, the heirs of LEMUEL H SULLIVAN,

JOHN SULLIVAN, JULIAN SULLIVAN + WILLIAM SULLIVAN.

TH#1/155: Mr. FRANCIS HANCOCK executor of JOHN CROMWELL late of Anne Arundel Co deceased. 21 October 1829. Sureties: JOHN HANCOCK + FRANCIS WILLIAMS. Thirds of the balance to: ROBERT BOONE in right of his wife RHODA, who was the widow of the deceased; ELEANOR CROMWELL; PATIENCE CROMWELL.

TH#1/156: Mr. CHARLES G WORTHINGTON executor of BRICE J G WORTHINGTON late of Anne Arundel Co deceased. 27 October 1829. Sureties: FRANCIS CROSS + JOHN WARFIELD. Thirds of the balance to: WILLIAM H WORTHINGTON, ACHSAH ANN WORTHINGTON + MARY WORTHINGTON.

TH#1/157: Mr. BARUCH FOWLER administrator de bonis non of SAMUEL MINSKY late of Anne Arundel Co deceased. 3 June 1828. No sureties indicated. ANN M MINSKY, widow's third; fourths of the remaining balance to: HANSON MINSKY, ROBERT MINSKY, JOHN S MINSKY + HARRIET R MINSKY.

TH#1/158: Mr. BENJAMIN MCCENEY administrator de bonis non of ZACHARIAH MCCENEY late of Anne Arundel Co deceased. 28 October 1829. Sureties: JOHN CLAYTON + JACOB MCCENEY. Fifths of the remaining balance to: SARAH OWENS, BENJAMIN MCCENEY, JACOB MCCENEY, MARY CLAYTON + EDWARD MCCENEY.

TH#1/159: Mr. JAMES ANDERSON administrator of ANDREW ANDERSON late of Anne Arundel Co deceased. 17 November 1829. No sureties indicated. ANN ANDERSON, widow's third; sevenths of the remaining balance to: JESSE ORME, JOSEPHUS BISHOP, CALEB BERRY, BENJAMIN PENN, FRANCIS ANDERSON, JAMES ANDERSON + LEONARD ANDERSON.

TH#1/160: Mr. JOHN LAWTON executor of NICHOLAS HALLOWAY late of Anne Arundel Co deceased. 18 November 1829. Sureties: RICHARD MARSH + ELIJAH GRAY. RUTH GRAY, half; the remaining half shared by: LANDY HANCOCK, MARY LINSTED, ELIZABETH BOONE + JOHN HANCOCK.

TH#1/161: Mr. RICHARD L STOCKETT administrator of WILLIAM J STOCKETT late of Anne Arundel Co deceased. 23 November 1829. Sureties: JOSEPH N STOCKETT + JOHN STOCKETT. Mrs. MARY STOCKETT, widow's third; ninths of the remaining balance to: RICHARD L STOCKETT, WILLIAM J STOCKETT, JOHN H STOCKETT, JAMES B STOCKETT, GEORGE E STOCKETT, NICHOLAS A STOCKETT, JOSEPH N STOCKETT, WESLEY STOCKETT + THOMAS N STOCKETT.

TH#1/162: Mr. ENOS SHIPLEY administrator of DAVID MEEK Jr late of Anne Arundel Co deceased. 20 November 1829. Sureties: RICHARD PHELPS + WILLIAM SHIPLEY. Mrs. ELIZABETH MEEK, widow's third; fourths of the remaining balance to: ANN MEEK, JOHN MEEK, DAVID B MEEK + LOUISA MEEK.

TH#1/163: Mr. SAMUEL JONES administrator with will annexed of RICHARD SCOTT late of Anne Arundel Co deceased. 18 December 1829. Sureties: JOHN S SELBY + ROBERT S BRYAN. Legatees: JANE SCOTT, RICHARD SCOTT + TEMPERANCE COUCH.

TH#1/163: Mr. WILLIAM W SEEDERS administrator de bonis non of RICHARD WEEDON late of Anne Arundel Co deceased. 22 December 1829. Sureties: ROBERT MOSS + HENRY HALL (of ELISHA). Fourths of the balance to: RICHARD WEEDON, MARY WEEDON, HARRIET WEEDON + ELIZABETH WEEDON.

TH#1/164: Mr. THOMAS W WATKINS administrator de bonis non with the will annexed of NICHOLAS WATKINS late of Anne Arundel Co deceased. 30 December 1829. Sureties:

NICHOLAS WATKINS Jr + GASSAWAY WATKINS. Half of the balance to: LAFAYETTE WAT-KINS; the remaining half of the balance to the heirs of WILLIAM PITT WATKINS: HARRIET WATKINS (widow of WILLIAM P WATKINS, a third), WILLIAM T WATKINS, HAR-RIET ANN WATKINS, MANELIA WATKINS + OLIVE P WATKINS.

TH#1/165: Mr. BENJAMIN MCCENEY administrator de bonis non with will annexed of ZACHARIAH MCCENEY late of Anne Arundel Co deceased. 29 January 1830. Sureties: JOHN CLAYTON + JACOB MCCENEY. Fifths of the balance to: SARAH OWENS, BENJAMIN MCCENEY, JACOB MCCENEY, MARY CLAYTON (wife of JOHN CLAYTON) + EDWARD MCCENEY.

THOMAS J HALL one of the administrators of JOHN H TILLARD late of Anne Arundel Co deceased, 17 February 1830. Sureties: WILLIAM WEEMS + WILLIAM H HALL. Thirds of the balance to: EMMELINE DUVALL (formerly TILLARD), MARY E TILLARD + JANETTA H TILLARD.

TH#1/166: Mr. JOHN SELLMAN administrator of WILLIAM FISHER late of Anne Arundel Co deceased. 16 February 1830. Sureties: JOHN IGLEHART + JOHN S SELBY. HENRI-ETTA FISHER (now ROGERS), widow's third; fifths of the remaining balance to: JOHN H FISHER, WILLIAM FISHER, MARY A FISHER, HEZEKIAH FISHER + SUSANNA FISHER.

TH#1/167: Messrs BASIL BURGESS + THOMAS D BURGESS administrators of VACHEL BUR-GESS late of Anne Arundel Co deceased. 16 March 1830. Sureties: HENRY WELLING + NICHOLAS D WARFIELD. Mrs. REBECCA BURGESS, widow's third; tenths of the remain-ing balance to: ANN D BURGESS, PEREGRINE BURGESS, JULIET BURGESS, ELIZABETH HINES, HARRIET WATKINS, MARY V BURGESS, THOMAS D BURGESS, REBECCA O BURGESS, HETTY W BURGESS + VACHEL BURGESS.

TH#1/168: Mr. RICHARD MERCIER executor of ANDREW MERCIER late of Anne Arundel Co deceased. 19 April 1820. Sureties: ANDREW MERCIER + RICHARD MERCIER. RUTH MERCIER, widow's third; fourths of the remaining balance to: JOHN MERCIER, RICH-ARD MERCIER, the heirs of JOSHUA MERCIER + ANDREW MERCIER.

TH#1/169: Mr. RICHARD MERCIER administrator of JOSHUA MERCIER late of Anne Arun-del Co deceased. 19 April 1830. Sureties: MICHAEL IGLEHART + JOHN W RINGROSE. ELIZA MERCIER, widow's third; fourths of the remaining balance to: RUTH MERCIER, JOHN W MERCIER, MARY MERCIER + AZEL MERCIER.

TH#1/170: Mr. ROBERT MOSS executor of JAMES MOSS late of Anne Arundel Co deceased. 20 April 1830. Sureties: JAMES MOSS + ELIE DUVALL. Thirds of the balance to: JAMES MOSS, MARY ANN MOSS + HAMILTON P MOSS.

TH#1/171: Mr. NATHAN DAY administrator de bonis non with will annexed of JOHN DAY late of Anne Arundel Co deceased. 20 April 1830. Sureties: EDWARD BALDWIN + JOHN E QUESENBURY. Fourths of the remaining balance to: SAMUEL DAY, JOHN DAY, MARY DAY + ANN ELIZA DAY.

TH#1/172: Mr. RICHARD H MERRIKEN one of the executors of HENRY HAMMOND late of Anne Arundel Co deceased. 21 April 1830. Sureties: BASIL SHEPHERD + ZACHARIAH MERRIKEN. HENRIETTA HAMMOND, widow's third; thirds of the remaining balance to: HENRY HAMMOND, NATHAN HAMMOND + JOHN THOMAS HAMMOND.

TH#1/173: Mr. HEZEKIAH LINTHICUM administrator of ZACHARIAH LINTHICUM late of Anne Arundel Co deceased. 22 April 1830. Sureties: WILLIAM LINTHICUM + SETH SWEETSER. Eighths of the balance to: THOMAS NORWOOD, LICIOUS L X O'BRIAN, SARAH L LINTHICUM, MATTHIAS LINTHICUM, ELIZABETH LINTHICUM, CHARLES G LINTHICUM + RA-CHEL A LINTHICUM.

TH#1/174: Mrs. ANN JANETTA WATERS administratrix of WILLIAM M WATERS late of
Anne Arundel Co deceased. 10 June 1830. Sureties: Dr. WILLSON WATERS + RAM-
SAY WATERS. ANN JANETTA WATERS, widow's third; thirds of the remaining balance
to: REBECCA WATERS, JOHN WILLSON WATERS + MARIA WATERS.

TH#1/174: Mr. THOMAS W WATKINS administrator with will annexed of MARY HOWARD
late of Anne Arundel Co deceased. 14 June 1830. Sureties: HENRY WELLING +
NICHOLAS WATKINS Jr. Major legatee: MARY ANN WATERS; remainder shared equally
by: MARY ELIZABETH HOWARD, JOSEPH HOWARD WATERS, WASHINGTON WATERS, RACHEL HOW-
ARD WATERS + ISABELLA E O MADDEN WATERS.

TH#1/175: Mr. THOMAS W WATKINS administrator of WILLIAM P WATKINS late of Anne
Arundel Co deceased. 14 June 1830. Sureties: NICHOLAS WATKINS Jr + GASSAWAY
WATKINS. HARRIET WATKINS, widow's third; fourths of the remaining balance to:
WILLIAM T WATKINS, JULIA WATKINS, MANELIA E WATKINS + OLIVER P WATKINS.

TH#1/175: Mr. BERRY GRIFFITH administrator of HORATIO TILLY late of Anne Arundel Co deceased. 18 September 1829. Sureties: SAMUEL GRIFFITH + JAMES HUNTER.
Thirds of the balance to: BERRY GRIFFITH, SARAH TILLY + LUCRETIA TILLY.

TH#1/176: Mr. NICHOLAS C GILL administrator of WILLIAM GILL late of Anne Arun-
del Co deceased. 13 August 1830. Sureties: CHARLES GRIFFIN + JOHN MATTHEWS.
Eighths of the balance to: ELIZABETH GENT, NICHOLAS C GILL, MARY GILL, JOSHUA
GILL, STEPHEN GILL, BENNETT GILL, WILLIAM GILL + WILLIAM PALMER.

TH#1/176: Mr. RICHARD SELLMAN administrator of ELIZABETH WATKINS late of Anne
Arundel Co deceased. 20 August 1830. Sureties: WILLIAM J HALL + JOSEPH N
STOCKETT. Halves of the balance to: THOMAS B HALL in right of his (unnamed)
wife + RICHARD SELLMAN in right of his (unnamed) wife.

TH#1/177: Mr. JAMES IGLEHART administrator of FREDERICK HARWOOD late of Anne
Arundel Co deceased. 26 August 1830. Sureties: JOHN IGLEHART + LEONARD IGLE-
HART. Balance divided by: MARY E HARWOOD (mother); siblings: RICHARD HARWOOD,
JOHN T HARWOOD, ANN WATKINS, ELEANOR WATKINS + MARGARET WATKINS; and JOHN SEF-
TON in right of his (unnamed) wife, RICHARD STEWART in right of his (unnamed)
wife + JOSEPH STEWART in right of his (unnamed) wife; + the heirs of WILLIAM
HARWOOD (brother of the deceased).

TH#1/177: Mr. FRANCIS WELCH administrator of JOSEPH NORMAN late of Anne Arundel
Co deceased. 3 September 1830. Sureties: JOHN NORMAN + RICHARD PARKINSON.
Thirds of the balance to: FRANCIS WELCH, SAMUEL EVANS + JOHN LAMB.

TH#1/178: Mr. THOMAS J HALL administrator of JESSE LEITCH late of Anne Arundel
Co deceased. 14 September 1830. Sureties: JOHN SELLMAN + WILLIAM NORMAN. Ninths
of the balance to: the heirs of THOMAS LEITCH, the heirs of DRAYDON FOWLER,
WILLIAM LEITCH, ANN ELLIS, the heirs of JAMES LEITCH, the heirs of BENJAMIN LEITCH,
the heirs of ELLENDER SMITH, the heirs of MARY BALL + ELIZABETH TRUEMAN.

TH#1/178 + 179: Mr. JOHN S E NUTWELL administrator of JAMES NUTWELL late of
Anne Arundel Co deceased. 15 September 1830. Sureties: WILLIAM HALL Jr + THOM-
AS HARDESTY. TOMERSON NUTWELL, widow's third; fifths of the remaining balance to:
JOHN S E NUTWELL, GASSAWAY WINTERSON, MARY NUTWELL, GEORGE W NUTWELL + SARAH NUT-
WELL.

TH#1/179: Dr. GUSTAVUS WARFIELD one of the administrators of CHARLES A WAR-
FIELD late of Anne Arundel Co deceased. 10 December 1830. Sureties: PERE-
GRINE WARFIELD + THOMAS HOOD. Sevenths of the balance to: RICHARD SNOWDEN in
right of his wife LOUISA, RICHARD SNOWDEN in right of his wife ELIZABETH, HENRY
R WARFIELD, CHARLES A WARFIELD, PEREGRINE WARFIELD, GUSTAVUS WARFIELD + SAMUEL
THOMAS.

TH#1/179 + 180: Mr. REZIN D. HEWITT + Mr. ELI HEWITT administrators of ELI
HEWITT late of Anne Arundel Co deceased. 14 December 1830. Sureties: UPTON D
WELCH + WASHINGTON GAITHER. Thirds of the balance to: REZIN D HEWITT, ELI
HEWITT + JACOB HEWITT.

TH#1/180: Mr. ABNER LINTHICUM administrator of DAVID MEEK late of Anne Arundel
Co deceased. 16 December 1830. Sureties: SAMUEL YEALDHALL + JESSE CONWAY.
Tenths of the balance to: ANN PATTERSON, RACHEL PATTERSON, ELIZA PATTERSON,
ELEANOR BROWN, DEBORAH CONOWAY, SARAH LEATHERWOOD, ANN MEEK, JOHN MEEK, DAVID
B MEEK + LOUISA MEEK.

TH#1/181: Mr. FRANCIS SHEKELL administrator with will annexed of FRANCIS SHE-
KELL.late of Anne Arundel Co deceased. 13 January 1831. Sureties: WILLIAM
MCCENEY (of JOSEPH) + JOSEPH WARD. Thirds of the balance to: FRANCIS SHEKELL,
LEVI SHEKELL + RICHARD SHEKELL.

TH#1/181: Mrs. ELIZA MCCENEY surviving executrix of JOSEPH MCCENEY late of
Anne Arundel Co deceased. 13 January 1831. Sureties: REZIN ESTEP + JOHN CLAY-
TON. Fourths of the balance to: ELIZA MCCENEY, WILLIAM MCCENEY, GEORGE MCCENEY
+ HENRY MCCENEY.

TH#1/182: Messrs RICHARD M CHASE + RICHARD J CRABB administrators of MATILDA
CHASE late of Anne Arundel Co deceased. 9 November 1830. Sureties: HESTER A
CHASE + ANN CHASE. Thirds of the balance to: HESTER A CHASE, MATILDA CHASE +
FRANCES C T CHASE.

TH#1/182: Mr. JAMES IGLEHART administrator of MARGARET WATKINS late of Anne
Arundel Co deceased. 31 January 1831. Sureties: JOHN IGLEHART + LEONARD IGLE-
HART. Halves of the balance to: PARMELIA STEWART + MATILDA ANN STEWART; an
eighth to the heirs of MARIA STEWART; eighths of the remainder to: SOPHIA RIDG-
WAY, LOUISA CLAGETT, MARGARET WATKINS, ELEANOR WATKINS, MARY ELIZA WATKINS,
NICHOLAS G WATKINS + GEORGE WATKINS.

TH#1/183: Mr. WILLIAM J GREEN executor of MARY CALLAHAN late of Anne Arundel
Co deceased. 16 March 1831. Sureties: JONAS GREEN + SAMUEL MAYNARD. Eighths
of the balance to: SARAH DUVALL, ELIZA CALLAHAN, ANNE HARWOOD, RICHARD HARWOOD
(of THOMAS) in right of unnamed wife, SAMUEL MAYNARD in right of unnamed wife,
JOHN RIDGELY in right of unnamed wife, WILLIAM S GREEN in right of unnamed wife
+ THOMAS W LENDRUM in right of unnamed wife.

TH#1/184: Mr. JOHN SMITH administrator of SABIT SMITH late of Anne Arundel Co
deceased. 12 April 1831. Sureties: CHARLES R STEWART + JOSEPH HODGES. Sixths
of the balance to: JAMES SMITH, JOHN SMITH, ELLEN SMITH, JETHRO SMITH, RACHEL
SMITH + ANN SMITH.

TH#1/184: Mr. RICHARD H MERRIKEN administrator of WILLIAM H STINCHCOMB late of
Anne Arundel Co deceased. 13 April 1831. Sureties: GRAFTON B DUVALL + ZACHA-
RIAH MERRIKEN. SARAH STINCHCOMB, widow's third; fifths of the remainder to:
ELIZA ANN STINCHCOMB, THOMAS STINCHCOMB, WILLIAM STINCHCOMB, ALFRED STINCHCOMB
+ MARGARET STINCHCOMB.

TH#1/185: Mrs. MARY HOWARD administratrix of SAMUEL H HOWARD late of Anne Arundel Co deceased. 8 July 1831. Sureties: JOHN JOHNSON, NICHOLAS BREWER + DANIEL DELOZIER. MARY HOWARD, widow's third (she is a distributee of ANN HOWARD, a daughter of the deceased); remainder of balance to RICHARD W GILL, administrator de bonis non of SAMUEL HARVEY HOWARD.

TH#1/185: Messrs REZIN D HEWITT + ELI HEWITT administrators of ELI HEWITT late of Anne Arundel Co deceased. 19 July 1831. Sureties: UPTON D WELCH + WASHINGTON GAITHER. MARTHA HEWITT, widow's third; thirds of the remainder to: REZIN D HEWITT, ELI HEWITT + JACOB HEWITT.

TH#1/186: Mr. GASSAWAY PINDELL administrator of NICHOLAS PINDELL late of Anne Arundel Co deceased. 10 August 1831. Sureties: RINALDO PINDELL + EDWARD DUVALL. Sixths of the balance to: MARGARET PINDELL, ELIZABETH PINDELL, GASSAWAY PINDELL, PHILIP PINDELL, THOMAS PINDELL + JOHN PINDELL.

TH#1/187: Mr. JOHN P DAVIS administrator of DANIEL P JACOB late of Anne Arundel Co deceased. 14 September 1831. Sureties: JOSEPH HARWOOD + WILLIAM DAVIS. Thirds of the balance to: JOHN P DAVIS in right of (unnamed) wife, ARNOLD JACOB + the children of ROBERT JACOB, who were: SALLY HODGES, MARY ANN HARWOOD, SUSAN M JACOB, CAROLINE JACOB, MATILDA J JACOB, ELIZABETH JACOB, JULIANNA JACOB + EDWARD JACOB.

TH#1/187: Mr. WILLIAM W SEEDERS administrator of BASIL YEWELL late of Anne Arundel Co deceased. 19 September 1831. Sureties: WILLIAM SCOTT + THOMAS YEWELL. ELIZA YEWELL, widow's third; the remaining two-thirds to: JOHN T. YEWELL + BASIL YEWELL.

TH#1/187 + 188: Mrs. RACHEL HOWARD administratrix of CORNELIUS HOWARD late of Anne Arundel Co deceased. 12 October 1831. Sureties: AZEL WATERS + RODERICK BURGESS. Thirds of the balance to: RACHEL HOWARD (widow), MARY E HOWARD + SARAH E HOWARD.

TH#1/188: Mr. JOHN J DAVIDSON administrator with will annexed of CHARLES WALLACE late of Anne Arundel Co deceased. 26 October 1831. Sureties: SAMUEL J DAVIDSON + FRANCES DONALDSON. Thirds of the balance to: the children of REBECCA HANSON, the children of CATHARINE LATIMER + the children of REBECCA CAMPBELL.

TH#1/188: Messrs JOHN HANCOCK + STEPHEN W HANCOCK administrators de bonis non of SARAH JACOBS late of Anne Arundel Co deceased. 8 November 1831. Sureties: ROBERT BOONE + JOHN M WELCH. Thirds of the balance to: SARAH JACOBS, JOHN JACOBS + ZACHARIAH JACOBS.

TH#1/189: Mr. THOMAS FRANKLIN surviving executor of JOHN SHAW late of Anne Arundel Co deceased. 5 December 1831. Sureties: DANIEL HART + DENNIS CLAUDE Jr. Fifths of the balance to: THOMAS SHAW, MARY SHAW, JAMES SHAW (deceased), GEORGE SHAW (deceased) + THOMAS FRANKLIN in right of his wife ELIZABETH.

TH#1/189 + 190: Messrs JOHN HANCOCK + STEPHEN W HANCOCK administrators de bonis non of JOHN JACOBS late of Anne Arundel Co deceased. 6 January 1832. Sureties: ROBERT BOONE + JOHN M WELCH. Fourths of the balance to: ANN E JACOBS, ZACHARIAH JACOBS, JOHN JACOBS + SARAH JACOBS.

TH#1/190: Mr. JOHN H BROWN administrator of HENRIETTA BROWN late of Anne Arundel Co deceased. 10 January 1832. Sureties: THOMAS J STOCKETT + REZIN HAMMOND. Eighths of the balance to: HENRY H BROWN, JOHN H BROWN, JAMES NEWBORN in right of his (unnamed) wife), GEORGE G GAMBRILL in right of his (unnamed) wife, THOMAS J

STOCKETT in right of his (unnamed) wife, REZIN BROWN, PHILIP BROWN + WILLIAM BROWN.

TH#1/191: Mr. RICHARD BROWN administrator of RICHARD BROWN late of Anne Arundel Co deceased. 18 January 1832. Sureties: MORGAN HILL + ELIZABETH BROWN. Sixths of the balance to: ALTHEA HILL, RICHARD BROWN, HENRY C BROWN, WILLSON BROWN, ROBERT BROWN + ELIZA ANN BROWN.

TH#1/191 + 192: Mrs. LAURIANA FAULKNER guardian of LLOYD TUCKER minor late of Anne Arundel Co deceased. 28 March 1832. Sureties: BARUCH WHEELER + HORACE W WATERS. Halves of the balance to: LAURIANA FAULKNER + GASSAWAY FAULKNER, brother of the deceased.

TH#1/192: Mr. JEREMIAH SMITH administrator with will annexed of DANIEL SMITH late of Anne Arundel Co deceased. 18 April 1832. Sureties: LANE DENNIS + CHARLES FREELON. Thirds of the balance to: JEREMIAH SMITH, ABRAHAM SMITH + DANIEL SMITH.

TH#1/192 + 193: Mrs. SUSAN BARBER administratrix of JOHN T BARBER late of Anne Arundel Co deceased. 21 September 1831. Sureties: JAMES WILLIAMSON + WILLIAM WARFIELD. SUSAN BARBER, widow's third; the remainder of the balance to: JOHN T BARBER, GEORGE W BARBER + GUSTAVUS R BARBER.

TH#1/193: Messrs AMOS DORSEY + CHARLES G WORTHINGTON executors of MARY DORSEY late of Anne Arundel Co deceased. 28 Mary 1832. Sureties: THOMAS CROSS + J____ G____ WORTHINGTON. Fourths of the balance to: SAMUEL N RIDGELY in right of his wife DOBORAH, CHARLES C RIDGELY in right of his wife ELIZABETH, AMOS DORSEY + CHARLES G WORTHINGTON in right of his wife MARY.

TH#1/194: Mr. JOHN HALL administrator of EZEKEIL STEWART late of Anne Arundel Co deceased. 28 Mary 1832. Sureties: CHARLES PUMPHREY + CHARLES FRIZEL. Fourths of the balance to: WILLIAM PUMPHREY, MARY STEWART, SUSAN STEWART + ELEANOR STEWART.

TH#1/194: Mrs. HARRIET MARRIOTT administratrix of JOHN MARRIOTT late of Anne Arundel Co deceased. 30 June 1832. Sureties: HENRY MAYNADIER + JOSHUA HALL. HARRIET MARRIOTT, widow's third; fourths of the balance to: JOSHUA H MARRIOTT, ELIZABETH E MARRIOTT, ELVIRA MARRIOTT + JOHN MARRIOTT.

TH#1/194 + 195: Mr. JOHN THOMAS + Dr. JAMES CHESTON Jr administrators of JAMES DOOLEY late of Anne Arundel Co deceased. 10 July 1832. Sureties: WILLIAM M LANSDALE + JAMES CHESTON. Mrs. MARGARET GALE, widow's third; remainder of the balance to ISABELLA DOOLEY, daughter of the deceased.

TH#1/195: Mr. JOHN S E NUTWELL administrator of JAMES NUTWELL late of Anne Arundel Co deceased. 17 July 1832. Sureties: WILLIAM H. HALL Jr + THOMAS HARDESTY. TOMERSON NUTWELL, widow's third; fifths of the remaining balance to: JOHN S E NUTWELL, GASSAWAY WINTERSON in right of his (unnamed) wife, MARY NUTWELL, GEORGE W NUTWELL + SARAH NUTWELL.

TH#1/196: Mr. WILLIAM O'HARA administrator of EDWARD STEWART late of Anne Arundel Co deceased. 6 September 1832. Sureties: GEORGE MCNEIR + ISRAEL DAVIDSON. Beneficiaries: widow SARAH STEWART, BENJAMIN STEWART, JOHN STEWART, JOSEPH STEWART, CALEB STEWART, EDWARD STEWART, JAMES STEWART, MARY HARWOOD, JOHN COBERTH and (unnamed) wife, CHARLES STEWART + WILLIAM STEWART.

TH#1/197: Messrs ELIJAH WILLIAMS + BENJAMIN THOMAS administrators of HENRY WIL-LIAMS late of Anne Arundel Co deceased. 23 October 1832. Sureties: FRANCIS HAN-COCK + ORLANDO HANCOCK. LOUISA WILLIAMS, widow's third; fourths of the balance to: SARAH A WILLIAMS, MARY E WILLIAMS, OLIVER H WILLIAMS + LOUISA M WILLIAMS.

TH#1/197 + 198: Mr. GEORGE S. PORTER administrator of NATHAN PORTER Sr late of Anne Arundel Co deceased. 23 October 1832. Sureties: MCLANE BROWN + WESLEY LINTHICUM. Eighths of the balance to: GEORGE S PORTER, NATHAN PORTER, WILLIAM PORTER, WASHINGTON PORTER, DAVID A PORTER, JANE PORTER (who is married), MARY ANN PORTER + MARTHA E PORTER.

TH#1/198: Mr. WILLIAM BROWN (of BENJAMIN) administrator of BENJAMIN BROWN Sr late of Anne Arundel Co deceased. 25 October 1832. Sureties: THOMAS FURLONG + FRANKLIN F IJAMS. Mrs. ANN BROWN, widow's third; sevenths of the remaining bal-ance to: ELIZABETH FURLONG, WILLIAM BROWN (of BENJAMIN), BENJAMIN BROWN Jr, the heirs of SARAH ANN HATHERLY(?), HENRIETTA PETTIBONE, HARRIET IJAMS + DEBORAH BROWN.

TH#1/199: Mr. RICHARD BROWN administrator of JOHN FRANCIS WEEKES late of Anne Arundel Co deceased. 26 October 1832. Sureties: ISRAEL DAVIDSON + VACHEL SEVERN. Fifths of the balance to: HARRIET HARDESTY, MARGARET A WARD, ALFRED WEEKS, WIL-LIAM H WEEKS + MARY E WEEKS.

TH#1/200: Mr. MORTIMER DORSEY administrator of ANNE DORSEY late of Anne Arundel Co deceased. 27 November 1832. Sureties: BELA WARFIELD + TILGHMAN D WARFIELD. Elevenths of the balance to: MORTIMER DORSEY, ELIZA A DORSEY, CAROLINE WHEELER, JOHN DORSEY, CALEB DORSEY, LOUISA HOOD, MARY GIST, ACHSAH DORSEY, HANSON DORSEY, HENRY DORSEY + SEPTIMUS DORSEY.

TH#1/200: Mr. GASSAWAY WINTERSON administrator with will annexed of BENJAMIN WINTERSON late of Anne Arundel Co deceased. 20 December 1832. Sureties: WILLIAM O'HARA + BENJAMIN WELLS. Halves of the balance to: GASSAWAY WINTERSON + GEORGE T DITTY.

TH#1/201: Mr. RICHARD H HALL administrator de bonis non with will annexed of HENRY HALL late of Anne Arundel Co deceased. 21 December 1832. Sureties: ROBERT W. KENT + THOMAS W HALL. RACHEL S HALL, widow's third; sevenths of the remaining balance to: the estate of JOSEPH HALL, RICHARD G STOCKETT, BASIL WARREN, THOMAS W HALL, THOMAS H HALL, RICHARD H HALL + OSBORN S HALL.

TH#1/201 + 202: Dr. JOHN B. WELLS administrator of ANN JACKSON late of Anne Arun-del Co deceased. 21 December 1832. Sureties: JAMES WILLIAMSOND(?) + GEORGE WELLS. Halves of the balance to: CATHARINE WILLIGMAN + WILLIAM FOXCROFT Jr.

TH#1/202: Mr. JOHN SELLMAN administrator of WILLIAM FISHER late of Anne Arundel Co deceased. 21 December 1832. Sureties: JOHN IGLEHART + JOHN S SELBY. HENRI-ETTA ROGERS, widow's third; fifths of the remainder to: JOHN H FISHER, WILLIAM FISHER, MARY A FISHER, HEZEKIAH FISHER + SUSANNA FISHER.

TH#1/203 + 204: Dr. RICHARD W GILL administrator de bonis non of SAMUEL H. HOWARD late of Anne Arundel Co deceased. 8 January 1833. Sureties: DAVID STEWART + CHARLES S W DORSEY. Legatees: JOHN EDMONDSON, ARCHIBALD GOLDER, SAMUEL MOALE + RICHARD W GILL. Mention is made of the first administrator, Mrs. MARY HOWARD, who appears to be deceased as she does not figure in the above distribution.

TH#1/204 + 205: Mr. GRAFTON B DUVALL administrator with will annexed of EDWARD

BALDWIN late of Anne Arundel Co deceased. 15 January 1833. Sureties: RICHARD
H. MERRIKEN + ELI DUVALL. Eighths of the balance to: HENRY BALDWIN, JAMES T.
BALDWIN, JOSEPH M TATE, MARY H BALDWIN, HENRIETTA M BALDWIN, JOHN BALDWIN, ED-
WARD BALDWIN + ELIZA ANN BALDWIN.

TH#1/206: Mr. JOHN HAMMOND administrator of JOHN H. DORSEY, a minor, late of
Anne Arundel Co deceased. 29 January 1833. Sureties: CHARLES HAMMOND + JAMES
HUNTER. Halves of the balance to: JOHN HAMMOND in right of his (unnamed) wife
+ JOHN HALL in right of his (unnamed) wife.

TH#1/206: Mr. THOMAS J. HALL one of the administrators of JOHN H. TILLARD late
of Anne Arundel Co deceased. 15 January 1833. Sureties: WILLIAM WEEMS + WIL-
LIAM H HALL. Thirds of the balance to: ALEXANDER DUVALL in right of his (unnamed)
wife, MARY E TILLARD + JANNETTA H TILLARD.

TH#1/206: Mr. CHARLES R STEWART administrator of HENRY EVANS late of Anne Arun-
del Co deceased. 5 February 1833. Sureties: BENJAMIN ROBINSON + ABNER LINTHI-
CUM. CATHARINE EVANS, widow's third; remainder of the balance divided among:
ELIZABETH EVANS, CHARLES R STEWART in right of his (unnamed) wife, MARY EVANS,
CAROLINE EVANS, ACHSAH EVANS + MAREEN DUVALL in right of his (unnamed) wife.

TH#1/207: Mr. CHARLES H. LANE administrator de bonis non of MARY LANE late of
Anne Arundel Co deceased. 12 February 1833. Sureties: THOMAS G. WATERS +
GEORGE MCNEIR. Thirds of the balance to: EDWARD W BELT, CHARLES H LANE, RE-
BECCA LANE.

TH#1/207: Mrs. JANE M RAWLINGS (formerly BARBER) administratrix of GEORGE W. BAR-
BER late of Anne Arundel Co deceased. 26 February 1833. Sureties: WILLSON WATERS
+ RAMSAY WATERS. JANE M RAWLINGS, widow's third; thirds of the remainder to:
the deceased's mother, SUSAN BARBER; and the deceased's brothers, JOHN T BARBER
+ GUSTAVUS R BARBER.

TH#1/208: Mr. JOHN WARFIELD (of JOSHUA) administrator with will annexed of
RALPH DORSEY late of Anne Arundel Co deceased. 4 March 1833. Sureties: SAMUEL
BROWN + NICHOLAS WATKINS Jr. Sevenths of the balance to: MARIA M DORSEY, JOSHUA
A DORSEY, RINALDO W DORSEY, MARY A J DORSEY, RALPH J DORSEY, RICHARD G DORSEY +
BENJAMIN H DORSEY.

TH#1/208 + 209: Mr. HOWARD ELLICTT administrator of JOHN JUBB late of Anne Arundel Co deceased. 19 March 1833. Sureties: MOSES LAURENCE + DORSEY JACOB. Thirds
of the balance to: widow MARY ANN KNOTTS, WILLIAM JUBB + JOHN JUBB.

TH#1/209: Mr. JAMES HOOD (of JOHN) administrator with will annexed of JOHN
HOOD (of JOHN) late of Anne Arundel Co deceased. 20 March 1833. Sureties: WIL-
LIAM SHIPLEY, RICHARD DORSEY + THOMAS HOOD. Legatees: WILLIAM G HOOD; MARY G
HOOD; the children of BENJAMIN HOOD: MARY ANN HOOD, JOSHUA HOOD, CHARLES W. HOOD,
BENJAMIN HOOD, JOHN HOOD; the children of THOMAS HOOD: KITTY D PASCAULT, JOHN
HOOD, ELIZABETH ANN WATERS, HENRY W HOOD, RACHEL H HOOD (deceased)--twelfths.

TH#1/210: Mr. THOMAS ALLEIN administrator of BENJAMIN CARR late of Anne Arundel
Co deceased. 29 March 1833. Sureties: JAMES TONGUE + ELIZABETH ALLEIN. Fifths
of the balance to: ELIZABETH CARR, ELLEN CARR, RICHARD F CARR, BENJAMIN CARR +
ARTRIDGE CARR.

TH#1/211: Mr. THOMAS ALLEIN administrator of HENRY DEALE late of Anne Arundel

Co deceased. 29 March 1833. Sureties: JOSEPH ALLEIN + RICHARD DEALE. Fifths of the balance to: RICHARD DEALE, JOHN WELLS, RICHARD WELLS, ELLEN DEALE + HENRY DEALE.

TH#1/211 + 212: Mr. BENJAMIN WATKINS administrator of MARY E HARWOOD late of Anne Arundel Co deceased. 9 May 1833. Sureties: SAMUEL A CLAGETT + RICHARD STEWART. Legatees: RICHARD HARWOOD; JOHN _ HARWOOD; ELEANOR WATKINS; ANN WATKINS; JOHN SEXTON; JOSEPH STEWART; RICHARD STEWART; the heirs of WILLIAM HARWOOD: SALLY HARWOOD, CAROLINE HARWOOD + SUSAN HARWOOD; + the heirs of MARGARET WATKINS: ELIZABETH WATKINS, MARGARET WATKINS, JAMES CLAGETT in right of his (unnamed) wife, ROBERT BROWN in right of his (unnamed) wife, OVERTON RIDGAWAY, NICHOLAS G WATKINS, GEORGE W WATKINS + JOSEPH STEWART in right of his (unnamed) wife.

TH#1/213: Mrs. ANN HOLLAND administratrix of JAMES HOLLAND late of Anne Arundel Co deceased. 11 May 1833. Sureties: RICHARD C HARDESTY + LUCRETIA HOLLAND. ANN HOLLAND, widow's third; ninths of the remainder to: LUCRETIA HOLLAND, SARAH ANN HOLLAND, RICHARD HARDESTY in right of his (unnamed) wife, ROSETTA HOLLAND, JAMES S HOLLAND, ELLENORA HOLLAND, ALFRED G HOLLAND, CHARLES HOLLAND + JOHN M HOLLAND.

TH#1/213 + 214: Mr. ROBERT BOONE administrator of JOHN GRAY late of Anne Arundel Co deceased. 14 May 1833. Sureties: JOHN S SELBY + LLOYD JOHNSON Jr. CHARLOTTE GRAY, widow's third; sixths of the remainder to: WILLIAM CLARK in right of his (unnamed) wife; ANN GRAY, GEORGE W GRAY, STEPHEN GRAY, ELI H GRAY + WESLEY GRAY.

TH#1/214: Mr. WILLIAM BROWN (of BENJAMIN) executor of ANNE BOONE late of Anne Arundel Co deceased. 28 May 1833. Sureties: JOHN MILLER + JAMES HUNTER. Thirds of the balance to: WILLIAM BROWN (of BENJAMIN) in right of his (unnamed) wife, JOHN S BOONE + ANN ELIZABETH HAMMOND.

TH#1/215: Mr. DAVID MACKENZIE executor of AARON MACKENZIE late of Anne Arundel Co deceased. 3 June 1833. Sureties: JOSHUA YOUNG + GEORGE BURGESS. Halves of the balance to: DAVID MACKENZIE + AARON MACKENZIE.

TH#1/215: Mrs. ARABELLA CRAWFORD administratrix of BASIL B CRAWFORD late of Anne Arundel Co deceased. 11 June 1833. Sureties: FRANCIS EARLONGHER + JOHN BUTLER. ARABELLA CRAWFORD, widow's third; ninths of the balance to: MARY CRAWFORD, SOPHIA CRAWFORD, ELIZABETH CRAWFORD, WILLIAM CRAWFORD, SAMUEL CRAWFORD, LUCRETIA CRAWFORD, HARRIET CRAWFORD, FRANCIS CRAWFORD + BASIL B CRAWFORD.

TH#1/216: Mr. ELI LUSBY executor of ROBERT LUSBY late of Anne Arundel Co deceased. 11 June 1833. Sureties: ROBERT WELCH (of BENJAMIN) + STEPHEN BEARD. MARY LUSBY, widow's third; fourths of the remainder to: ELI LUSBY, BENJAMIN LUSBY, BEALE LUSBY + JOHN M GAITHER.

TH#1/217: Mr. JOSEPH G HARRISON + Mr. ROBERT GRIFFITH executors of SAMUEL WOOD late of Anne Arundel Co deceased. 18 June 1833. Sureties: BENJAMIN CARR + LEWIS GRIFFITH. Halves of the balance to: EDWARD WYVILL + WILLIAM H WOOD.

TH#1/217 + 218: Mr. LEWIS REYNOLDS administrator of TOBIAS REYNOLDS late of Anne Arundel Co deceased. 23 July 1833. Sureties: JAMES REYNOLDS + ALLEN REYNOLDS. Eighths of the balance to: LEWIS REYNOLDS, ALLEN REYNOLDS, SARAH REYNOLDS, REBECCA STEWART, GOVEN REYNOLDS, JAMES DEAVER for the use of REZIN HOPKINS, LEONARD OSBORNE for the use of ANDREW ELLIOTT + MARGARET KELLY.

TH#1/218: Mrs. MARY HAWKINS + Mr. ISAAC HAWKINS executors of JOSHUA HAWKINS
late of Anne Arundel Co deceased. 6 August 1833. Sureties: WILLIAM PUMPHREY
+ RANDOLPH CROMWELL. MARY HAWKINS, widow's third; fourths of the remainder to:
JOHN W(?) HAWKINS, JOSHUA HAWKINS, WALLACE W HAWKINS + SARAH HAWKINS.

TH#1/219: Mr. SAMUEL MAYNARD executor of LEWIS NETH late of Anne Arundel Co deceased. 13 August 1833. Sureties: HARRIET NETH + RICHARD HARWOOD (of THOMAS).
Mrs. HARRIET NETH, widow's third; residuary legatee, LEWIS NETH.

TH#1/219: Mr. ZACHARIAH JOHNSON Sr. administrator of CHRISTOPHER JOHNSON late
of Anne Arundel Co deceased. 17 September 1833. Sureties: RICHARD CHANEY +
WILLIAM BURTON. Sevenths of the balance to: HELEN MCCOY, JOHN J JOHNSON, ALE-
THEA CHANEY, MARY JOHNSON, OWEN JOHNSON, SOPHIA JOHNSON + BEALE JOHNSON.

TH#1/220: Mr. JOHN D. MERRIKEN surviving administrator with will annexed of
BENJAMIN PHIPPS late of Anne Arundel Co deceased. 15 October 1833. Sureties:
ANDREW A LYNCH + JAMES M (surname not recorded). Halves of the balance to: WIL-
LIAM H BANGS + JOHN BANGS.

TH#1/221: Mr. SETH W WARFIELD administrator of SARAH WARFIELD late of Anne Arun-
del Co deceased. 28 October 1833. Sureties: JOHN G WORTHINGTON + JAMES R BROWN.
Fourths of the balance to: WARNER WELCH in right of his (unnamed) wife, FIELDER
WILSON in right of his (unnamed) wife, JOHN H WARFIELD + SETH W WARFIELD.

TH#1/221: Mr. GEORGE H WARFIELD administrator of WILLIAM SMITH late of Anne
Arundel Co deceased. 20 October 1833. Sureties: CHARLES WATERS + JOHN TYDINGS.
AILCEY SMITH, widow's third; halves of the balance to: MARTHA SMITH + WILLIAM
SMITH.

TH#1/222: Messrs CHARLES R STEWART + BENJAMIN ROBINSON administrators of CHARLES
ROBINSON late of Anne Arundel Co deceased. 30 October 1833. Sureties: RICHARD
LINTHICUM + ABNER LINTHICUM. Halves of the balance to: the heirs of HANNAH STEW-
ART: SARAH STEWART, SUSAN WALLER, CHARLES R STEWART, RACHEL LINTHICUM + MARY ANN
HOLLAND; + the heirs of THOMAS ROBINSON: BENJAMIN ROBINSON, THOMAS ROBINSON +
ANN ROBINSON.

TH#1/223: Mr. JOSIAS CROSBY administrator of JAMES G PRICE late of Anne Arundel
Co deceased. 5 November 1833. Sureties: WILLIAM SMITH + RICHARD MACKALL.
Thirds of the balance to: the deceased's mother, ANN MITCHELL; JOSIAS CROSBY in
right of his wife ANN; + the deceased's sister, LUCINDA PRICE.

TH#1/223 + 224: Mr. BENJAMIN PALMER one of the administrators of WILLIAM HINCKS
late of Anne Arundel Co deceased. 12 November 1833. Sureties: JOHN S WILLIAMS
+ CHARLES DENT. MARY HINCKS, widow's third; sixths of the remainder to: SAMUEL
HINCKS, CHARLES D HINCKS, MARY ANN HINCKS, CAROLINE HINCKS, MARY HINCKS + EDWARD
HINCKS.

TH#1/224: Mr. WILLIAM LINTHICUM executor of ANN WRIGHT late of Anne Arundel Co
deceased. 27 November 1833. Sureties: GUSTAVUS MCELHINEY + THOMAS WARFIELD.
Sixths of the balance to: ANN DEEMS (WEEMS intended?), ELIZABETH PEARCE, JOHN
PEARCE, FRANCIS PEARCE, NANCY PATTERSON + RACHEL PATTERSON.

TH#1/225: Mr. RICHARD J. COWMAN administrator with will annexed of SARAH BATTEE
late of Anne Arundel Co deceased. 27 January 1834. Sureties: RICHARD HARWOOD
(of THOMAS) + THOMAS FRANKLIN. Thirds of the balance to: RICHARD J COWMAN, RICH-
ARD H COWMAN + HENRIETTA COWMAN.

TH#1/225: Mr. WILLIAM PUMPHREY (of WILLIAM) administrator of GASSAWAY STEWART late of Anne Arundel Co deceased. 28 January 1834. Sureties: ABNER LINTHICUM + RICHARD LINTHICUM. Thirds of the balance to: MARY FREE, SUSAN STAMP + ELEA-NOR STEWART.

TH#1/226: Mr. GASSAWAY WINTERSON administrator with will annexed of BENJAMIN WINTERSON late of Anne Arundel Co deceased. 7 February 1834. Sureties: WIL-LIAM O'HARA + BENJAMIN WELLS. Halves of the balance to: GASSAWAY WINTERSON + GEORGE T DITTY.

TH#1/226: Mr. JOSEPH KIRBY administrator of HORATIO TYDINGS late of Anne Arundel Co deceased. 20 February 1834. Sureties: EDWARD HOLLAND + SELE KELLY. Fourths of the balance to: ELIZABETH TYDINGS, SALLY TYDINGS, RICHARD TYDINGS + SUSAN TYDINGS.

TH#1/227: Mr. CHARLES D WARFIELD executor of BANI WARFIELD late of Anne Arundel Co deceased. 21 February 1834. Sureties: REUBEN WARFIELD + ROBERT WELCH. Sixths of the balance to: CHARLES D WARFIELD, DANIEL WARFIELD, ALFRED WARFIELD, NICHOLAS D WARFIELD, MARGARET WARFIELD + NICHOLAS OWENS in right of his (unnamed) wife.

TH#1/227: Mr. EPHRAIM WARFIELD Jr. executor of EPHRAIM WARFIELD late of Anne Arundel Co deceased. 27 February 1834. Sureties: ROBERT WARFIELD + NIMROD WELCH. Halves of the balance to: JOHN D WARFIELD + ANNA WARFIELD.

TH#1/228: Mr. SAMUEL OWENS administrator of JOHN B ETCHERSON late of Anne Arundel Co deceased. 15 April 1834. Sureties: JOHN CLAYTON + RICHARD M FOGGETT. ARABELLA ETCHERSON, widow's third; fifths of the remaining balance to: NANCY ETCHERSON, ELIZABETH ETCHERSON, ELIZA ETCHERSON, SALLY ETCHERSON + MARY ETCH-ERSON.

TH#1/228 + 229: Mr. JAMES F. EICHELBERGER one of the executors of JOHN EICHEL-BERGER late of Anne Arundel Co deceased. 6 May 1836. Sureties: NICHOLAS DOR-SEY (of LLOYD) + NOAH DUVALL. MARY EICHELBERGER, widow's third; fifths of the remaining balance to: JAMES F EICHELBERGER, MARIA EICHELBERGER, JOHN W EICHEL-BERGER, EMANUEL W EICHELBERGER + CHARLES W EICHELBERGER.

TH#1/229 + 230: Mr. THOMAS FLEMING administrator of CHARLES MULLENAUX late of Anne Arundel Co deceased. 13 May 1836. Sureties: ELI MOLESWORTH + THOMAS MUL-LENAUX. ELIZABETH MULLENAUX, widow's third; elevenths of the remaining balance to: JOSHUA MULLENAUX, AMELIA FLEMING, ASHBURY MULLENAUX, CHARLTON MULLENAUX, JESSE MULLENAUX, ELEANOR MULLENAUX, ELIZABETH MULLINAUX, JASON MULLENAUX, CARO-LINE MULLENAUX, RHODA A MULLENAUX + ANDREW MULLENAUX.

TH#1/230: Mr. ELIAS BREWER one of the executors of SARAH PUMPHREY late of Anne Arundel Co deceased. 8 July 1834. Sureties: DORSEY JACOBS + DORSEY STEWART. Five-dollar legacy to be shared by CHARLES PUMPHREY, WILLIAM PUMPHREY + ANN BREWER; sevenths of the remaining balance to: SARAH ANN STEWART, ZACHARIAH PUMP-HREY, WILLIAM PUMPHREY, JOHN J PUMPHREY, CHARLES P BREWER, EDWARD P BREWER + ELIAS N B BREWER.

TH#1/231: Mr. MICHAEL IGLEHART (who intermarried with MARY HOPKINS, widow + administratrix of SAMUEL HOPKINS late of Anne Arundel Co deceased). 15 July 1834. No sureties indicated. Balance shared by: MICHAEL IGLEHART in right of his wife + the deceased's (unnamed) children.

TH#1/232: Mr. JOHN IGLEHART administrator of THOMAS IGLEHART late of Anne Arundel Co deceased. 29 July 1834. Sureties: LEONARD IGLEHART + JAMES IGLEHART. ANN IGLEHART, widow's third; fourths of the remainder to: MARTHA ANN IGLEHART, MARY L IGLEHART, THOMAS IGLEHART + JAMES IGLEHART.

TH#1/232: Mr. SAMUEL THOMAS + Mr. WILLIAM SHIPLEY executors of JOHN R. THOMAS late of Anne Arundel Co deceased. 2 September 1834. Sureties: ABNER LINTHICUM Jr + WILLIAM LINTHICUM. Fifths of the balance to: ANN C THOMAS, JOHN R THOMAS, JAMES E THOMAS, BENJAMIN F THOMAS + CAROLINE M THOMAS.

TH#1/231 (sic): Mr. ALEXANDER OWENS administrator of NICHOLAS OWENS late of Anne Arundel Co deceased. 16 December 1834. Sureties: SAMUEL SHEPHERD + JAMES S OWENS. SUSANNA OWENS, widow's third; sevenths of the remaining balance to: ALEXANDER OWENS, MARY WELCH, GASSAWAY OWENS, DENNIS OWENS, FIELDER OWENS, HORATIO OWENS + ENOCH OWENS.

TH#1/231 + 232: Messrs ELI DUVALL + RICHARD H MERRIKEN executors of JEMIMA DUVALL late of Anne Arundel Co deceased. 16 December 1834. Sureties: GRAFTON B DUVALL + RICHARD DUVALL. Halves of the remainder to: MARY MERRIKEN + MARGARET DUVALL.

TH#1/232: Mrs. SARAH STINCHCOMB administratrix of NATHANIEL STINCHCOMB late of Anne Arundel Co deceased. 21 April 1835. Sureties: JOHN TYDINGS + LEWIS ROBINSON. SARAH STINCHCOMB, widow's third; fifths of the remainder to: THOMAS W STINCHCOMB, RICHARD A STINCHCOMB, SARAH STINCHCOMB, HENRIETTA R STINCHCOMB + WILLIAM V STINCHCOMB.

TH#1/233: Mr. GEORGE BRADFORD administrator of ZACHARIAH BROWN late of Anne Arundel Co deceased. 22 April 1835. Sureties: JOSHUA D BROWN + WILLIAM JENKINS. SARAH A BROWN, widow's third; fourths of the remainder to: JOSHUA D BROWN, BERNARD MCGINN, LLOYD BROWN + ZACHARIAH BROWN.

TH#1/233: Mr. BENJAMIN GAITHER administrator of EVAN GAITHER late of Anne Arundel Co deceased. 5 Mary 1835. Sureties: ANN B GAITHER + RACHEL M GAITHER. Sevenths to: BENJAMIN GAITHER, JOHN M GAITHER, the heirs of JULIA BICKNELL, the heirs of AGNES OWENS, the heirs of ELIZABETH MULLIKEN, ANN R GAITHER + RACHEL M GAITHER.

TH#1/234: Mr. CHARLES H. LANE administrator de bonis non of MARY LANE late of Anne Arundel Co deceased. 1 June 1835. Sureties: THOMAS G WATERS + GEORGE MCNEIR. Thirds of the balance to: EDWARD W BELT, CHARLES H LANE + REBECCA LANE.

TH#1/235: Mr. HUMPHREY DORSEY executor of MARGARET OWINGS late of Anne Arundel Co deceased. 21 July 1835. Sureties: ROBERT WELCH (of BENJAMIN) + GUSTAVUS WARFIELD. Fourths of the balance to: HUMPHREY DORSEY, RICHARD DORSEY, MARGARET GAITHER + JOHN DORSEY.

TH#1/235: Mr. JOSEPH E COWMAN executor of HENRIETTA HALL late of Anne Arundel Co deceased. 4 August 1835. Sureties: JOHN CLAYTON + THOMAS J DORSETT. Fourths of the balance to: PRICILLA HALL, THOMAS W HALL, ELEANOR W COWMAN + JOSEPH E. COWMAN.

TH#1/236 + 237: Mr. HENRY H HARWOOD administrator of BENJAMIN HARWOOD late of Anne Arundel Co deceased. 23 September 1835. No sureties indicated. Twenty-sixths of the balance to: RICHARD HARWOOD (of THOMAS); WILLIAM S GREEN and MARY,

his wife; LEWIS DUVALL + wife SARAH; ELIZABETH JONES; MARY WARFIELD; THOMAS
LYLES + wife MARGARET; WALTER JONES + wife ELIZABETH; CARDWELL BREATHETT +
wife REBBA; JOHN H HARWOOD: HENRY HARWOOD; ODLE TALBOT + wife MARY ANN; MARY
ALEXANDER; HELEN M GILL; THEODRICK WARFIELD + wife ANN; SURENE W WATKINS +
ELEANOR, his wife; RICHARD G STOCKETT; JOSEPH N STOCKETT; ANN WATKINS; ELEA-
NOR WATKINS; JAMES IGLEHART administrator of FREDERICK HARWOOD; JAMES IGLEHART
administrator of MARGARET WATKINS; JOHN T HARWOOD; RICHARD STEWART + wife LOU-
ISA; JOHN SEFTON + wife MARY; RICHARD HARWOOD (of WILLIAM); + MARIA HARWOOD.

TH#1/237: Mr. THOMAS ALLEIN administrator of BENJAMIN CARR late of Anne Arun-
del Co deceased. 29 September 1835. Sureties: JAMES TONGUE + ELIZABETH AL-
LEIN. Fifths of the balance to: ELIZABETH WEIR, ELEANOR HOPKINS, RICHARD F
CARR, BENJAMIN CARR + ARTRIDGE CARR.

TH#1/238: Mr. JAMES IGLEHART administrator of MARGARET WATKINS late of Anne
Arundel Co deceased. 5 November 1835. Sureties: JOHN IGLEHART + LEONARD IGLE-
HART. Eighths of the balance to: the children of MARIA STEWART: PAMELIA STEW-
ART + MATILDA STEWART; SOPHIA RIDGWAY; LOUISA CLAGETT: MARGARET WATKINS; ELEA-
NOR WATKINS; MARY ELIZA WATKINS; NICHOLAS G WATKINS + GEORGE WATKINS.

TH#1/238 + 239: Mr. JAMES IGLEHART administrator of FREDERICK HARWOOD late
of Anne Arundel Co deceased. 5 November 1835. Sureties: JOHN IGLEHART + LEON-
ART IGLEHART. Ninths of the balance to: RICHARD HARWOOD (brother), JOHN T HAR-
WOOD (brother), ANN WATKINS (sister), ELEANOR WATKINS (sister), MARGARET WAT-
KINS (sister), JOHN SEFTON in right of his (unnamed) wife, RICHARD STEWART in
right of his (unnamed) wife, JOSEPH STEWART in right of his (unnamed) wife, +
the heirs of WILLIAM HARWOOD (brother).

TH#1/239: Mr. JOSEPH ATWELL executor of JOSEPH ATWELL late of Anne Arundel Co
deceased. 27 October 1835. Sureties: WILLIAM O'HARA + ROBERT DODSON. ELIZA-
BETH ATWELL, widow's third; thirds of the remainder: BENJAMIN ATWELL, ELIZABETH
ATWELL + PRISCILLA ROBINSON.

TH#1/240: Mrs. ANN JENKINS administratrix of FRANCIS JENKINS late of Anne Arun-
del Co deceased. 26 October 1835. Sureties: SAMUEL NICHOLS + JAMES WALTERS Jr.
ANN JENKINS, widow's third; thirds of the remainder to: ELIZA E JENKINS, MAR-
GARET A JENKINS + JAMES P JENKINS.

TH#1/240: Mr. RICHARD MERCIER administrator of JOSHUA MERCIER late of Anne
Arundel Co deceased. 26 October 1835. Sureties: MICHAEL IGLEHART + JOHN W
RINGROSE. ELIZA MERCIER, widow's third; fourths of the remainder to: RUTH
BARNES, JOHN MERCIER, MARY MERCIER + AZEL MERCIER.

TH#1/241: Mr. GEORGE W LINSTED administrator of WILLIAM LINSTED late of Anne
Arundel Co deceased. 29 December 1835. Sureties: RICHARD CHEYNEY + WALTER
PUMPHREY. JANE LINSTED, widow's third; thirds of the remaining balance to:
WILLIAM LINSTED, ANN ELIZA LINSTED + SARAH ANN LINSTED.

TH#1/241 + 242: Mrs. SARAH SIMMONS administratrix of GASSAWAY SIMMONS late of
Anne Arundel Co deceased. 12 January 1836. Sureties: JOSEPH SMITH + WILLIAM
WELLS. SARAH SIMMONS, widow's third; the remainder of the balance to: son
SAMUEL G. SIMMONS.

TH#1/242: Mr. JOHN TYDINGS executor of GEORGE ADAMS late of Anne Arundel Co
deceased. 8 March 1836. Sureties: CHARLES STEWART + LEWIS TYDINGS. Sevenths

of the balance to: THOMAS ADAMS, MARGARET ADAMS, ROBERT ADAMS, ALBERT ADAMS, SUSAN ADAMS, LUNDY LINSTED in right of (unnamed) wife, + the children of MATILDA WELCH.

TH#1/242 + 243: Mr. RAMSAY WATERS executor of Dr. WILLSON WATERS late of Anne Arundel Co deceased. 9 March 1836. Sureties: WILLIAM BROGDEN + RICHARD MARRIOTT. MARGARET WATERS, widow's third; thirds of the remainder to: RAMSAY WATERS, MARIA LOUISA WATERS + JOHN WILLSON WATERS.

TH#1/243: Mr. HENRY PURDY one of the administrators of JOHN PURDY late of Anne Arundel Co deceased. 18 March 1836. Sureties: THOMAS PURDY + N(R?) WELCH (of BENJAMIN). SUSAN PURDY, widow's third; fifths of the remaining balance to: HENRY PURDY, THOMAS PURDY, GALEN PURDY, JOHN PURDY + JACOB PURDY.

TH#1/244: Mr. RINALDO PINDELL surviving administrator with will annexed of PHILIP PINDELL late of Anne Arundel Co deceased. 29 March 1836. Sureties: WILLIAM H HALL + WILLIAM WEEMS. Thirds of the balance to: RINALDO PINDELL, EMMELINE DUVALL + PHILIP P WEEMS.

TH#1/244: Mr. ROBERT NEILSON an executor of RICHARD RIDGELY late of Anne Arundel Co deceased. 20 April 1836. Sureties: WILLIAM O'HARA + JOHN KNIGHTON. Legacy to RICHARD H RIDGELY; fifths of the remaining balance to: RICHARD H. BATTEE, NATHANIEL C DARE, MICHAEL T BAER, ROBERT NEILSON + EDWARD D RIDGELY.

TH#1/245: Mr. ROBERT NEILSON administrator of EDWARD D RIDGELY late of Anne Arundel Co deceased. 20 April 1836. Sureties: RICHARD H BATTEE + NATHANIEL C DARE. Sevenths of the balance to: RICHARD H BATTEE in right of his (unnamed) wife; NATHANIEL C DARE in right of his (unnamed) wife; MICHAEL T BAER in right of his (unnamed) wife; ROBERT NEILSON in right of his (unnamed) wife; ELIZABETH RIDGELY; A_____ H_____ DUVALL; DANIEL RIDGELY; + RICHARD H RIDGELY.

TH#1/245 + 246: Mr. ROBERT NEILSON one of the executors of RICHARD RIDGELY late of Anne Arundel Co deceased. 20 April 1836. Sureties: WILLIAM O'HARA + JOHN KNIGHTON. Fourths of the balance to: RICHARD H BATTEE in right of his (unnamed) wife, NATHANIEL C DARE in right of his (unnamed) wife, MICHAEL T BAER in right of his (unnamed) wife, and ROBERT NEILSON in right of his (unnamed) wife.

TH#1/246: Mr. ENOCH SHEKELL administrator of SARAH SMITH late of Anne Arundel Co deceased. 21 April 1836. Sureties: EZRA SHEKELL + LEVI SHEKELL. Fourths of the balance to: the heirs of RICHARD SMITH, the heirs of AZARIAH SMITH, the heirs of WILLIAM SMITH + the heirs of SARAH SHEKELL.

TH#1/246 + 247: Mr. RICHARD J. COWMAN administrator of THOMAS J. COWMAN late of Anne Arundel Co deceased. 9 April 1836. Sureties: RICHARD HARWOOD (of THOMAS) + THOMAS FRANKLIN. MATILDA COWMAN, widow's third; fourths of the remaining balance to: THOMAS J. COWMAN, RICHARD H. COWMAN, HENRIETTA COWMAN + HENRY COWMAN.

TH#1/247: Mr. DENTON IGLEHART one of the administrators of JOHN IGLEHART late of Anne Arundel Co deceased. 24 Mary 1836. Sureties: SARAH COLE + JOEL IGLEHART. HARRIET IGLEHART, widow's third; ninths of the remaining balance to: SARAH COLE, JOEL IGLEHART, DENTON IGLEHART, JARBIN(?) IGLEHART, RUFUS IGLEHART, EZRA IGLEHART, MARY ANN IGLEHART, MARGARET IGLEHART, + CAROLINE IGLEHART.

TH#1/248: Mr. SETH W WARFIELD + Mr. LORENZO G. WARFIELD administrators of JOHN H WARFIELD late of Anne Arundel Co deceased. 23 August 1836. Sureties: EDWARD DORSEY (of RICHARD) + FIELDER WILSON. Thirds of the balance to: LORENZO G. WAR-

FIELD, SARAH A. WARFIELD + CATHARINE ANN WARFIELD.

TH#1/248 + 249: Mr. HENRY WELLING administrator of WILLIAM WELLING late of Anne Arundel Co deceased. 24 August 1836. Sureties: HENRY H. OWINGS + WILLIAM WELLING. POLLY WELLING, widow's third; sixths of the remaining balance to: WILLIAM WELLING, JAMES W. WELLING, HENRY WELLING, ELIZABETH YOUNG (wife of LEVI), REBECCA MORRIS (wife of JAMES), + MARY WELLING.

TH#1/249: Mr. CHARLES A. WATERS administrator of JACOB WATERS late of Anne Arundel Co deceased. 30 August 1836. Sureties: CHARLES WATERS + STEPHEN BEARD. Sixths of the balance to: ANN BEALMEAR, GEORGE A. WARFIELD, THOMAS R. BEARD, CHARLES A. WATERS, JAMES W. WATERS, + JACOB WATERS.

TH#1/249 + 250: Mr. CHARLES R. STEWART administrator of CAROLINE EVANS late of Anne Arundel Co deceased. 13 September 1836. Sureties: BASIL OSBORNE + SARAH STEWART. Fifths of the balance to: CATHERINE EVANS, ELIZABETH EVANS, CHARLES R. STEWART, ACHSAH EVANS + MAREEN M. DUVALL.

TH#1/250: Mr. CHARLES R. STEWART administrator of MARY EVANS late of Anne Arundel Co deceased. 13 September 1836. Sureties: WILLIAM PUMPHREY + JOSHUA STEWART. Fifths of the balance to: CATHARINE EVANS, ELIZABETH EVANS, CHARLES R. STEWART, ACHSAH EVANS, + MAREEN M. DUVALL.

TH#1/251: Mr. FREDERICK G. HARMAN administrator of GEORGE HARMAN late of Anne Arundel Co deceased. 20 December 1836. Sureties: LARKIN SHIPLEY + SAMUEL MC-PHERSON. Sixths of the balance to: ANN HARMAN, ELIZABETH L. HARMAN, FREDERICK G. HARMAN, PETER A HARMAN, LOUISA A HARMAN, + AMELIA J. HARMAN.

TH#1/251: Mr. BUSHROD W. MARRIOTT administrator of SAMUEL WATERS late of Anne Arundel Co deceased. 21 December 1836. Sureties: NATHAN WATERS + FRANKLIN WATERS. Fourths of the balance to: MARY LOUISA WATERS, MARTHA E WATERS, AR-TRIDGE WATERS, + ANN L WATERS.

TH#1/252: Mr. WILLIAM S. MCPHERSON administrator de bonis non with will annexed of LEWIS NETH late of Anne Arundel Co deceased. 13 December 1836. Sureties: JOHN MCPHERSON + JOHN SELLMAN. Third of the balance to WILLIAM S. MCPHERSON in right of his wife HARRIET; the remainder of the balance to LEWIS NETH, infant son of the deceased.

TH#1/252: Mr. RICHARD SELLMAN administrator of BENJAMIN HARWOOD late of Anne Arundel Co deceased. 10 January 1837. Sureties: ALFRED SELLMAN + RICHARD COW-MAN. PEGGY H. HARWOOD, widow's third; fifths of the remaining balance to: LUCINDA M. SELLMAN, ANN C. HARWOOD, HENRIETTA HARWOOD, BENJAMIN HARWOOD, + MARY D. HARWOOD.

TH#1/253: Mr. ANDREW MERCIER executor of RUTH MERCIER late of Anne Arundel Co deceased. 17 January 1837. Sureties: ARCHIBALD MERCIER + CORNELIUS MERCIER. Half of the balance to ANDREW MERCIER; the remaining half of the balance to be shared by: the heirs of JOSHUA MERCIER, RUFUS BARNES in right of his wife RUTH, JOHN W. MERCIER, MARY MERCIER, + AZEL MERCIER.

TH#1/253 + 254: Mr. THOMAS FRANKLIN administrator of JACOB FRANKLIN late of Anne Arundel Co deceased. 24 January 1837. Sureties: DANIEL HART + GEORGE E. FRANKLIN. Legatees: THOMAS FRANKLIN (brother); ANN FRANKLIN (sister); SAMUEL H. BEALL, in right of his wife HARRIET, the widow of JACOB FRANKLIN; the children of MARY DEALE (sister): ANN ELIZABETH GILL, MARY F. PINKNEY, JAMES DEALE Jr., + JACOB F. DEALE; + the children of SAMUEL FRANKLIN (brother): RACHEL

-93-

WATERS, HARRIET LANSDALE, NANCY FRANKLIN, + MARIA FRANKLIN.

TH#1/254: Mr. SOLOMON G. CHANEY executor of ELIJAH CHANEY late of Anne Arundel Co deceased. 30 January 1837. Sureties: ROBERT W. KENT + JOHN S. SELLMAN. SARAH CHANEY, widow's third; fifths of the remaining balance to: ELIJAH CHANEY, RICHARD CHANEY, RIGNEL CHANEY, JOHN KNIGHTON, + HENRIETTA GROVES CHANEY.

TH#1/255: Mr. JOHN IGLEHART executor of ANN IGLEHART late of Anne Arundel Co deceased. 31 January 1837. Sureties: JAMES IGLEHART + LEONARD IGLEHART. Fifths of the balance to: JOHN IGLEHART, JAMES IGLEHART, LEONARD IGLEHART, the (unnamed) children of THOMAS IGLEHART (deceased), + MARY LUCKETT IGLEHART (deceased). The heirs of MARY LUCKETT IGLEHART are: JAMES H. WATKINS, THOMAS S. IGLEHART, JAMES A. IGLEHART, + ANN IGLEHART.

TH#1/256: Mr. RICHARD SELLMAN administrator of PEGGY H. HARWOOD late of Anne Arundel Co deceased. 31 January 1837. Sureties: ALFRED SELLMAN + RICHARD HARMAN. Halves of the balance to children: BENJAMIN HARWOOD + MARY DRYDEN HARWOOD.

TH#1/256 + 257: Mr. FREDERICK RAWLINGS administrator with will annexed of PRISCILLA STEWART late of Anne Arundel Co deceased. 7 February 1837. Sureties: CHARLES HAMMOND + MAREEN M DUVALL. Halves of the balance to: REBECCA PERRY + ANN STEWART.

TH#1/257: Mrs.(?) MARY T. RUSSELL executrix of ELIJAH PAIN late of Anne Arundel Co deceased. 21 March 1837. Sureties: JOHN PUMPHREY + OWEN DORSEY. Legacies to: HENRY WATTS (family Bible), OWEN DISNEY, GEORGE R.(?) WEBB, ELIZABETH TUCKER, + AQUILA BARBER.

TH#1/258: Mrs. MARGARET ANN RAY administratrix of JOSEPH J. RAY late of Anne Arundel Co deceased. 18 March 1837. No sureties indicated. MARGARET ANN RAY, widow's third; remaining two-thirds of the balance to son JOSEPH J. RAY.

TH#1/258: Mr. JAMES IGLEHART administrator of HENRY PURDY late of Anne Arundel Co deceased. 30 March 1837. Sureties: LEONARD IGLEHART + JOHN IGLEHART. SARAH PURDY, widow's third; fifths of the remaining balance to: (unnamed) children of WILLIAM PURDY (deceased), JOHN PURDY, ALFRED PURDY, SAMUEL PURDY, + RICHARD MITCHELL in right of his wife MARY ANN.

TH#1/259: Mr. SOMERVILL PINKNEY administrator of JONATHAN PINKNEY late of Anne Arundel Co deceased. 24 April 1837. Sureties: WILLIAM STEWART + ALEXANDER C. MAGRUDER. Eighths of the balance to: ANN PINKNEY, MARY PINKNEY, SOMERVILL PINKNEY, SOMERVILLE PINKNEY trustee of JOHN W. HAMMOND in right of his wife SALLY, ELLEN PINKNEY, EDWARD SPARKS, EDWARD SPARKS in right of his wife SOPHIA, + JONATHAN PINKNEY.

TH#1/259: Mr. RICHARD GAMBRILL administrator of JOSEPH MATTINGLY late of Anne Arundel Co deceased. 23 May 1837. Sureties: RICHARD IGLEHART + ELIZABETH GAMBRILL. Thirds of the balance to: DOROTHY MATTINGLY, JOHN F. MATTINGLY, + ELIZABETH A. MATTINGLY.

TH#1/260: Mr. LLOYD SELBY executor of JOHN DEMPSEY late of Anne Arundel Co deceased. 13 June 1837. Sureties: ADAM DELANDER + JAMES SMITH. Fourths of the balance to: ANN SIDES, FREDERICK DEMPSEY, JANE PERRY SIDES, + ADELAIDE MARIA SIDES.

TH#1/260: Mr. JOHN S. SELBY administrator de bonis non of JOHN W WEEMS late of Anne Arundel Co deceased. 13 June 1837. Sureties: BASIL SHEPHERD + HARRIET

SELBY. MARIA A. WILLIAMS, widow's third; fifths of the remainder to: EDWARD C. WILLIAMS, JOHN W. WILLIAMS, EDITHA WILLIAMS, JOSEPH S. WILLIAMS, + MARY A. W. WILLIAMS.

TH#1/261: Mr. JOHN S. SELBY administrator of MARIA ANN WILLIAMS late of Anne Arundel Co deceased. 13 June 1837. Sureties: JOHN MILLER + WILLIAM W. SEEDERS. Fourths of the balance to: JOHN W. WILLIAMS, EDITH(A?) WILLIAMS, JOSEPH S. WIL- LIAMS, + MARY A. W. WILLIAMS.

TH#1/261 + 262: Mr. JAMES SHIPLEY administrator with will annexed of NEHEMIAH MOXLEY late of Anne Arundel Co deceased. 28 June 1837. No sureties indicated. Legatees: REZIN MOXLEY; JOSHUA MOXLEY; NEHEMIAH MOXLEY; JOHN MOXLEY; WILLIAM MOXLEY; EZEKIEL MOXLEY; SARAH MOXLEY during natural life then to children of JACOB MOXLEY (deceased): STEPHEN MOXLEY, SUSANNA OWENS, MARY MOXLEY + ELIZA- BETH WILSON; the children of JOSHUA MOXLEY: HARRIET WATERS, grandson _____ MOXLEY, EMILY MOXLEY, + JOHN MOXLEY; + the children of JOHN MOXLEY: CHARLES MOXLEY, LLOYD MOXLEY, EVELINE TENAIN (deceased), LUTHER MOXLEY, JERUSA MOXLEY, + CECELIA IJAMS.

TH#1/262: Mr. WILLIAM W. SEEDERS(WEEDER?) administrator of HENRY HALE late of Anne Arundel Co deceased. 13 July 1837. Sureties: WILLIAM S. WEEDER + JAMES T. YEWELL. MARY ANN HALE, widow's third; thirds of the remaining balance to: WILLIAM T. HALE, NICHOLAS E. HALE, + ZACHARIAH L. HALE.

TH#1/263: Mrs. HENRIETTA H. NORWOOD administratrix of THOMAS NORWOOD late of Anne Arundel Co deceased. 24 October 1837. Sureties: WILLIAM SHIPLEY + MAT- THIAS LINTHICUM. HENRIETTA H. NORWOOD, widow's third; sixths of the remaining balance to SAMUEL NORWOOD, ROBERT NORWOOD, LUCRETIA L. NORWOOD, MATTHIAS L. NORWOOD, CAMILLA E. NORWOOD, + HENRIETTA H. NORWOOD.

TH#1/263: Mr. CHARLES R. STEWART executor of WILLIAM PUMPHREY late of Anne Arundel Co deceased. 24 October 1837. Sureties (sic): CHARLES WATERS. Halves of the balance to: WILLIAM S. PUMPHREY + JOHN E. J. PUMPHREY.

TH#1/264: Mr. BENJAMIN WARFIELD (of RICHARD) administrator of RICHARD WARFIELD late of Anne Arundel Co deceased. 25 October 1837. Sureties: RICHARD B. WAR- FIELD + JESSE PUMPHREY. Elevenths of the balance to: JESSE PUMPHREY, THOMAS B. WARFIELD, BENJAMIN WARFIELD (of RICHARD), RICHARD B. WARFIELD, THOMAS WARFIELD in right of his (unnamed) wife, WILLIAM L. WARFIELD, JOHN WELLHAM in right of his (unnamed) wife, JONATHAN S. WARFIELD, ELLEN WARFIELD, ENOCH WARFIELD, + CALEB WARFIELD.

TH#1/265: Mrs. PATIENCE MACCUBBIN administratrix of HENRY MACCUBBIN late of Anne Arundel Co deceased. 7 November 1837. Sureties: BENJAMIN ROBINSON + JOHN HANCOCK. PATIENCE MACCUBBIN, widow's third; PATIENCE MACCUBBIN is also the mother and representative of deceased son JAMES MACCUBBIN and of deceased son JOSEPH MACCUBBIN; remainder of the balance to GEORGE W. MACCUBBIN + LYDIA MAC- CUBBIN.

TH#1/265: Mr. ROBERT GRIFFITH administrator of ARIMENTA WOOD late of Anne Arun- del Co deceased. 21 November 1837. Sureties: JOSEPH G. HARRISON + BENJAMIN CARR. Thirds of the balance to: SAMUEL WOOD, ELEANOR CHALK, + LEVI WEBB in right of his wife ELIZA.

TH#1/266: Mrs. MARY LINSTED administratrix of GEORGE W. LINSTED late of Anne Arundel Co deceased. 2 December 1837. Sureties: ORLANDO HANCOCK + CHARLES

BOONE. MARY LINDSTED, widow's third; fourths of the remaining balance to:
ANN MARIA LINSTED, ELIZABETH LINSTED, JOHN LINSTED, + GEORGE ELLEN (sic)
LINSTED.

TH#1/266: Mr. FREDERICK RAWLINGS administrator of JOSHUA RAWLINGS late of
Anne Arundel Co deceased. 5 December 1837. Sureties: CHARLES HAMMOND + MA-
REEN M DUVALL. ELIZABETH RAWLINGS, widow's third; fifths of the remaining
balance to: JOSHUA RAWLINGS, FREDERICK RAWLINGS, JAMES RAWLINGS, ROBERT BOCK-
MILLER, + SAMUEL DORSEY in right of his wife ELIZABETH.

TH#1/267: Mr. JAMES C. HITCHCOCK administrator of JOSHUA YOUNG late of Anne
Arundel Co deceased. 12 December 1837. Sureties: TRUE PUTNEY + CALEB DAVIS.
ORPHA YOUNG, widow's third; tenths of the remaining balance to: JASON YOUNG,
CATHARINE HITCHCOCK, ORPHA MILLER, ELIZABETH HITCHCOCK, JOSHUA YOUNG, WILLIAM
YOUNG, SAMUEL ROBINSON, JAMES C. HITCHCOCK, JOHN ROBERTS, + WILLIAM MCMEEKEN.

TH#1/268: Mr. WILLIAM CRANDALL + Mr. JOSEPH CRANDALL administrators of ABEL
CRANDALL late of Anne Arundel Co deceased. 2 January 1838. Sureties: THOMAS
CRANDALL + WILLIAM O'HARA. SARAH CRANDALL, widow's third; elevenths of the
remaining balance to: THOMAS CRANDALL, WILLIAM CRANDALL, JOSEPH CRANDALL,
ELIZABETH ATWELL, FRANCES CRANDALL, HARRISON CRANDALL, REBECCA CRANDALL, MARY
ANN CRANDALL, PRISCILLA CRANDALL, SALLY CRANDALL, + HARRIET CRANDALL.

TH#1/268 + 269: Mr. JOHN S. SELLMAN administrator of SAMUEL MAYNARD late of
Anne Arundel Co deceased. 9 January 1838. Sureties: GEORGE WELLS + WILLIAM
S. MCPHERSON. Fourths of the balance to: WILLIAM S. MCPHERSON, JOHN S. SELL-
MAN, EDWARD MAYNARD, + SAMUEL MAYNARD.

TH#1/269: Mr. JOHN KNIGHTON one of the executors of GASSAWAY KNIGHTON late of
Anne Arundel Co deceased. 12 January 1838. Sureties: CHARLES CLAGETT, THOMAS
DAVIDSON + JOSEPH NICHOLSON. Fourths of the balance to: JOHN KNIGHTON, NICHO-
LAS KNIGHTON, THOMAS KNIGHTON, + FRANCIS BRASHEARS in right of his wife ELEANOR.

TH#1/269 + 270: Mr. FRANCIS BIRD one of the administrators of WILLIAM BIRD
late of Anne Arundel Co deceased. 23 January 1838. Sureties: WILLIAM O'HARA
+ JOSEPH ATWELL. Halves of the balance to: ELIZABETH FARRELL + ANN NICHOLS.

TH#1/270: Mr. JAMES R. BROWN administrator with will annexed of ELISHA BROWN
(of SAMUEL) late of Anne Arundel Co deceased. 23 January 1838. Sureties:
JOHN G. WORTHINGTON + LUCRETIA BROWN. Thirds of the balance to: JAMES R. BROWN,
LUCRETIA BROWN, + ELIZABETH BROWN.

TH#1/270: Mr. HOWARD M. DUVALL administrator with will annexed of HOWARD DUVALL
late of Anne Arundel Co deceased. 21 February 1838. Sureties: WASHINGTON G.
TUCK + JOHN KNIGHTON. SUSAN DUVALL, widow's third; sixths of the remainder to:
CATHARINE H. + HARRIET C. DUVALL, NICHOLAS D. DUVALL, JULIA A. DUVALL, ENOCH DU-
VALL, HOWARD M. DUVALL, + ELIZABETH A. GARDNER.

TH#1/271: Mr. JOHN BEARD Jr. administrator of ELIZABETH H. WATSON late of Anne
Arundel Co deceased. 5 March 1838. Sureties: THOMAS R. BEARD + THOMAS G.
WATERS. Elevenths of the balance to: THOMAS G. WAYMAN in right of his wife MARY,
JOHN GARDINER in right of his wife ANNE, BENJAMIN ELLIOTT in right of his wife
MARY, WILLIAM WATSON, JULIANNA WATSON, RUTLAND WATSON, THOMAS WATSON, RACHEL
WATSON, ELIZABETH WATSON, EMILY WATSON, + MARIA L. WATSON.

TH#1/272: Mr. JOHN S. SELLMAN administrator of SAMUEL MAYNARD late of Anne Arun-

del Co deceased. 15 February 1838. Sureties: GEORGE WELLS + WILLIAM S. MC-
PHERSON. Fourths of the balance to: WILLIAM S. MCPHERSON in right of his wife
HARRIET, JOHN S. SELLMAN in right of his wife SALLY, EDWARD MAYNARD, + SAMUEL
MAYNARD.

ADAMS:
Albert, 92; Elizabeth, 15, 49;
George, 15, 38, 45, 91; Margaret,
92; Robert, 92; Susan, 92; Thomas,
92.

ADDISON:
Henrietta Maria, 33; John, 68;
Thomas G., 33.

AILSWORTH:
Ann, 42.

ALDRIDGE:
Zachariah, 9.

ALEXANDER:
Ann, 76; Jane, 76; John H., 76;
Mary, 73, 91; Mary H., 76; Thomas
S., 76; William, 38, 76.

ALLEIN:
Ann, 3, 47; Artridge, 3; Benjamin,
3, 20, 43, 47; Elizabeth, 47, 69;
86, 91; Harriet, 47; Jacob, 3;
Joseph, 3, 47, 87; Juliet, 47;
Mary, 3; Mary Ann, 47; Rachel, 3,
47; Thomas, 47, 86, 91.

ALLEN:
Azel, 39; Dinah, 17; Jane, 17;
John, 29; Joseph, 78; Lindy, 11;
Martha, 17; Ruth, 29; Susanna, 29;
William, 11, 17.

ALLISON:
James, 65.

ALLWELL, ALWELL:
Ann, 50, 54; Eliza, 50, 54; Jacob,
15; John, 15; Nathan, 15; Nathaniel, 50; Nicholas, 15; Rebecca,
15; Rhoda, 50, 54; Sarah, 15; Wesley, 50, 54; William, 15.

ANDERSON:
Absalom, 33; Andrew, 33, 77, 79;
Ann, 29, 33, 77, 79; Asa, 73; Edward, 17, 31, 38, 54, 60; Eleanor Weylie, 53; Elizabeth, 33;
Elizabeth Edwards, 11; Frances,
77, 79; James, 31, 32, 33, 53, 77,
79; Joshua, 33; Leonard, 77, 79;
Lydia, 33; Robert, 33; Samuel, 31,

33, 38; Sarah, 29, 59; Thomas, 33,
76; William, 11, 31, 33, 38.

ANGLING:
Zachariah, 11.

ANKERS:
Snowden, 31.

ANTIST:
Nancy, 41.

ARMIGER:
_____, 72; Ann, 26, 30, 72;
Benjamin, 23, 26, 52; James, 26;
Jesse, 23; John, 23, 52, 72; John
Francis, 52; Joseph, 26; Leonard,
23, 26, 30, 72; Mary, 52; Mary
Ann, 72; Rachel, 52; Rezin, 26;
Richard, 52; Samuel, 52; Sarah
Ann, 52; Susannah, 52; Thomas, 52;
William, 23, 52.

ARNOLD:
John, 60, 62, 67, 78; Richard, 70;
Robert, 70; Sarah, 70; William, 75.

ASHLAND,
John, 20.

ASHLEY:
Zachariah, 5, 9, 11.

ASHPAW:
Ann, 12, 39; Catherine, 67, 68;
Elizabeth, 67; Francis, 39; George,
67, 68; Henry, 1, 12; John, 12, 23,
36, 39, 68; Joseph, 67, 68.

ATKINSON:
Catherine, 9; Elizabeth, 9, 43;
Francis, 9; Joseph, 42; Nathan,
9; Rachel, 9; Thomas, 9.

ATWELL, ATTWELL:
Benjamin, 16, 39, 61, 91; Catherine, 39; Daniel, 39; Elizabeth,
91, 96; Elizabeth Rawlings, 18,
45; John, 16, 46; Joseph, 16, 39,
91, 96; Margaret, 16; Mary, 39,
42; Nathan, 14; Onerah Wells, 51;
Rachel, 16; Robert, 39, Samuel,
39; Sarah, 16; Thomas, 51, 59;
William, 16, 39, 45.

AUGLIN:
Zachariah, 29.

AUSTIN:
Sarah, 35.

BABBS:
Nancy, 24; Thomas, 24.

BAER:
Michael T., 92.

BAKER:
Nancy, 67.

BALDWIN:
Edward, 45, 80, 85-86; Eliza Ann, 86; Elizabeth, 15; Ellender, 45; Henrietta M., 86; Henry, 15, 86; James, 15, 19, 33, 45; James T., 86; John, 35, 86; John, 25, 86; Mariam, 15; Mary, 57; Mary H., 86; Nicholas, 24, 25; Rezin D., 24, 25, 74, 78; Samuel, 25; Sarah, 15; Thomas, 25; Tyler, 24, 25; William, 15; Zachariah, 25.

BALL:
Henry, 77; John, 46; Mary, 73, 81.

BANDA:
Daniel, 78; Emilia, 78.

BANGS:
John, 88; William H., 88.

BANKS:
Eleanor, 36; Samuel, 36.

BARBER:
Aquila, 94; George W., 84, 86; Gustavus R., 84, 86; Jane M., 86; John, 38; John T., 84, 86; Susan, 84, 86; Susanna Rawlings, 38.

BARNES:
Benjamin, 62; Cordelia, 67; Elizabeth, 62; Harry, 62; James A., 62; John, 62; Marcela, 62; Rhoda, 62; Rufus, 62, 93; Ruth, 91, 93; Thomas, 62.

BARNEY:
Caleb, 77.

BARRETT:
Eleanor, 4; John, 4; Joseph, 4;

BARRETT, continued:
William, 4.

BARRY:
Elisha, 67; Jacob, 67; James, 67; Rachel, 67.

BASFORD:
Ann Plummer, 23; Benjamin, 3, 9; Dinah Cheney, 45; Elizabeth Shekell, 9; Frederick, 3; Henry, 61; Jacob, 61; Jemima, 3; John, 3, 34, 61; Rachel, 3; Richard, 3; Thomas, 3, 61; Zachariah, 3.

BASIL:
Elizabeth, 14.

BATEMAN:
Amzi, 19; Ann, 19; Benjamin, 19; Elizabeth, 19; Henry, 19; Lemuel, 19; Rachel, 19.

BATSON:
Elizabeth, 7; John, 7; Thomas, 7, 8, 66.

BATTEE:
Ann, 70; Elizabeth, 52; Ferdinando, 52; Matilda, 70; Richard, 32, 70; Richard H., 92; Samuel, 75; Sarah, 70, 88.

BEACRAFT:
John, 54.

BEALL:
Eleanor, 54, 57; Eleanor Deaver, 18; Harriet, 93; Isabella, 23; John, 54; Joseph, 4; Margaret D., 54; Mary, 54; Rachel Howard, 4; Samuel H., 93.

BEALMEAR:
Absalom, 72; Ann, 93; Elizabeth Anderson, 33; Francis, 29, 33, 42; John, 29; Lewis, 29; Samuel, 29.

BEARD:
Catherine, 12; Elizabeth, 5, 53; John, 52, 53, 63, 70, 71, 96; John W., 71; Jonathan, 5; Joseph, 12; Luranah, 5; Mary, 5, 53; Mathew, 10; Rebecca, 53; Richard, 5; Stephen, 5, 7, 12, 24, 32, 36, 42, 45, 52, 53, 55, 71, 87, 93; Sus-

BEARD, continued:
anna, 52; Susanna Rawlings, 45;
Thomas, 5; Thomas R., 93, 96.

BECK:
Mary, 19.

BELT:
Basil, 57; Benjamin, 57, 73; Dorothy, 57; Edward W., 86, 90; James,
57; John, 57, 78; John Sprigg, 44,
54; Joseph, 57; Osborn, 57; Richard, 57.

BENSON:
Ann S., 63; Basil S., 63; Elizabeth, 14, 63; Harriet, 78; John,
14, 77; Joseph S., 63; Margaret,
78; Rachel, 14; Richard, 14, 63,
77; Samuel, 77; Sarah, 14; Thomas,
14, 51, 63, 77; William, 14.

BENTLEY:
Harriet Dorsey, 58.

BERRY:
Caleb, 79; Jeremiah, 71, 74; Mary,
55; Philip, 41; Sarah, 6.

BETHRAY:
William, 23.

BEVANS:
George O., 68; John, 75, John T.,
68; Laura, 68, 75; Mary, 75; Mary
R., 68.

BICKNELL:
Julia, 90; Thomas, 2, 10, 12, 15,
21, 22, 29, 36, 40, 58, 64.

BIRCKHEAD:
Christianna, 61; Eleanor, 61; E-
lizabeth, 40, 61; John J., 61;
Mary, 52; Mary Drury, 49; Mary E.,
61; Nehemiah, 40, 52; Nehemiah
Richardson, 52; Samuel, 40, 61;
Sarah, 40, 52, 61; Sarah R., 52.

BIRD:
Ann, 17, 46; Ann Green, 13; Elizabeth, 76, Francis, 69, 75, 96; Jacob W., 75; John, 75; Lemuel, 75;

BIRD, continued:
Margaret, 75; Mary, 75; Richard,
75; Thomas, 75; William, 13, 17,
96.

BISHOP:
Josephus, 77, 79.

BLACK:
Christopher, 53; Eli A., 53; Elizabeth, 53; James, 53; John, 53;
Joshua, 53; Rebecca, 53; William,
53.

BLACKISON:
Rebecca, 35.

BLOWERS:
Ann Ray, 44; Jonathan, 44, 73.

BLUNT:
Edward, 47; Rebecca, 33.

BOCKMILLER:
Robert, 96.

BONNER:
John, 58.

BOONE:
Ann, 31, 41, 45, 48, 59, 87; Ann
E., 48; Burley G., 12, 45, 48, 59;
Charles, 12, 13, 31, 33, 37, 45,
48, 59, 95-96; Charlotte, 36, 57;
Charlotte Burley, 12; Eleanor, 36;
Eliza, 45, 48, 59; Elizabeth, 12,
48, 79; Elizabeth Stansbury, 13;
Henry, 45; James, 45, 48; John, 36,
45, 48, 57; John H.D., 48, 59; John
S., 87; Margaret, 48, 59; Margaret
S., 45, 48; Mary Ann, 48; Nicholas,
36, 57; Rhoda Cromwell, 79; Robert,
31, 41, 79, 83, 87; Sarah, 34, 45,
48, 59; Stephen, 31, 41, 62, 66.

BOWSE:
Caesar, 36; Catherine, 36; Edward,
36; Esther, 36; James, 36; John,
36.

BOYD:
James P., 26.

BOYER:
John Adam, 22.

BRADFORD:
George, 75, 90; Margaret, 57; Nathan, 75; Samuel, 75; Sarah, 75; Sarah Stansbury, 68.

BRASHEARS:
Jesse, 12; Judson, 12; Levi, 12; Lilburn, 12; Margery, 12; Nancy, 12; Waymack, 12; Wilkerson, 1.

BRAY:
John, 12; Joseph, 12; Mary, 12.

BREATHETT:
Cardwell, 73, 91; Rebba, 91.

BREWER:
Ann, 3, 89; Ann Odle, 4; Charles P., 89; Edward P., 89; Eleanor, 25, 96; Elias, 24, 89; Elizabeth, 3, 24, 26, 52; Ellin, 12; Francis, 96; John, 3, 4, 30, 50, 52; Joseph N., 25, 70; Joseph Nathaniel, 4; Joseph Newton, 52; Juliet, 24; Lot, 3, 10; Mary, 40, 52, 62; Mary Jane, 52; Mary Newton, 4; Nathaniel, 4; Nicholas, 3, 4, 24, 29, 30, 35, 50, 52, 73, 74, 83; Peggy, 54; Rachel, 10, 25; Rebecca, 52; Rhoda, 10; Richard, 71; Roady, 3; Sarah Ann, 52, Susannah, 4; William, 52, 62, 73; 74; William Wootton, 25.

BRICE:
Jacob, 6; Kitty Lewin, 6.

BRIGHT:
Hamutel, 42; Mary Ann, 49.

BROGDEN:
David M., 74; William, 21, 92.

BROOKS:
Ann, 77; John, 77.

BROTHERS:
Nancy, 77.

BROWN:
Achsah, 47; Alley, 13; Althea, 32, 37; Ann, 13, 15, 18, 32, 85; Ann

BROWN, continued:
Burton, 51; Basil, 37, 38, 45, 57; Benjamin, 85, 87; Clarissa, 47, 57; Darkus, 57; Deborah, 85; Eleanor, 82; Elisha, 46, 96; Eliza, 47, 57; Eliza Ann, 84; Elizabeth, 47, 84, 96; Elizabeth Deroch, 33; Ely, 27; Harriet, 13; Henrietta, 57, 76, 83; Henry C., 84; Henry G., 47; Henry H., 47, 57, 76, 83; James R., 88, 96; Jennett, 13; John, 9, 13; John H., 47, 57, 76, 83; John R., 47; Joshua, 2, 9; Joshua D., 90; Julian, 71; Juliana, 47, 57; Kitty Ann, 47; Lloyd, 90; Louisa, 47; Lucretia, 96; McLane, 85; Mary Ann, 47; Obadiah, 32, 37; Philip, 47, 76, 84; Philip H., 57; Rachel, 3, 13, 32; Rezin, 47, 76, 84; Rezin H., 57; Richard, 13, 32, 37, 84, 85; Robert, 32, 87; Samuel, 47, 86, 96; Sarah, 47; Sarah A., 90; Thomas, 1; Vachel, 71; William, 1, 46, 47, 76, 84, 85, 87; William H., 57; Willson, 84; Zachariah, 90.

BROWNING:
Achsah, 43.

BRUCE:
Affa, 16; James, 16.

BRYAN:
Elizabeth, 45; John, 45; Lydia, 45; Robert S., 79.

BUCKMAN:
Ann, 38; Benjamin, 38; David, 38; Deborah, 38; Edmund, 38; Esther, 38; John, 38; Oliver, 38; Thomas, 44.

BURGESS:
Absalom, 55; Ann, 21; Ann D., 80; Basil, 7, 55, 66, 71, 75, 80; Caleb, 6, 31; Deborah, 31; Eleanor Dorsey, 7; Elizabeth, 6, 21; Elizabeth Warfield, 50; George, 87; Hetty W., 80; Husley, 10; John, 31; John Brice, 18; Joseph, 55; Joshua, 55; Juliet, 80; Margaret Ann, 50; Mary, 55; Mary V., 80; Matilda, 31, 63; Michael, 55; Peregrine, 55, 80; Rebecca, 55, 80; Rebecca O., 80;

BURGESS, continued:
Richard, 50; Roderick, 55, 83; Samuel, 31; Samuel West, 50; Sarah, 55; Susanna, 31; Thomas, 55; Thomas D., 80; Vachel, 44, 80; West, 50; William, 55.

BURLEIGH:
Ann, 76; Eleanor, 75, 76; Thomas, 75, 76.

BURNESTON:
Joseph, 14.

BURTON:
Ann, 51; Charles, 28, 49; Edmond, 51; Edward, 28; Elizabeth, 28; John, 7, 15, 18, 28, 34, 50, 51; Louisa, 51; Mary, 28, 51; Nancy, 15, 28; Patsy, 51; Sarah, 28, 51; William, 28, 51, 88.

BUSEY:
Ann, 25; Benjamin, 18; Charles, 25; Daniel, 25; Henry, 22, 25; Jane, 18; Joseph, 18; Mary, 18, 25; Nelly, 25; Paul, 18; Samuel, 18, 22; Sarah, 18; William, 18.

BUTCHER:
Samuel, 15; Sarah, 15.

BUTLER:
John, 87.

CADLE:
Eleanor, 40; Elizabeth, 3, 40; James, 9; Priscilla, 40; Samuel, 40; Thomas, 40; William, 40; Zachariah, 2.

CALLAHAN:
Eliza, 82; Elizabeth, 56; James, 56; John, 56; Margaret, 56; Maria, 56; Mary, 56, 82; Nancy, 56; Thomas, 12, 56.

CALVERT:
George, 17.

CAMPBELL:
Rebecca, 83.

CAMPER:
Mary, 69.

CANADY:
Elizabeth, 33; Susanna, 8.

CAREY:
James, 26.

CARR:
Abigail, 35; Artridge, 86, 91; Benjamin, 6, 26, 54, 57, 77, 86, 87, 91, 95; Catherine, 16; Elizabeth, 86; Ellen, 86; Jacob, 77; Jane Russell, 15; John, 3, 16, 77; Lucy, 57; Martha, 17; Mary, 17, 77; Mary Armiger, 52; Mary Burgess, 55; Mary E., 71; Pamelia, 17; Rachel, 16; Richard, 54; Richard F., 86, 91; Robert, 32, 60; Samuel, 15; Walter, 72, 77; William, 16, 77.

CARROLL:
Charles, 41; James, 41; John, 71.

CARTER:
Ann, 17, 31; Ann Lewin, 6; John, 6; Mary, 72.

CARVILL:
Elizabeth, 10; John, 10; Mary, 10.

CECIL:
Margery, 55; Philip, 73; Samuel, 59, 73; Zachariah, 73; Zepheniah, 73.

CHAIRS:
Rhoda, 67.

CHALK:
Alexander, 5; Eleanor, 95; Margaret, 65; Minah, 5; Rebecca, 5; Sarah, 5.

CHAMBERS:
Achsah, 48; Amelia, 48; Amos, 48; Edward, 48; James, 10; John, 10, 11, Joshua, 48; Mary, 27; Nancy, 48; Senatha, 48; Thomas, 48.

CHANDLER:
John, 60.

CHANEY, CHENEY:
Abel, 9, 37, 44; Abraham, 45; Achsah Rizel, 34; Alethea, 88; Ann, 9; Benjamin, 9, 45, 77; Charles,

CHANEY, CHENEY, continued:
19; Delilah, 9; Dinah, 45; Elijah,
92; Elizabeth, 9, 31, 45; Cassaway, 45; Henrietta Groves, 94;
Hezekiah, 9; John, 14; Joseph, 45;
Mary, 45; Nancy, 35; Richard, 9,
88, 91, 94; Rignel, 94; Ruth, 22;
Samuel, 45; Sarah, 94; Solomon G.,
94; Sophia, 9; Susanna, 9; Thomas,
9, 44; William, 19.

CHARD:
Cornelius, 5, 7; Oliver, 5; Rebecca,
5, Rhoady Robinson, 53.

CHASE:
Ann, 82; Cecilia, 58; Frances C.T.,
82; Hester A., 82; Matilda, 82;
Richard M., 56, 82.

CHESTON:
Ann, 21, 24; Francina Augustina,
21; James, 21, 84.

CHEW:
Nathaniel, 13, 75.

CHILDS:
Ann, 8, 32, 33, 34, 73; Barbary,
8, Benjamin, 10, 32; Betsy, 32;
Cephas, 18, 20, 32, 34, 35; Eleanor, 51, 60, 71; Elijah, 34; Elizabeth, 8, 34; Henry, 32, 37, 39, 51,
61, 67, 78; Henry L., 60; Henry
Lloyd, 51; John, 32; Jonathan, 51,
62; Joseph, 32, 35, 51; Julianna,
51, 60, 62; Martha P., 32; Mary,
8, 34, 37, 51, 60; Mary E., 62;
Mordecai, 34; Nathan, 60, 62, 71;
Nathan S., 51; Nelly, 8; Obadiah,
34; Samuel, 32; Sarah, 8, 34; Sephas, 8; Sophia, 34; William, 34,
44, 51, 60, 62; William P., 71;
Zachariah, 8.

CHISHOLM:
Archibald, 5, 44; Catherine, 44;
Charlotte, 44; Elizabeth, 44; Emi-
ly, 44.

CLAGETT:
Charles, 96; Edmund, 64; Elizabeth,
64; James, 87; John, 64; Mary E.,

CLAGETT, continued:
65; Louisa, 82, 91; Richard, 64-65;
Samuel, 64, 87; Thomas, 64; William, 64, 65.

CLARIDGE:
Achsah, 28; Elizabeth, 44; Solomon, 44.

CLARK, CLARKE:
Amos, 28; Benjamin D., 28, 33; Dor-
cas, 28; Fanny Lewin, 6; Henry, 28;
Jacob, 28; Joseph, 16; Josiah, 28;
Peter, 6; Rachel, 28; William, 87.

CLAUDE:
_____, 26; Abraham, 1, 2, 7, 8,
19; Dennis, 1, 19, 83; Elizabeth,
19; John, 1, 19; Nancy, 1.

CLAYTON:
John, 76, 79, 80, 82, 89, 90; Mary,
79; Mary McCeney, 80; Philip, 65.

CLEARY:
James, 8, 26; S_____, 26; Sarah
Maccubbin, 8.

CLEMENTS:
Francis T., 63, 70.

COBERTH:
John, 84.

COE:
William, 6.

COALE, COLE:
Alfred, 18; Ann Wilson, 23; Anna
Maria, 18; Charles Ridgely, 18;
Harriet, 18; John, 55; Joseph, 55;
Joseph, 55; Sarah, 18, 92; Susanna,
77; Thomas, 18, 55; Wesley, 77.

COLLINS:
Anne, 38; James, 9; Josias, 37; Patience, 38; Rachel, 38; Richard, 9,
37; Ruth, 38; Sarah, 14, 17.

COLLISON:
Alse, 13; Ann, 69; Benjamin, 13, 41;
Charity, 13; Edward, 13, 41, 56;
John, 13, 35, 41; Mary, 13; Sarah,
13; William, 13, 41.

COLMWOOD:
Rachel, 65.

COMPTON:
Evalina, 50; John Willson, 50; Julia Ann, 50; Mary, 50; Susanna, 50; William, 50.

CONAWAY, CONWAY:
Amelia, 3; Area, 3; Deborah, 82; George, 3, 10, 23; Jesse, 82; John, 6; Margaret, 6; Rachel, 3; Vachel, 3, 5.

CONNER, CONNOR:
Mary, 20, 75; Mary Gott, 24; Susanna, 56.

CONTEE:
Elizabeth Cassaway Sanders, 26; Richard, 26.

COOGLE:
Mary, 21; Rosanna, 21.

COOK:
Ann, 68; Elisha, 68; John, 68; Larkin, 68; Thomas, 1, 68.

COOLEY:
Ann, 4; Margaret, 4; Thomas, 4.

COOPER:
George, 14.

CORD:
Ann, 9; Catherine, 9; George, 9; Hellen, 9; Henry, 9; James, 9; Jesse, 9; John, 9; Rebecca, 9; Sarah, 9; Sophia, 9.

COWLEY:
Charles, 19, Elizabeth, 15; Elizabeth Deale, 19; Joseph, 19; William, 22.

COWMAN:
Henrietta, 88, 92; Henry, 92; John, 53; Joseph, 1, 64; Joseph E., 90; Matilda, 92; Richard, 93; Richard H., 88, 92; Richard J., 65, 88, 92.

GOYLE:
Eliza, 44.

CRABB:
Richard J., 82.

CRAGGS:
Elizabeth, 65; George, 65; John, 21; Joseph H., 65; Mary A., 65.

CRAMLICK:
Andrew, 27; Elizabeth, 27; Frederick, 27; Jacob, 27; John, 27; Michael, 27; Stephen, 27; Thomas, 27.

CRANDALL:
Abel, 96; Adam, 13; Ann, 67; Elizabeth Caroline, 54; Frances, 96; Harriet, 96; Harrison, 96; Henry, 43, 46; Hester, 54; Joseph, 96; Mary Ann, 96; Priscilla, 20, 96; Priscilla Gott, 24; Rebecca, 96; Richard, 43; Sally, 96; Sarah, 76, 96; Thomas, 43, 54, 96; William, 96.

CRANE:
Caleb, 43; John, 35, 43; Lydia, 75; Reuben, 35; Samuel, 35, 43.

CRAWFORD:
Adam, 23; Arabella, 87; Basil B., 87; Elizabeth, 37, 87; Francis, 87; Harriet, 87; Julian, 37; Lucretia, 87; Mary, 87; Nathaniel, 37; Samuel, 87; Sarah, 37; Sophia, 37, 87; William, 87.

CRAYCROFT:
Andrew, 30; Ann, 51; Benjamin, 51; Bladen, 30; Charles, 30; Eleanor, 30; Elizabeth, 30; George, 51; Gerard, 51; Gerret S., 25; Joseph, 30; Mary, 30, 51; Richard, 30; Samuel, 30; Sarah, 30; Susanna, 30.

CROMWELL:
Ann, 41; Charlotte Williams, 49; Ebenezer, 33, 97; Eleanor, 79; Francis, 12, 14, 17, 35, 55; Harriet, 73, 75; Henrietta, 41; John, 11, 35, 38, 46, 55, 73, 74, 79; John G., 45, 50, 53; Joseph, 38; Joshua, 38; Levi, 38; Margaret, 73, 75, 97; Mary, 35, 55; Michael, 38; Nancy, 38; Oliver, 26, 33, 38, 50, 54; Oneal, 73, 74; Patience,

CROMWELL, continued:
73, 75, 79; Patience Jacob, 27; Rachel, 38, 54; Randolph, 88; Richard, 32, 50, 54; Sarah, 35, 38, 75; Thomas, 7, 38, 54; William, 11, 35, 38, 42; Zachariah, 35, 40, 41, 49, 61, 64, 73.

CROSBY:
Ann Price, 88; Elizabeth, 77; John, 3; Josias, 3, 12, 20, 23, 88; Rachel, 3; Richard, 3, 32.

CROSS:
Abetha, 67; Dennis, 67; Elizabeth, 62, 67, 68; Emma, 67; Fielder, 66; Francis, 79; Isaiah, 67; Jemima, 52, 62; Jeremiah, 67; John, 47, 52, 62; Joseph, 67; Lydia, 67; Mary Ann, 62, 68; Rebecca, 62, 68; Sarah, 61; Stephen, 67, Thomas, 84; Walter, 72.

CROUCH:
Ann, 8; John, 8.

CROW:
Lydia, 63; Mary, 41.

CRUCHLEY:
Jesse, 12; Mary Ann, 19.

DADDS:
Emanuel, 65; Mary, 65.

DANIELSON:
Elizabeth, 17; Joseph, 17; Samuel, 17.

DARE:
Nathaniel C., 92.

DARNALL:
Elizabeth, 50, 59; Francis, 50, 59; Henry, 44, 50, 59; Nicholas, 44; Philemon, 59; Philip, 50, 52.

DAVIDSON:
Ezekiel, 74; Henrietta, 74; Israel, 71, 74, 84, 85; James, 29; John, 34, 74; John J., 83; Samuel J., 83; Thomas, 31, 96; William, 20.

DAVIS:
Ann, 2; Eleanor, 43; Elizabeth, 7; Henry, 7; John P., 70, 83; Mary, 25; Mary Beard, 53; Nancy, 7; Orpha, 43; Richard, 25; Robert, 43; Ruth, 26; Ruthy, 43; Samuel, 32, 35; Sarah, 7; Sarah Ditty, 54; Sarah Jacob, 43; Thomas, 23, 25, 43, 52, 63; William, 83; William M., 43; Zachariah, 14.

DAWKINS:
Thomas, 77.

DAWSON:
Elizabeth, 55.

DAY:
Ann Eliza, 80; Israel, 40; John, 71, 80; Mary, 80; Nathan, 80; Nicholas, 40; Rebecca, 40; Samuel, 80; William, 40.

DEALE:
Ann, 27; Elizabeth, 19, 48, 53; Ellen, 87; Henrietta, 20; Henry, 86, 87; Jacob F., 93; James, 19, 52, 55, 64, 93; John, 6; Joseph, 64; Margaret Lewin, 6; Martin, 48, 53, 55; Mary, 58, 93; Nathan, 19, 64; Rachel, 19, 20, 35, 37, 55, 56; Rachel Gott, 24; Richard, 87; Samuel, 19, 64; Sarah, 19; Thomas, 19; William, 6, 48, 53, 55, 64.

DEAN:
Micha, 39; Richard, 39.

DEAVER, DEVER:
Ann, 18, 31; Basil, 77; Benjamin, 31, Deborah, 77, Eleanor, 18, Henry, 18, 57, 77; James, 87; Joseph, 31, 77; Lucy, 18; Margaret, 18; Philip, 77; Richard, 77; Samuel, 77; Sarah, 18; Stephen, 18, 77.

DEEMS (WEEMS?)
Ann, 88.

DEFORD:
Ann, 46, 49; Benjamin, 46, 49; Charlotte, 46, 49; Maria, 46.

DELANDER:
Adam, 74, 94.

DELOZIER:
Daniel, 83.

DEMPSEY:
Frederick, 94; John, 94.

DENNIS:
Lane, 84.

DENNY:
Ellen, 55; Mary, 46; Mary Norris, 33; Matilda, 55; Robert, 26; Thomas, 33; Thomas B., 55; Thomas D., 46.

DENT:
Charles, 88; Eleanor, 36, 37; Elizabeth Maria, 37; Erasmus, 37; John, 36, 37; Richard, 37; Walter, 37.

DEW:
Jesse, 77; Samuel, 77.

DILLWORTH:
William, 6.

DISNEY:
Arry, 23; Elizabeth, 62; James, 38; John, 62; Lilly, 48; Margaret, 62; Mary, 38, 64, 67; Mordecai, 23; Owen, 94; Richard, 24; Sarah, 67; William, 31, 62, 64, 67.

DITTY:
George P., 54; George T., 85, 89; John, 54; Roger, 54; Samuel, 54; Sarah, 54; Thomas R., 54.

DODSON:
Robert, 91.

DONALDSON, DONALSON:
Francis, 22, 83; Hezekiah, 22; Margaret, 22; Richard, 22; Sarah, 22.

DOOLEY:
Isabella, 84; James, 74, 84.

DORSEY:
Achsah, 78, 85; Amelia, 5; Amos, 16, 84; Andrew, 48, 58; Ann, 5, 7,

DORSEY, continued:
17, 36, 39, 41, 63, 70, 78, 85; Archibald, 54; Ariana, 5; Baker, 69; Benedict, 44; Benjamin, 68; Benjamin H., 66, 86; Betsey, 41, 63; Caleb, 5, 26, 27, 29, 30, 42, 63, 70, 71, 78, 85; Catherine, 5, 7, 36; Charles, 29; Charles B., 63; Charles S.W., 85; Charles Worthington, 42; Daniel H., 58; Daniel Horatio, 48; Deborah, 16; Edward, 63, 70, 92; Eleanor, 7; Eliza Ann, 30, 85; Elizabeth, 5, 7, 16, 30, 39, 41, 44, 48, 69, 96; Ezekiel, 48, 58; Fanny, 63; George, 36, 39, 44, 55, 63; Hammond, 69; Hanson, 78, 85; Harriet, 17, 20, 58, 66; Henrietta, 5; Henry, 78, 85; Humphrey, 29, 62, 63, 78, 90; James Ireland, 48, 58; John, 5, 6, 7, 17, 26, 29, 36, 39, 58, 63, 69, 78, 85, 90; John H., 20, 68, 86; John Henry, 17; John Ireland, 48; John Worthington, 27; Joshua, 5; Joshua A., 66, 86; Julia, 63; Juliana, 41, 63; Lancelot, 6, 7, 21; Larkin, 40; Larkin Sheredine, 69; Lloyd, 89; Louisa, 48, 58; Lucy, 41; Margaret, 29, 58; Margaret A., 63; Maria M., 68, 86; Mary, 63, 69, 78; Mary A.J., 66, 68, 86; Mary Ann, 16; Michael, 6, 7, Mortimer, 30, 78, 85; Nacky, 63; Nancy, 6; Nathan, 48; Nica, 69; Nicholas, 89; Owen, 94; Patience, 12; eggy, 30; Philemon, 5, 7, 36, 63; Polly, 16, 41; Priscilla, 69; Rachel, 5, 28, 41, 63, 71, 75; Ralph, 68, 86; Rebecca, 20, 48, 58, 69; Richard, 11, 12, 21, 23, 25, 27, 28, 30, 39, 40, 41, 52, 63, 66, 68, 69, 70, 71, 78, 86, 90, 92; Richard G., 86; Rinaldo W., 66, 68, 86; Robert, 40; Roderick, 58, 66; Ruth, 6, 7; Sally, 63; Samuel, 39, 48, 58, 96; Sarah, 5, 8, 29, 42, 69; Sarah A., 58; Sarah Ann, 48; Sarah Eleanor, 52; Septimus, 78, 85; Stephen B., 58; Stephen Boone, 29; Thomas, 44; Thomas B., 41, 42; Thomas Beall, 27; Thomas H., 58, 61, 70, 71; Thomas Hall, 19; Thomas J., 90; Vachel, 7, 17, 21, 28, 48; Washington, 44, William, 18, 24, 26, 63.

DOVE:
Alice, 9, Elizabeth, 9; Joseph, 9;
Mary, 9; Sarah, 9; Thomas, 9; William, 9.

DOWELL:
Ann, 35; Elizabeth, 52; Nica, 78;
Priscilla, 78.

DOWLEY:
Deborah, 9.

DRANE:
James, 17; Sarah Gwinn, 32, 36.

DRURY:
Ann Ijams, 51; Charles, 15, 18, 21,
22, 32, 34, 39, 46, 49; Elizabeth,
49; Elizabeth Ijams, 51; Ethelda,
49, Harriet, 49; Henry C., 46, 49,
52; Hester, 15; Jerningham, 13, 15,
18, 20, 40, 46, 51, 63; John, 49;
Joseph C., 46; Margaret, 46, 49;
Mary, 49; Matilda, 61, Samuel, 15,
20, 22, 46, 49, 51; Sarah, 49;
Susan, 77; Thomas, 17, 49; William,
13, 15, 22, 49, 51.

DUCKETT:
Eliza, 59, Richard, 59; Sophia, 27.

DULANY:
Walter, 21.

DUNBAR:
Henry, 44, 46.

DUNHAM:
John, 17.

DUNN:
Elizabeth Cheney, 9, Jean, 14; Michael, 9.

DUVALL:
A____ H____, 92; Alexander, 86;
Basil, 50; Catherine H., 96; Edward, 50, 83; Elie, 42, 80, 90;
Elisha, 50; Elizabeth, 27, 28, 51;
Emmeline, 80, 92; Enoch, 96; Enos,
10; Ephraim, 10, 12, 20, 27, 37, 56;
Garrard, 50; Grafton, 42; Grafton
B., 82, 85; Grafton D., 90; Harriet

DUVALL, continued:
C., 96; Henry, 42, 44, 46, 58, 59,
62; Howard, 66, 96; Howard M., 96;
Jemima Hazell, 27; Jesse, 25, 50;
John, 18, 45; Julia A., 96, Leonard, 50; Lewis, 36, 40, 42, 56,
63, 66, 70, 73, 91; Mareen, 50,
86; Mareen M., 93, 94, 96; Margaret, 42, 50, 90; Mary, 50, 73;
Nicholas D., 96; Noah, 89; Rachel,
29; Rebecca Rawlings, 18, 45;
Richard, 90; Sally, 37; Samuel, 37,
50; Samuel E., 70; Sarah, 10, 56,
82, 91; Susan, 96; Thomas, 29; William, 45, 48, 50; Zachariah, 2, 10,
37, 42, 44, 47, 49.

EARLE:
Thomas, 22.

EARLONGHER:
Francis, 87.

EARP:
Joshua, 42.

EDELEN:
Carel W., 63; Edward, 63; Thomas,
63; Thomas H., 63.

EDMONDSON:
John, 85.

EDWARDS:
Cadwallader, 6, 11, 27; Edward,
10; Elizabeth, 11; Jonathan, 11,
13; Margaret, 11; Mary, 11; Sarah,
11; William, 4, 10, 11.

EICHELBERGER:
Charles W., 89; Emanuel W., 89;
James F., 89; John, 89; John W.,
89; Maria, 89; Mary, 89.

ELDER:
Hellen, 6; Owen, 56; Providence,
6; Sarah, 18.

ELLENDER:
Margaret, 61.

ELLIOTT:
Amelia, 59; Andrew, 87; Ann, 3, 73,

ELLIOTT, continued:
59; Aquila, 59; Benjamin, 49, 96;
Howard, 48, 49, 59, 86; Jacob, 59;
James, 3; John, 9; Margery, 59;
Mary, 96; Richard, 59; Robert, 3,
9; Samuel, 6, 9; Sarah, 3, 56, 59;
Sarah Johnson, 49; Thomas, 3, 49;
William, 3, 9.

ELLIS:
Ann, 77, 81.

ERRICKSON:
Elizabeth, 30, Matthew, 30.

ESTEP:
Rezin, 50, 59, 66, 71, 74, 76, 77,
82; Richard, 65.

ETCHESON, ETCHISON:
Ann, 43; Arabella, 89; Eliza, 89;
Elizabeth, 89; John B., 89; Mary,
89; Nancy, 89; Rachel, 43; Sally,
89.

EVANS:
Achsah, 86, 93; Caroline, 86, 93;
Catherine, 86; Elizabeth, 27, 86,
93; Henry, 27, 28, 86; Jemima, 11;
Joseph, 14, 27, 28, 62; Mary, 2,
86; Samuel, 81.

FAIRBROTHER:
Ann, 5; Elfrida, 5; Francis, 5.

FARIS:
Priscilla, 34, 35; William, 34, 35.

FARRELL:
Elizabeth, 96.

FAULKNER:
Gassaway, 84; Lauriana, 84.

FELL:
Ann, 78.

FENNELL:
Ann, 33; Caleb, 9; Dorcas, 33; Eleanor, 33; Elisha, 33; William,
22, 33.

FERGUSON:
Abraham, 6; Elizabeth, 23; Jane

FERGUSON, continued:
Norman, 6.

FIGANSER:
John, 37.

FISH:
Benjamin, 7; Richard, 7, 37, 41-42,
45; Sarah, 45; William, 7.

FISHER:
Abraham, 6; Eleanor, 8; Elizabeth,
8; Elizabeth Childs, 8; Elizabeth
Lewin, 6; Fanny, 8; Henrietta, 71,
80; Hezekiah, 71, 80, 85; John H.,
71, 80, 85; Joshua, 24; Lewis, 8,
28; Martin, 5, 28; Mary A., 71, 80,
85; Mary Childs, 8; Rebecca Chalk,
5; Susanna, 71, 80, 85; William,
8, 71, 80, 85.

FITZHUGH:
Eleanor, 44.

FLEHARTY, FLUHARTY:
Freeborn, 44; Hopkins, 44; James,
44; Matthew, 44; Richard, 44; Susanna, 44.

FLEMING:
Amelia, 89; Richard, 43; Thomas,
89.

FOGGETT:
Richard M., 89.

FONERDON:
John, 11; Margaret Edwards, 11.

FORD:
John, 55.

FOREMAN:
Ann, 39; Ann C. Thomas, 60; Ellen-
der Hancock, 45; Henry, 45, 49;
John, 1; Joseph, 5, 39; Leonard, 1;
Mary, 39; Samuel, 39.

FOSTER:
Joseph, 19; Nathaniel, 16, 19; Susanna, 19.

FOWLER:
Achsah, 22, Baruch, 17, 49, 59, 76,

FOWLER, continued:
77, 79; Benjamin, 57; Daniel, 57;
Drayton, 73, 77, 81; George, 57;
Hannah, 31; John, 22, 31, 75; Jub,
31; Mark, 22, 26; Mary, 57; Priscilla, 22; Thomas, 22.

FOX:
Charles, 44; George, 50.

FOXCROFT:
William, 31, 85.

FRANKLIN:
Ann, 52, 58, 93; Artridge, 35, 41;
Benjamin, 52, 58; Charity, 35, 41;
Elizabeth, 20, 43; Elizabeth Gott,
24; Elizabeth Shaw, 83; George E.,
93; Isabella, 35, 56; Jacob, 3, 27,
39, 42, 58, 93; John, 21, 43; Maria, 94; Mary, 21, 35; Nancy, 94;
Robert, 20, 55, 65; Samuel, 43,
52, 58, 93; Sarah, 35, 41, 56;
Susan, 35; Thomas, 42, 52, 58, 83,
88, 92, 93.

FRAZIER:
Alexander, 7; Richard, 22.

FREE:
Mary, 89.

FREEBURGHER:
Ann Fennell, 33.

FREELAND, FREELON:
Charles, 84; Francis, 2.

FRENCH:
William, 3.

FRIZELL, FRIZZELL:
Achsah, 20; Charles, 20, 34, 67,
84; Elizabeth, 20, 34; John, 20;
Nelly, 20, 34.

FROST:
Ann, 68; Harriet, 68; James, 2,
68; John, 27; Mary, 68; William,
68.

FUNDENBURG:
David, 50.

FURLONG:
Elizabeth, 85; Thomas, 57, 85.

GAITHER:
Agnes, 62; Ann B., 90; Ann R., 90;
Beale, 17, 36; Benjamin, 37, 56,
61, 90; Edward, 38, 62; Elizabeth
Ann, 65; Ephraim, 47; Evan, 32, 38,
90; Greenbury, 38; Henry C., 47;
James, 38; Jane, 65; John, 25, 38;
John M., 87, 90; John R., 62; Lucy,
38; Margaret, 63, 90; Mary, 62;
Nancy, 32, 62; Patience, 23; Ra-
chel, 38; Rachel M., 90; Samuel,
32, 62; Sarah, 32, 38; Vachel, 22,
27, 32, 62; Washington, 82, 83;
Zachariah, 32, 38, 62.

GALE:
Margaret Dooley, 84.

GALLOWAY:
Benjamin, 21; John, 21, 24; Joseph,
24; Samuel, 24.

GAMBRILL:
Augustine, 28, 57; Augustus, 11;
Benjamin, 41; Elizabeth, 94;
George G., 76, 83; John, 11, 42;
Joseph, 41, 45; Juliana Brown, 57;
Mary, 11; Miriam Baldwin, 15; Nan-
cy, 42; Peggy, 42; Richard, 29, 94;
Ruth, 42; Sarah Fish, 45; Stephen,
42; Stevens, 11, 12, 21, 23, 38;
Thomas, 11; William, 28.

GANTTS:
Sarah H., 64.

GARDINER, GARDNER:
Ann, 33, 46, 66, 96; Ann Riston,
56; Charles, 46, 66, 70; Edward,
33; Elizabeth, 1; Elizabeth Ann,
96; George, 1, 30, 33; Henry, 46;
James, 1, 33; John, 1, 33, 46, 66,
70, 96; Joshua Merriken, 46; Martha, 33; Mary, 1, 33, 36; Richard,
1, 46, 66, 70; Samuel, 55, 58, 60;
Sarah, 1; Thomas, 34; Willamina,
33; William, 1, 33.

GARNER:
Robert, 78.

GARTRELL:
Margaret, 57; Samuel, 57; Stephen, 57.

GARY:
Deborah, 4; Everard, 4; Gideon, 4; Leonard, 4, 16, 34, 46, 51, 53, 54, 61; Lloyd, 4; Mary, 4.

GASSAWAY:
Brice J., 9, 44, 47; Catherine, 9; Charles, 9; Dinah, 29; John Brice, 14; Thomas, 9.

GASTON:
Nancy, 16; Susanna, 16; Thomas, 16.

GENNERS:
Elizabeth, 4; Mary, 4.

GENT:
Elizabeth, 81.

GEOGHAGEN:
Denton, 64; Henrietta, 34.

GHISELIN:
Ann Roboson, 25; Reverdy, 25.

GIBBS:
Cassandra, 73; Julia, 73; Mary, 44, 73; Thomas, 64.

GILL:
Ann Elizabeth, 93; Bennett, 81; Helen M., 91; Joshua, 81; Mary, 81; Nicholas C., 81; Richard W., 83, 85; Stephen, 81; William, 81.

GILLHAM:
Lydia, 12.

GIST:
John Smith, 23; Mary, 85.

GIVENS:
John, 7; William, 7.

GLOVER:
William, 25.

GOLDER:
Archibald, 42, 85; George, 42; Hen-

GOLDER, continued:
ry, 64; Susan, 64; William, 59.

GOLDSMITH:
William, 11.

GOODWIN:
Ara, 15; Ellinder, 15; John, 15; Mary, 15; Richard, 15, 50; Richard Rawlings, 50; Sarah, 50; Thomas, 12, 15.

GOOTEE:
Frederick, 46.

GOTT:
Edwin, 20; Eleanor, 27; Eliel, 20; Elizabeth, 20, 24, 65; Ezekiel, 3, 20; Henrietta, 24; Joseph, 20, 24; Mary, 24; Priscilla, 24; Rachel, 24; Rizpah, 24; Samuel, 20; Sarah, 41; Susanna S., 20.

GOVER:
Samuel, 70.

GRANGER:
Clement, 65; Edward, 65; James, 65; William, 65.

GRAVES:
Solomon, 51; William, 66.

GRAY:
Ann, 5, 87; Charles, 17; Charlotte, 87; Charlotte Brown, 57; Eli H., 87; Elijah, 43, 45, 57, 79; Elizabeth, 5, 49, 59; George, 66; George W., 87; Gideon, 2, 41; Greenbury, 9; Henry, 17; John, 1, 5, 9, 17, 57, 58, 59, 63, 66, 87; Joshua, 66; Leonard, 12; Linch, 12; Mary, 66; Rebecca, 12; Richard, 66; Ruth, 79; Sarah, 9, 35; Stephen, 87; Susan, 5; Susanna Cheney, 9; Wesley, 87; William, 10; Zachariah, 5, 10, 59.

GREEN:
Ann, 13; Benjamin, 37; Elijah, 2, 4; Elizabeth, 2, 13; Elizabeth Drury, 49; Frederick, 6, 26; Jacob, 2, 13; Jonas, 82; Lancelot, 2, 3, 13, 17, 18, 37; Maria, 37; Mary, 56,

GREEN, continued:
90; Mary Selby, 3; Samuel, 5; Sarah, 2, 17, 37; William J., 82;
William S., 56, 73, 82, 90.

GREENWELL:
Charles, 8; Rachel, 72.

GRIFFIN:
Benjamin, 35; Charles, 81.

GRIFFIS:
Elizabeth, 67; John, 67; William,
67.

GRIFFITH:
Agnes, 17; Amelia, 41; Ann, 20;
Ann Dorsey, 17; Basil, 33; Berry,
81; Betsey, 63; Catherine, 29;
Charles, 28, 33, 78; Elizabeth,
78; Fanny, 76; Henry, 2, 29; John,
33; John H., 58; Joshua, 63, 71;
Lewis, 87; Lyde, 20, 41; Mary, 78;
Rebecca, 33; Remus, 63, 75; Richard,
78; Robert, 33, 45, 87, 95; Samuel,
81; William R., 63.

GWINN:
Achsah, 26; Ann, 26, 36; Caleb,
26; Edward, 26; Elizabeth, 32, 36,
43, 46, 47; Esther, 32, 36; Francis,
9, 32; Henry, 36; John, 43, 46, 47;
Joseph, 36, 52; Rebecca, 27; Sarah,
32, 36.

HALE:
Daniel, 45; Edward, 8; Henry, 95;
Mary Ann, 95; Mordecai, 17; Nicholas E., 95; William T., 95; Zachariah L., 95.

HALL:
Ann Anderson, 33; Charlotte Johnson, 49; Daniel, 12, 23, 27; Delilah Williams, 49; Elisha, 12, 47,
79; Eliza, 47; Elizabeth, 12, 23,
27; Elizabeth Dorsey, 48; Harriet,
36; Henry, 36, 42, 47, 79, 85; Hester, 42; Jane, 47; Jesse, 12; John,
12, 23, 27, 28, 42, 67, 73, 74, 79,
84, 86; Joseph, 59, 85; Joshua, 3,
36, 84; Margaret, 59; Martha, 42;
Nathaniel, 11; Osborn S., 85; Patience, 12, 13; Priscilla, 90; Ra-

HALL, continued:
chel S., 85; Richard H., 85; Richard Jacob, 12; Sarah, 12, 13, 23,
27; T___ A___, 65; Thomas, 36;
Thomas B., 77, 81; Thomas H., 85;
Thomas Henry, 4; Thomas J., 73, 74,
77, 80, 81, 86; Thomas W., 59, 85,
90, William, 36, 81; William H.,
61, 80, 84, 86, 92; William J., 77,
81.

HALLOWAY:
Nicholas, 79.

HAMMOND:
___, 71; Andrew, 50; Ann E.,
87; Ann R., 76; Charles, 29; Elizabeth Brown, 47, 57; Hannah, 17;
Henrietta, 42, 80; Henry, 42, 44,
46, 56, 71, 75, 80; John, 13, 17,
86; John Thomas, 80; John W., 94;
Lloyd, 44; Mary, 76; Matthias, 49;
Nathan, 80; Philip, 17, 50, 57, 60;
Rezin, 17, 76, 83; Sally, 94; William, 22, 37.

HANCE:
Ann, 55.

HANCOCK:
Abraham, 49; Absalom, 41; Anne, 41;
Elijah, 45; Elizabeth, 45; Ellender, 45; Francis, 30, 41, 49, 50,
53, 54, 55, 59, 73, 75, 79, 85;
John, 45, 79, 83, 95; Landy, 45,
79; Mary, 45; Nathaniel, 9, 43, 45;
Orlando, 85, 95; Rhoda, 49; Ruth,
43; Sophia Cheney, 9; Stephen, 3,
23, 31, 36, 41, 49; Stephen W., 83.

HANDS:
Achsah, 16; Catherine, 16; Ephraim,
16; John, 16; Lancelot, 16; Margaret, 16; Mary, 16; Nicholas, 16;
Sarah, 16; William, 16.

HANSON:
Rebecca, 83.

HARDESTY, HARDISTY:
Achsah Simmons, 60; Agnes, 30; Eleanor W., 48; Eleanor Whittingham,
59; Elias, 30; Elizabeth, 30; Harriet, 30, 85; John, 29; Mary, 30;

HARDESTY, HARDISTY, continued:
Richard, 30, 87; Thomas, 81, 84;
William P., 48, 59; William T., 58,
60.

HARMAN:
Amelia J., 93; Andrew, 66; Ann, 93;
Caroline, 64, 66; Elizabeth, 93;
Eva, 66; Frederick G., 93; George,
64, 93; John, 64, 66; John M., 64;
Julian, 64; Kitty, 66; Louisa A.,
93; Mary, 64, Peter, 64; Peter A.,
93; Richard, 94.

HARPER:
Elsey, 41.

HARRIS:
Clair, 27; Joseph, 43, 46; Samuel,
8; Thomas, 43, 46, 47; William, 4.

HARRISON:
Benjamin, 18, 20, 24, 33, 44; Eleanor, 24; Ellen, 33; J____ G____,
62; Joseph, 24, 33, 60, 61, 87, 95;
Kitty, 67; Mary, 24, 33; Mary Norris, 1; Rachel Deale, 19; Richard,
1, 24; Samuel, 70, 73.

HART:
Daniel, 83, 93.

HARTMAN:
Mary Price, 22; Paul, 22.

HARWOOD:
____ S., 45; Ann, 56, 66, 82;
Ann C., 93; Benjamin, 73, 90, 93,
94; Caroline, 87; Frederick, 73,
81, 91; Henrietta, 93; Henry, 56,
91; Henry H., 73, 90; Henry S., 66;
James, 66; John, 73, 87; John H.,
91; John T., 73, 81, 91; Joseph,
83; Maria, 73, 91; Mary, 84; Mary
Ann, 83; Mary D., 93; Mary Dryden,
94; Mary E., 81, 87; Nancy Callahan, 56; Nicholas, 56, 66, 73;
Peggy H., 93, 94; Richard, 31, 32,
56, 73, 81, 82, 87, 88, 90, 91, 92;
Richard H., 29; Sally, 87; Samuel,
73; Sarah, 56; Susan, 87; Thomas,
73, 82, 88, 90, 92; William, 5, 17,
73, 81, 87, 91.

HASLIP:
William, 78.

HATHERLY:
Benjamin, 2; John, 2; Nathan, 2;
Sarah Ann, 2.

HAWKINS:
Aaron, 38; Caleb, 11; Charles, 11;
Catherine, 97; Isaac, 88; James,
10; John, 11, 88; Joseph, 26, 38,
78; Joshua, 64, 88; Mary, 88; Mary
Yealdhall, 50; Nicholas, 11; Ralph,
26, 54; Rebecca, 11; Rezin, 11, 24;
Ruth, 11; Samuel, 38, 64; Sarah,
88; Thomas, 11, 26; Wallace W., 88;
William, 11.

HAYES, HAYS:
Margaret, 44; William, 9, 15.

HAYWARD:
John, 6; William, 6.

HAZELL:
Ann, 20; Jemima, 27.

HEATH:
Mary, 15; Nancy, 78; Rachel, 60;
Robert, 60, 67, 78; Sarah, 15.

HENSHAW:
Amelia, 15; Elizabeth, 15.

HENWOOD:
Charles, 15; Elizabeth, 15; Joshua,
15; Mary, 15, 55; Mertilda, 15;
Nancy, 12, 55; Rachel, 15; Robert,
15, 54; Sarah, 15; Vachel, 15; William, 6, 7, 12, 15.

HERBUTT:
George, 28.

HEWITT:
Edmond, 40; Eleanor, 10; Eli, 82,
83; Jacob, 82, 83; James, 40; Jane,
10; Margaret, 40; Martha, 83; Mary
Ann Jane, 40; Rezin D., 82, 83;
Sarah Ellen, 40; Thomas, 40; Thomas W., 40; Thomas William, 10; William, 40.

HIGGINS:
George W., 27.

HILL:
Abel, 15, 27, 28, 32, 39; Althea,
84; Joseph, 18, 21, 28, 39; Morgan,
28, 39, 84; Sarah, 27; Susanna, 39.

HILTON:
Eleanor, 31; John, 31, 47.

HINCKS:
Caroline, 88; Charles D., 88; Edward, 88; Jemima, 24; Mary, 88;
Mary Ann, 88; Mary Wood, 24; Samuel,
88; Sarah Wood, 24; William, 24, 88.

HINES:
Elizabeth, 80.

HINTON:
Thomas, 5.

HITCHCOCK:
Catherine, 96; Elizabeth, 96; James
C., 96.

HOBBS:
Achsah, 72; Caleb, 67; Eleanor Louisa, 49; Elizabeth, 72; Gerrard, 67,
Henry, 53, 72; Henry Cornelius, 29;
Horatio, 49; Joseph, 67; Lancelot,
21; Lydia, 21; Maria, 21; Mary Ann,
49; Rachel, 21; Ruth, 21; Samuel,
21; Thomas, 30, 36, 67; William, 21.

HODGES:
Charles D., 29, 37; Delilah Pumphrey, 58; Henry, 67; Joseph, 67,
73, 82; Martha Ann, 67; Rebecca,
67; Sally, 83; Sarah, 15, 70; Thomas, 37, 77.

HOGG:
William H., 31.

HOLLAND:
Alfred G., 87; Ann, 40, 87; Charles,
87; Delilah Sands, 40; Edward, 53,
89; Ellenora, 87; Hannah, 47; Isaac,
40; James, 87; John M., 87; Lucretia, 87; Margaret, 34; Mary Ann, 88;
Rosetta, 87; Sarah Ann, 87.

HOLLAWAY, HOLLWAY:
Daniel, 9, 43; Nicholas, 43; Sarah,
43.

HOLLIDAY:
Ann, 16; John, 51, 53; Mary, 51;
Nicholas, 51; Richard G., 51;
Thomas, 51.

HOLMES:
Delilah Cheney, 9; James, 9; Susanna Beard, 53.

HOOD:
Benjamin, 13, 24, 52, 86; Charles
W., 86; Elizabeth, 13, 14, 24;
Hannah, 24; Henry Gaither, 24; Henry W., 86; James, 13, 14, 24, 52,
86; John, 13, 24, 52, 86; Joshua,
13, 86; Louisa, 78, 85; Mary Ann,
86; Mary G., 86; Rachel, 41; Rachel H., 86; Sarah, 41, 67; Thomas, 13, 24, 52, 64, 82, 86; William G., 86.

HOOPER:
John, 9; Mary Dove, 9.

HOPKINS:
_____ (Mrs.), 16; Ann Maria Snow-
den, 51; Anne, 1; Catherine, 68;
David, 68; Edward, 16; Eleanor, 91;
Eliza, 53, 68; Elizabeth, 1, 16,
71; Gerrard, 53; Hannah, 53; Han-
nah Hammond, 17; Hester, 33; Johns,
1, 16, 53; Jonathan, 68; Jonye, 71;
Joseph, 1, 16, 71; Joseph J., 53;
Joseph R., 51; Mahlon, 53; Margaret,
1, 16, 53, 71; Mary, 1, 53, 68, 89;
Philip, 16, 33, 53, 71; Rachel, 1;
Rezin, 87; Richard, 1, 16, 17; Sam-
uel, 16, 33, 53, 57, 71, 89; Sam-
uel S., 53; Sarah, 16, 53, 68, 71;
William, 16, 45, 71.

HOOPER:
Susanna, 21.

HORNER:
Benjamin, 54.

HOUGHTON:
John, 6; Sarah, 6.

HOWARD:
Achsah, 18; Ann, 19, 20, 29, 83;
Brice, 13, 19, 29, 49; Brice Worth-
ington, 19, 20; Brutus, 18; Cathe-

HOWARD, continued:
rine, 59; Charles, 29; Cornelius, 4, 20, 72, 83; Eleanor, 59; Elizabeth, 18; Ephraim, 6, 7, 18, 19, 20; George, 19, 20; Gustavus, 49; Harriet, 19, 20; Henry, 18, 19, 20, 29, 38; Jeremiah Brice, 19, 20; John, 1, 28; Joseph, 4, 55, 72; Margaret, 19, 20; Margery, 59; Martha, 59; Mary, 29, 72, 81, 83, 85; Mary E., 81, 83; Nancy, 27; Rachel, 4, 83; Rispah, 49; Robert, 49; Samuel, 48; Samuel H., 83, 85; Samuel Harvey, 83; Sarah, 4, 49; Sarah E., 83; Thomas, 29, 49; Thomas Cornelius, 13, 29; Thomas Worthington, 19, 20, 29; William, 4, 19, 49.

HOWSE:
Ellender, 22; Elizabeth, 22; Jonathan, 22; Mary, 22; Sarah, 22; Thomas, 22; William, 22; Zacharish, 22.

HUDSON:
Horatio, 39; Priscilla, 11; Robert, 11.

HUNTER:
Henry, 43; James, 43, 53, 81, 86, 87; John, 43, 49, 74; Sarah, 43; Thomas, 43.

HURST:
Bennett, 72; John, 16, 64.

HUSBAND:
Samuel E., 56.

HUTTON:
Ann, 34; Henry, 34; Jonathan, 66; Joshua, 34; Mary, 34; Mary Armiger, 52; Richard, 39; Richard C., 52, 55; Richard G., 49, 50, 59; Richard Geoghagen, 34; Richard S., 66; Samuel, 10; Sarah, 34.

HYDE:
Sarah, 72.

IGLEHART:
Ann, 90, 94; Caroline, 92; Denton, 92; Ezra, 92; James, 34, 52, 61, 62,

IGLEHART, continued:
65, 68, 70, 71, 81, 82, 90, 91, 94; Jane, 56; Jarbin, 92; Joel, 92; John, 17, 50, 65, 70, 80, 81, 85, 90, 91, 92, 94; Leonard, 71, 81, 82, 90, 94; Margaret, 92; Martha Ann, 92; Mary Hopkins, 68, 89; Mary L., 90; Mary Luckett, 94; Michael, 80, 89, 91; Richard, 31, 94; Rufus, 92; Samuel, 70; Thomas, 70, 90, 94.

IJAMS:
Ann, 51; Cecelia, 95; Elizabeth, 51, Franklin F., 85; Harriet, 85; John, 23, 24, 78; Plummer, 22, 51; Rachel, 54; Ruth, 22; Thomas, 8.

IRELAND:
Elizabeth, 58.

ISAAC:
Elsey, 57.

ISRAEL:
Robert, 13.

IVORY:
Elizabeth, 31; Thomas, 31.

JACKSON:
Ann, 85; Elizabeth, 12; Matilda, 12; Robert, 12; Sarah, 12; Susanna, 12.

JACOB, JACOBS:
Achsah, 36; Ann, 30, 40, 70; Ann E., 83; Arnold, 43, 83; Benjamin, 70; Caroline, 70, 83; Daniel P., 43, 54, 83; David Love, 30; Dorsey, 11, 12, 13, 14, 17, 23, 27, 36, 40, 59, 86, 89; Edward, 70, 83; Elizabeth, 30, 70, 83; Ezekiel, 30; Harriet, 36; James, 37; John, 31, 32, 83; Joseph, 13, 23; Julian, 70, Juliana, 83; Margaret, 23; Mary Ann, 70; Matilda, 70; Matilda J., 83; Patience, 13, 27; Priscilla, 30, 35; Rachel, 35; Richard, 20, 34, 36, 40; Robert, 43, 70, 83; Samuel, 9, 13, 43; Sarah, 23, 43, 83; Susan M., 83; Susanna, 70; Zachariah, 7, 11, 12, 15, 23, 36, 59, 83.

JAMES:
Catherine, 2; Elizabeth, 73; Susanna Lusby, 14; Walter, 73; William, 14, 31, 58.

JARVIS:
John, 19, 38, 42; Sarah, 42, 54.

JEAN:
Joseph, 39.

JENIFER, JENNIFER:
Ann, 38; Joseph, 17, 19, 33, 38.

JENKINS:
Ann, 91; Eliza E., 91; Francis, 91; James P., 91; Margaret A., 91; William, 90.

JOHN, JOHNS:
Ann, 18, 22, 25, 49, 50, 75; Ara, 48, 58; Archibald, 18, 50; Baker, 49; Beale, 88; Betty, 48; Catherine, 59; Charles, 9, 10, 11, 14, 15, 18, 22, 25; Charlotte, 27, 49; Christopher, 20, 40, 48, 88; Delia Lusby, 14; Elijah, 22; Eliza, 75; Elizabeth, 15, 22, 48, 58; Ezekiel F., 74-75; Garret, 49; Gerrard, 58; Grafton, 49, 58, 60; Greenbury, 58; Harriet, 49, 58, 60; Henrietta, 2; Henry, 2, 39, 43, 74; Horatio, 49, 58, 60, Garret, 60; John, 14, 19, 20, 22, 58, 83, 88; Joseph, 49; Joshua, 22, 33, 40, 48; Lancelot, 28; Leander, 48; Lloyd, 20, 22, 25, 33, 49, 51, 58, 60, 87; Mahala, 49, 58, 60; Margaret, 11; Mary, 22, 67, 88; Mary Ann, 78; Mary Welch, 75; Nancy, 22; Nancy Burton, 28; Oneal, 18, 25, 50; Orlando, 22; Owen, 88; Patience, 22, 48; Rachel, 22, 48; Ralph, 60, 67; Rebecca, 27, 67, 78; Rebecca Traverse, 55; Rinaldo, 22; Robert, 2; Samuel, 2; Sarah, 49, 55; Sarah Burton, 51; Sarah Deale, 19; Silas; 55; Solomon, 7, 22, 25; Sophia, 88; Thomas, 25, 60, 75, 78; Vachel, 2; William, 18, 19, 31, 38, 74; Zachariah, 2, 22, 48, 49, 50, 58, 66, 88.

JOINER:
Elizabeth, 44.

JONES:
Anne, 36; Benjamin, 75; Elizabeth, 35, 43, 55, 66, 91; Elizabeth Thompson, 19; Esther, 4; Hansbury, 4; Henry, 49; Isaac, 4; Jacob, 44; Jason, 19; John, 75; Lewis, 35; Martha Tillard, 49; Mary, 8; Rachel, 4, 39; Samuel, 79; Susannah, 4; Walter, 91; William G., 66, 75.

JOYCE:
Abel, 28; Caroline, 3; Elijah, 1; Henry, 42, 45; John, 45; Joshua, 45; Nicholas, 24; Phillis, 33; Richard, 1; Sarah, 3, 33, 45; William, 1, 7, 33.

JUBB:
John, 86, William, 86.

KELLEY, KELLY:
Ann, 42; Margaret, 87; Mordecai, 43; Richard, 15, 60; Sele, 89.

KENT:
Robert W., 85, 94.

KER, KERR:
Elrida Fairbrother, 5; John, 5, 22.

KILLMAN:
John, 1.

KING:
Ann, 68, 71, 74; Henry H., 68, 71, 74; Letha, 68; Samuel, 68; Sarah, 68, 71, 74; Thomas, 68; William, 57; William H., 68, 71, 74.

KINGSBURY:
Elizabeth, 1.

KIRBY:
James, 44; John, 44; Joseph, 89; Nathan, 44; Robert, 44; Sarah, 44; William, 44.

KNIGHTON:
Artridge, 52; Gassaway, 76, 96; Jane, 62, John, 52, 76, 92, 94; 96; Mary Ann, 86; Nicholas, 52, 96; Rachel, 38; Richard, 52, 77; Samuel, 52; Sarah, 46, 52, 62; Susanna, 77; Thomas, 96; William, 77.

LACKLAND:
Joshua, 3.

LAKE:
Bennett, 44.

LAMB:
John, 81.

LAMBETH:
Elizabeth, 16.

LANE:
Charles H., 86, 90; Elizabeth, 44;
Harrison, 44; John, 13, 32, 35;
Joseph, 44; Mary, 86, 90; Rebecca,
13, 86, 90; Richard, 44; Thomas,
44; Wilemina, 44.

LANSDALE:
Harriet, 94; William M., 84.

LARIMORE:
James, 47, 56, 70.

LARK:
Greenbury, 15, 45, 47; Mary, 15;
Sarah, 45; Stephen, 15, 45.

LATIMER:
Catherine, 83.

LATTIN:
Mary, 65; Plummer, 65; Thomas, 65.

LAURENCE:
Moses, 86.

LAVEY:
Mary, 39.

LAWRENCE:
Caleb, 40-41; Caroline, 41; Francis,
53; Hammond, 41; John, 41; Larkin,
41; Levin, 40; Moses, 41, 66; Rebecca, 41; Sally, 26; Sally Ann, 41;
Sarah, 40.

LAWREY:
Margaret, 73.

LAWTON:
John, 79.

LEADINHAM:
Mary, 76.

LEATHERWOOD:
Ann, 41; Mary, 41; Priscilla, 41;
Samuel, 41; Sarah, 82; Thomas, 41.

LEDNUM, LENDRUM:
Mary, 46; Thomas W., 82.

LEE:
Deborah, 16; Edward, 4, 16, 33,
58; Elizabeth, 33, 58; Henrietta,
33, 58; John, 40; Joseph, 40, 58;
Joseph Edward, 33; Margaret, 33,
38, 58; Mary, 16; Sarah, 16; Stephen, 16; Thomas, 32.

LEEKE:
Ann, 14; Henry, 14; Joseph, 14.

LEGG:
James, 27; John, 27.

LEITCH:
Benjamin, 73, 77, 81; James, 73,
77, 81; Jesse, 73, 77, 81; Mary,
56; Thomas, 73, 77, 81; William,
73, 77, 81.

LEWIN:
Ann, 6; Elizabeth, 6; Fanny, 6;
Henrietta, 6; Kitty, 6; Lewis, 6;
Margaret, 6; Mary, 6; Richard, 6;
Samuel, 6; Sarah, 6.

LEWIS:
Ann, 5; Catharine, 22; Elizabeth,
5; Hellen, 5; Isaac, 22; Jesse, 22;
John, 22; Mary, 5; Nicholas, 5;
Rachel, 61, 64; Rebecca, 5; Sam-
uel, 22, 69; Sarah, 5; Thomas, 5;
Thomas William Henry, 5; William, 5.

LINSEY:
Daniel, 28; Sarah Marsh, 28.

LINSTED:
Ann Eliza, 91; Ann Maria, 96;
Elizabeth, 96; George Ellen, 96;
George Washington, 63, 73, 75, 91,
95; Jane, 91; John, 63, 75, 96;
Lundy, 92; Mary, 79, 95, 96; Sarah
Ann, 91; Susannah, 63; William, 63,
75, 91.

LINTHICUM:
Abner, 19, 20, 34, 39-40, 47, 48,
51, 54, 58, 62, 74, 82, 86, 88,

LINTHICUM, continued:
89, 90; Adaline, 77; Ann Robinson,
47; Anrose, 77; Catharine, 66;
Charles, 77; Charles G., 80; Elizabeth, 63, 77, 80; Elizabeth Beard,
53; Elizabeth Dorsey, 39; Hezekiah,
77, 80; John, 11, 18; John F., 63;
Joshua, 17, 52, 63; Lot, 66; Matthias, 77, 70, 95; Mary, 33-34, 63;
Mary A., 77; Mary Edwards, 11; Nancy, 54; Rachel, 22, 34, 88; Rachel
A., 80; Rebecca, 63; Richard, 54,
58, 62, 88, 89; Richard B., 63;
Sarah A., 63; Sarah L., 77, 80; Stephen, 63; Thomas, 14; Thomas F., 63;
Wesley, 85; William, 80, 88, 90;
William A., 77; Zachariah, 77, 80.

LINTON:
Hannah, 38.

LITCHFIELD:
Eleanor, 41.

LITTLE:
James, 1.

LONG:
John, 11.

LOR___:
Rezin, 48.

LOWE:
James, 37; Lloyd M., 29; Sarah, 55.

LOWMAN:
Elizabeth, 55; Mary, 22; William,
55.

LOWREY:
Joseph, 27; Margaret, 32.

LUCAS:
Rachel, 57; Sarah Bradford, 75.

LUSBY:
Ann, 29; Baldwin, 6; Beale, 87; Benjamin, 87; Catherine, 11; Deborah,
3, 36; Deborah Lee, 16; Debra, 6;
Delia, 14; Edward, 3, 11, 14, 36;
Eli, 87; Elizabeth, 6; Hellender,
14; Henry, 3, 36; James, 3, 36;

LUSBY, continued:
John, 6, 14, 33; Mary, 23, 36, 87;
Mary Rawlings, 18; Nancy, 14; Peggy,
6, 14; Polly, 3; Rebecca Beard, 53;
Robert, 3, 6, 14, 16, 31, 87, Samuel,
3, 4, 36; Samuel R., 63; Sarah Marsh,
28; Solomon, 14; Susanna, 3, 6, 14;
Vincent, 29; William, 3, 36.

LYLES:
Margaret, 73, 91; Thomas, 73, 91.

LYNCH:
Andrew A., 88.

MCCAULEY:
Anne, 2, 6; Delia, 6; Francis, 6;
Jehosophat, 6; John, 78; Nancy, 6;
Nancy Lusby, 14; Sarah, 2; Thomas,
6, 8, 14, 21; Zachariah, 2.

MCCENEY:
_____, 35; Benjamin, 16, 76, 79,
80; Edward, 76, 79, 80; Eliza, 82;
George, 82; Henry, 82; Jacob, 76,
79, 80; Joseph, 29, 49, 66, 82; Martha, 76; William, 82; Zachariah, 79,
80.

MCCOY:
Alexander, 54; Amos H., 54; Dorcas,
54; Helen, 88; Henry, 54; Isaac, 54;
Maria, 66; Sarah, 54; Stephen, 3.

MCELHINEY:
Gustavus, 88.

MCGILL:
Anne, 3; Delilah, 3; Hellen, 73;
James, 2; John, 2; Margaret, 3;
Mary, 3; Thomas, 2, 50.

MCGINN:
Bernard, 90.

MCKAY:
Stephen, 15.

MCMEEKEN:
William, 96.

MCNEIR:
George, 84, 86, 90.

MCPARLIN:
William, 61.

MCPHERSON:
Alexander, 28; Harriet, 93, 97; John, 93; Margaret, 78; Mary, 78; Robert H., 78; Samuel, 93; Thomas, 78; William H., 78; William S., 93, 96, 97.

MCQUILLAIN:
Eliza, 47; Elizabeth, 47; James, 47; Mary, 47.

MACCUBBIN:
Ann, 17, 28, 36; Ann Merriken, 36; Caroline, 52; Caroline L., 57, 58; Charity, 38; Charlotte, 20, 29; Dorcas, 20, 29; Eleanor, 28; Eleanor M., 52, 57, 58; Elizabeth, 2; Frances, 74; Frederick, 52; George, 52; George W., 95; Henry, 95; James, 12, 42, 52, 57, 58, 61, 95; John, 5; John H., 76, 77; John Henry, 35, 36; John Mercer Stevens, 38; Joseph, 12, 20, 29, 95; Julian E., 52, 57, 58; Lydia, 95; Martha R., 52, 57; Mary, 2, 42, 52, 57, 58; Moses, 2; Nicholas, 8, 20, 26, 29; Nicholas Zachariah, 8; Patience, 95; Ruth, 74; Sarah, 8, 60, 67, 78; William, 5 37.

MACE:
Amerlia, 30, 31; Elizabeth, 30, 31; Harriet, 30, 31; James (Joseph?), 12; Joseph, 19, 30; Lydia, 30, 31; Richard, 30, 63; Sarah, 19, 30, 31; Sarah Jackson, 12.

MACKALL:
Richard, 88.

MACKELY:
Susan, 77.

MACKENZIE:
Aaron, 87; David, 87.

MAGOWAN:
Elizabeth, 28.

MAGRUDER:
Alexander C., 94; Rebecca, 9.

MAHAND:
Charles, 77; Daniel, 77; Sarah, 77.

MAHONY:
Barnett, 72; Daniel, 71; Henry, 72; James, 72; Robert, 71, 72.

MALLONEE:
Sally, 33.

MANNING:
Sarah Elliott, 59.

MARE:
Richard, 59.

MARKEL:
Ann, 51; John, 51; Stephen, 51.

MARRIOTT:
Achsah, 21; Anne, 37; Augustine, 11, 21; Bushrod, 93; Caleb, 11; Elizabeth, 11, 19, 21, 67, 84; Elvira, 84; Emanuel, 11; Ephraim, 17, 31, 38; Harriet, 84; Henrietta, 21, 56; Homewood, 54; James H., 31, 38, 54; James M., 54; Jane, 37; John, 8, 14, 18, 84; Joseph, 11, 21; Joshua, 23, 54; Joshua H., 84; Kitty, 21; Martha, 11, 21; Mary, 11, 21, 37; Rachel, 11, 19; Rezin, 37; Richard, 19, 37, 92; Ruth, 19; Thomas, 21, 54; William, 37, William H., 61, 63, 64, 65, 66, 71.

MARSH:
Ann, 14, 56; Charity, 14; Elizabeth, 14; Mary, 14; Patience, 56; Richard, 28, 79; Sarah, 28; William, 14.

MARSHALL:
Edward, 11; Mary, 46; Robert, 50.

MASH:
Ann, 35, 37; Joseph, 37; Patience, 37.

MASON:
Sarah, 43.

MATTHEWS:
John, 81.

MATTINGLY:
Dorothy, 94; Elizabeth A., 94; John

MATTINGLY, continued;
F., 94; Joseph, 94.

MATTOCKS:
Charity, 1; Charles, 1; Jacob, 1;
Jonathan, 1; Susannah, 1.

MAYNADIER:
Henry, 45, 59, 84.

MAYNARD:
Ann, 56; Edward, 96, 97; Samuel,
38, 56, 82, 88, 96, 97.

MAYO:
George, 17; Hannah, 32, 38; Henrietta, 1, 4, 38; Isaac, 1, 17; James,
4, 32, 36, 38; John, 1, 4, 32, 38;
Joseph, 1, 13; Joshua, 1, 26; Mary,
14; Philip, 26; Sarah, 17; Sarah
Ann, 17; Thomas, 14; William, 32,
38.

MEAD:
Samuel, 16, 25.

MEDCALF:
Susanna, 32, 36.

MEDFORD:
Charlotte, 65.

MEEK:
Ann, 79, 82; David, 79, 82; David
B., 79, 82; Elizabeth, 66, 79;
James, 5; John, 79, 82; Louisa, 79,
82; Mary, 5; Samuel, 8; Wastel, 5.

MEGUINES:
Margaret, 8.

MENSHAW:
Archibald, 67; Nathan, 15.

MERCER, MERCIER:
Andrew, 11, 17, 80, 93; Archibald,
93; Azel, 80, 91, 93; Cornelius, 93;
Eliza, 80, 91; Francis, 49; John, 11,
80, 91; John W., 93; Joshua, 80, 91,
93; Mary, 80, 91, 93; Richard, 80, 91;
Ruth, 80, 93.

MERIWEATHER:
Eleanor, 30, 44; Elizabeth, 30, 44;

MERIWEATHER, continued:
Elizabeth, 30, 44, 52; John, 52;
Louisa, 30, 44; Mary, 44; Nicholas,
30; Polly, 30; Reuben, 30; Sally,
30, Sarah, 27, 30; Thomas Beall Dorsey, 30.

MERRIKEN:
Ann, 1, 20; Charles, 20, 44; Eleanor, 49; Eliza, 42; Elizabeth, 20,
44, 54; Jacob, 20; James, 44; John,
1, 3 5, 12, 14, 20, 23, 25, 29, 44,
54; John D., 88; John Dorsey, 20;
Joseph, 1; Joshua, 5, 7, 8, 13, 25,
44; Margaret, 42; Mary, 42, 90;
Mary Ann, 42; Nicholas, 44; Richard,
25, 42; Richard H., 73, 80, 82, 86,
90; Robert 1; Sarah, 1, 20, 27, 28,
44; Sarah Talbott, 4; Thomas, 1;
William, 4, 27, 28, 44; Zachariah,
42, 80, 82.

MIDDLETON:
Gilbert, 11.

MILES:
Margaret, 20; Mary, 20; Richard, 20.

MILLER:
Caleb, 67; Denton, 67; Eleanor, 43;
Elizabeth Ann, 21; Elizabeth Shriver, 11; Enoch, 67; George Washington,
59; Henrietta, 59; James, 66; Jesse,
11; John, 14, 53, 87, 95; Louisa,
67; Mary, 36, 43; Nehemiah, 66; Nicholas, 66, 67; Orpha, 96; Peter, 53;
Rachel, 21; Rachel Marriott, 11; Samuel, 11; Susanna, 24.

MILLS:
Achsah, 18; Ann, 18, 31; Elizabeth,
18; Frederick, 18; Jane, 43; Rachel
Vore, 26; Samuel, 26.

MINSKY:
Ann M., 59, 76, 77, 79; Hanson, 76,
77, 79; Harriet R., 76, 77, 79;
John S., 76, 77, 79; Robert, 76, 77,
79; Samuel, 59, 77, 79; Sophia, 13.

MITCHELL:
Alexander, 46, 54; Ann, 88; Harriet,
50; Mary Ann, 94; Richard, 94.

MOALE:
Samuel, 85.

MOCKABEE, MOCKBEE:
Caleb, 60; Sarah, 28; Stephen, 28,
30.

MOLESWORTH:
Amelia Chambers, 48; Eli, 48, 78,
89; George, 78; Harriet, 78; Henrietta, 78; James, 78; Joseph, 78;
Nancy, 78; Samuel, 78; Senatha Chambers, 48.

MOORE:
Frances Moxley, 69.

MORRIS:
James, 93; Rebecca, 93.

MORTON:
Joseph, 60.

MOSS:
Charles, 15; Delilah, 1, 3; Elizabeth, 8, 15; Hamilton P., 80; James,
5, 8, 80; John Thomas, 8; Joseph,
15; Mary Ann, 80; Monica, 8; Nathan,
1; Rachel, 2; Richard, 2, 15, 35,
66; Robert, 15, 79, 80; Samuel Skidmore, 8; Sarah, 2, 15, 35; Thomas,
8; Willoby, 2, 35.

MOXLEY:
_____, 95; Amelia, 39, 69; Angelina,
39, 69; Basil, 39, 69; Caroline, 39;
Ceceilia, 69, 76; Charles, 39, 69,
76, 95; Emily, 95; Eveline, 69, 76;
Ezekiel, 95; Frances, 39, 69, 76;
Jacob, 95; Jerusha, 69, 76, 95;
John, 38, 39, 41, 69, 76, 95; Joshua,
95; Lloyd, 39, 69, 76, 95; Luther,
69, 76, 95; Mary, 39, 95; Nehemiah,
39, 69; Rezin, 71, 95; Sarah, 95;
Stephen, 95; Thomas, 38, 39, 69;
William, 95.

MUIR:
John, 37.

MULLIKEN:
Ann D., 27; Baruch, 27; Basil D.,
27; Belt, 27; Benjamin Hall, 19, 20,
27; Elizabeth, 90; Kitty D., 27;

MULLIKEN, continued;
Margaret, 27; Mary, 27; Richard
D., 27; Rignal, 27.

MULLINAUX:
Andrew, 89; Ashbury, 89; Caroline,
89; Charles, 89; Charlton, 89; Elea-
nor, 89; Elizabeth, 89; Jason, 89;
Jesse, 89; Joshua, 89; Rhoda A., 89;
Thomas, 54, 89.

MUNROE:
Alexander, 56; Ann, 72; Charles, 72;
Elizabeth, 72; Grafton, 72; Horatio
G., 56, 61, 63, 64, 65, 66, 67;
James, 31, 72; John, 30, 40, 56,
61, 63, 64, 65, 66, 67; Jonathan,
72; Major, 56; Mary, 72; Rebecca,
72; Thomas, 56, 61, 63, 64, 65, 67,
72; William, 56, 64; William T., 61,
63, 65, 66, 67.

MURRAY:
Harriet Woodward, 18; William, 18,
21.

MUSGROVE:
Achsah, 36; Anthony, 36; Jemima, 36;
Margaret, 36; Mary, 36; Samuel, 36;
Stephen, 36.

NEILSON:
Robert, 92.

NELSON:
Henry, 28; J____ M____, 61; John,
56; John M., 63, 64, 65, 66, 67; Rebecca Munroe, 56.

NETH:
Harriet, 88; Lewis, 57, 88, 93.

NEWBORN:
James, 76, 83.

NICHOLS:
Ann, 96; Isaac, 3; Rachel, 28;
Samuel, 91.

NICHOLSON:
Benjamin, 56, 60; Eleanor, 4; Esther, 4; James, 51; John, 36, 51;
Joseph, 51, 96; Mary, 4, 51; Nicholas, 4, 51.

NIVIS:
Margaret, 77.

NIXON:
Elizabeth, 22.

NORMAN:
Benjamin, 65; Eleanor, 8.

NUTWELL:
Elizabeth, 28; George W., 81, 84;
James, 28, 30, 81, 84; John S.E.,
81, 84; Levi, 28; Mary, 81, 84; Patsey, 28; Samuel, 28; Sarah, 28, 81,
84; Surrance, 17; Tomerson, 81, 84.

O'BRIAN:
Licious L.X., 80.

O'CONNOR:
Dennis, 31; Oneal, 31.

OGLE:
Benjamin, 75; Henry M., 75.

O'HARA:
William, 48, 52, 53, 72, 84, 85, 89,
91, 92, 96.

O'REILLY, O'RILEY:
Patrick H., 58, 60, 70.

ORME:
Jesse, 77, 79.

O'ROURKE:
James, 66.

OSBORNE:
Basil, 93; Leonard, 87.

OWENS:
Agnes, 90; Alexander, 90; Ann, 35,
56; Benjamin, 35, 39, 72, 78; Charles,
39, 73; Dennis, 90; Edward, 11; Elizabeth, 11, 39, 73; Enoch, 90; Fielder,
90; Gassaway, 90; Horatio, 90; Isaac,
32, 72, 78; James, 11, 35, 47, 72;
James S., 90; Joseph, 72, 76; Mary,
41; Nicholas, 32, 35, 72, 89, 90;
Priscilla, 65; Richard, 6; Samuel,
75, 89; Sarah, 79, 80; Susanna, 39,
90, 95; Thomas, 32, 39, 72; William,
32, 72.

OWINGS:
Elizabeth Hood, 47; Hannah, 47, 52;
Henry H., 93; Jesse, 47; John Hood,
47; Margaret, 90; Richard, 30; Thomas, 47.

PACA:
Ann Robinson, 74; James W., 74.

PACKER:
George, 2; Mary, 2.

PAIN:
Elijah, 94.

PAISLEY:
Elizabeth, 39.

PALMER:
Aaron, 16; Benjamin, 88; William,
81.

PARISH:
Isaac, 16; John, 16; Sarah, 16;
Susanna, 16.

PARKER:
Elizabeth, 26; Isaac, 26; Mary,
17; Priscilla, 26; Thomas, 17.

PARKINSON:
Richard, 81.

PARROTT:
Abraham, 53; Ann, 34; George, 53;
John, 53, 72; Knighton, 72; Mary,
53, 72, 76; Richard, 53; Samuel,
53; Sarah Norman, 46; Thomas, 10,
20, 27, 72.

PASCAULT:
Kitty D., 86.

PATTERSON, PATTISON:
Ann, 82; Eliza, 82; Elizabeth, 19;
Jacob, 19, 40, 69, 78; James, 7;
Jeremiah, 7; Mary, 69; Nancy, 88;
Rachel, 82, 88; Thomas, 7.

PEACO:
Samuel, 7, 24, 48, 63.

PEAKE:
Eliza, 69; Joseph, 69; William, 69.

PEARCE:
Abraham, 48; Elizabeth, 32, 36, 88;
Elizabeth Shelhamer, 21; Francis,
88; George, 48; James, 5; John, 48,
88; Matilda, 48; Philip, 48; Rachel,
48; Richard, 50; Sally, 48; Samuel,
21, 36, 59; Walter, 12; William, 9,
48.

PECKER:
George, 1.

PEDDICORD:
Amelia, 67; Elizabeth, 67; Jasper,
72.

PENN:
Benjamin, 77, 79; Caroline, 69; Jo-
seph, 8; Joshua, 8, 18; Mary, 8;
Peggy, 8; Rachel, 8; Sarah, 8.

PENNINGTON:
Elijah, 71; Mary, 71; Rebecca, 42,
71; William, 71.

PERRY:
Rebecca, 94.

PETTIBONE:
Charles, 48, 52, 62; Henrietta, 85;
John, 62; Philip, 62, 71.

PHELPS:
Basil, 9, 10; Deborah, 9; Esther
Gwinn, 32, 36; Ezekiel, 69; George,
9; Hester, 68; Joseph H., 68; Mar-
garet, 69; Mary, 9; Middleton, 69;
Nelson, 69; Richard, 10, 55, 69, 79;
Robert, 9; Sarah, 68; Walter, 69;
Wilson, 69; Zachariah, 9, 68.

PHILLIPS:
Benjamin, 11; Delilah, 11; Elizabeth, 74; Henrietta, 14; Humphrey,
29; John, 11; Mary, 11; Paul, 11;
Ruth, 11; Sarah, 11; Thomas, 1.

PHIPPS:
Ann, 63; Ann Foreman, 39; Benjamin,
88; John, 18; John Wilson, 63; Mary,
42; Mary Ann, 63; Nathaniel, 63;
Nicholas, 63; Randolph, 63; Sarah
Busy, 18; Susanna Jackson, 12;

PHIPPS, continued:
Thomas, 63.

PIERCE:
Benjamin, 65; Ezekiel, 31; Joseph,
32, 65; Mary, 65; Richard, 65;
William, 65.

PIERPONT:
Faithful, 6; Henry, 6.

PINDELL:
Elizabeth, 83; Gassaway, 32, 70,
83; John, 18, 83; Margaret, 15, 18,
83; Nicholas, 83; Philip, 30, 73,
83, 92; Rinaldo, 83, 92; Thomas, 83.

PINKNEY:
Ann, 94; Elizabeth, 56, 61; Ellen,
94; Jonathan, 56, 61, 63, 64, 65,
66, 67, 94; Mary, 94; Mary F., 93;
Somerville, 94; William E., 63, 64,
65, 66.

PIPER:
Ann, 10; Elizabeth, 10; Mary, 10;
Thomas, 10.

PITT:
Ann, 35.

PLATER:
Elizabeth, 37.

PLUMMER:
Ann, 23; Elizabeth, 23; Henry, 4, 9,
23; James, 23; Margaret, 23; Rachel, 23; Richard, 23; Samuel, 23;
Charles, 18, 28, 41; Charles P., 41;
Elizabeth, 41; Mary, 41; Sarah Burton, 28; Thomas, 41; Zachariah, 71.

POOLE:
Elizabeth Wood, 16; Jenny, 54; John,
46; John Whips, 12; Luke, 17; Marshall, 16; Peter, 12; Verlinda, 46.

PORTER:
David A., 85; George S., 85; Jane,
85; John, 23, 41; Martha E., 85;
Mary Ann, 85; Nathan, 85; Washington, 85; William, 85.

POWELL:
Henry, 15; William, 3.

PRESTMAN:
George, 13.

PRICE:
Ann, 54; Ann Armiger, 26; Benjamin, 54; Edward, 22-23; Elizabeth, 22; Harriet, 22; James, 26, 54; James G., 88; James Gassaway, 54; Letty, 23; Lucinda, 54, 88; Mary, 22; Smith, 30; Sophia, 22; Thomas, 22.

PRITCHARD:
Ann, 66; Arthur, 66; Eliza, 66; Isabella, 66; Margaret, 66; William, 66.

PUMPHREY:
Aminty, 7; Ann, 7; Aquila, 32; Catherine, 58; Charles, 41, 54, 58, 66, 67, 84, 89; Cockey, 41, 46; Cordelia, 47; Delilah, 58; Ebenezer, 12, 32, 97; Edward, 7, 37, 54, 57; Elizabeth, 7, 26, 37; Frederick, 7; Greenbury, 33; Jesse, 95; John, 94; John E.J., 95; John J., 89; Joseph, 7, 26; Joshua, 45; Margaret, 46, 47, 74; Mary, 7; Nacky, 7; Priscilla, 32; Rachel, 47; Rezin, 7, 26; Rhoady, 47; Sarah, 89; Silvanus, 26; Susanna, 97; Thomas, 78; Walter, 58, 91; William, 7, 12, 26, 47, 67, 74, 78, 84, 88, 89, 95, 97; William S., 95; Zachias, 7, 26, 37, 47, 89.

PURDY:
Alfred, 94; Elizabeth, 49; Galen, 92; Henry, 9, 32, 36, 92, 94; Jacob, 92; John, 92, 94; Mary, 36, 36; Mary Phelps, 9; Samuel, 94; Sarah, 65, 94; Susan, 92; Thomas, 92; William, 32, 94.

PURNALL:
Rachel Deale, 19; Thomas, 19.

PURVIANCE:
John, 26.

PUTNEY:
True, 96.

QUESENBURY:
John E., 80.

QUYNN:
Allen, 19.

RAINER, RAYNER:
Ann, 67; Benjamin, 50, 67; Nelson, 50; Rachel, 50; Rizdon, 50; Samuel, 50.

RANDALL:
Ann, 43; Aquila, 9, 27; Brice, 27; Bruce, 27; Christopher, 27; Edward, 55; John, 27, 34, 45, 63; Nathan, 27; Polly, 48; William, 48.

RAWLINGS:
Aaron, 18, 23, 45; Ann, 23, 38; E____ W____, 18; Eleanor, 6, 8; Eliza, 18; Elizabeth, 23, 45, 96; James, 96; Jane M., 86; John, 18, 23; Joshua, 96; Lurana, 8; Mary, 18, 23, 45; Moses, 18, 23, 45; Nathan, 18, 23; Rebecca, 18, 23, 45; Richard, 3, 8, 18, 23, 38; Sally, 38; Stephen, 8; Susanna, 18, 23, 38, 45; Thomas, 8.

RAY:
Ann, 25, 26, 44; Asa, 44; Catherine Beard, 12; Elizabeth, 25; George Washington, 44; James, 44; John, 12, 26; Joseph, 26, 44, 94; Margaret Ann, 94; Martha Ann, 44; Matthew, 25; Nicholas, 25, 26, 44; Priscilla, 25; Rebecca, 25; Sarah, 25; Susannah, 9; William 25, 26; William Alfred, 44.

REDMAN:
Elijah, 60, 62, 67; Rebecca, 62; Rebecca Riston, 56; Thomas, 62.

REED:
Eleanor, 17; James, 14; John, 10; Rebecca, 14, 17.

REES(?)
Sarah Timmons, 34.

RETALLIE:
Simon, 14.

REYNOLDS:
Allen, 87; Goven, 87; James, 87;

REYNOLDS, continued:
Lewis, 87; Sarah, 49, 87; Tobias, 87; Wilamenia, 43.

RICHARDS:
Edward, 31; Mary Burton, 28; Paul, 28; Sarah Tucker, 37.

RICHARDSON:
Deborah, 74; Elizabeth, 74; Elliott, 74; John S., 74; John Thomas, 18, 30, 33; Margaret, 74; Martha, 74; Miranda, 74; Rachel, 74; Richard, 18, 30; Sarah, 31; William, 30, 74.

RICHMOND:
Samuel, 39.

RICKORD, RICORDS:
Ann, 31; Mary, 34; William, 31.

RIDOUT:
Ann, 51; Horatio, 26, 44, 51, 57; John, 51; Samuel, 26, 44, 51.

RIDGELY:
Absalom, 2, 7, 10, 13, 22, 25, 38; Airy, 35; Ann, 33; Ann C., 56; Archibald, 78; Charles, 10, 25, 28; Charles C., 84; Charles G., 63, 71, 75; Cynthia, 63; Daniel, 92; David, 52, 60, 67, 78; David G., 28; Deborah, 84; Delilah, 25; Edward D., 92; Elizabeth, 7, 25, 84, 92; Emily C., 56; Fanny, 63; Francis, 7; Greenbury, 16, 25, 33; Harriet, 56; Henrietta, 28; Henry, 25, 28, 56; Hester T., 56; John, 16, 24, 25, 28, 56, 82; Joshua, 2, 7; Linda, 25; Lloyd, 63, 78; Lucy, 63; Mary. 12. 23; Mary Ann, 26; Mary Lewis, 5; Matilda, 56; Milo, 63; Milton, 63; Mordecai, 23, 25; Nicholas, 25, 28; Overton, 87; Patience, 22; Peregrine, 5, 10, 12, 23, 25; Philemon D., 71, 75; Philemon Dorsey, 63; Rachel, 28, 33; Rhoady, 23; Richard, 18, 24, 29, 51, 56, 92; Samuel, 36, 63, 77; Samuel Chase, 56; Samuel N., 84; Sarah, 2, 3, 7, 28, 29; Sarah Ann, 78; Sophia, 91; W_____ C_____, 78; William, 7, 23, 25, 28, 63, 71, 74;

RIDGELY, continued:
William G., 56; William P., 63.

RIDGWAY:
Sophia, 82.

RIELY:
John A., 72.

RIGBY:
Ann, 75; John, 40.

RIGGS:
Achsah Fowler, 22; Ninian, 22.

RIGHT:
Ellen, 17; Joshua, 17.

RINE:
Rachel, 76.

RINGROSE:
John W., 80, 91.

RISTON:
Rachel, 56, Rebecca, 56; Zachariah, 39, 56.

RIZEL:
Achsah, 34.

ROBERTS:
Edward, 22, 36; John, 96.

ROBINSON:
Ann, 47, 88; Ann Cheney, 9; Ann Talbott, 4; Benjamin, 47, 67, 86, 88, 95; Betty Johnson, 48; Charles, 2, 10, 13, 14, 15, 28, 34, 47, 48, 49, 50, 55, 58, 59, 66, 88; David, 20, 27, 48, 50, 51, 55, 56; Dennis, 9; Dorcas Maccubbin, 29; Eleanor, 53; Elijah, 4; Elizabeth, 47, 62; Flemming, 74; George, 39; George W., 70, 74; Hampton, 10, 11, 27; Hezekiah, 53; Isabella, 66; James, 47, 70, 74; Jane, 45; Jane Rockhold, 11; Jane Turner, 10; John, 10, 11, 20, 27, 75; John B., 70; John T., 54; John W., 74; Lewis, 66, 90; Luke, 20, 27; Mordecai S., 70; Patience, 66; Patience Johnson, 48; Priscilla, 91; Rhoady, 53; Richard, 20, 45;

ROBINSON, continued:
Samuel, 96; Sarah, 19, 74; Sarah
Ann, 70; Stewart, 74; Thomas, 15,
34, 47, 88; Thornton F., 70; Wesley, 70; William, 20, 66.

ROBOSON:
Ann, 25; Dorsey, 10, Elijah, 25;
Elizabeth, 10, 25; John, 10; Mary,
25; Sarah, 10; Thomas, 10; Vachel,
10.

ROCKHOLD:
Charles, 10, 11, 45; Charlotte,
63; Clark, 10; Elijah, 63, 75;
Elizabeth, 11; Jane, 11; John, 10;
Mary, 10; Rachel, 10; Sarah, 10;
Solorah, 10; Thomas, 6, 11, 20,
27, 35, 45; Thomas Clarke, 10;
Thomas Fields, 10.

RODGERS, ROGERS:
Ann, 9, 14; Catherine, 14; Charles,
14; Henrietta, 85; Henrietta Fish-
er, 71, 80; John, 14; Mary, 14;
Nicholas, 9; Nicholas G., 14;
Philip, 18; Rebecca Woodward, 18;
Samuel, 9, 14.

RODWELL:
Elizabeth, 15, Mary, 15; Sarah, 15.

ROWAN:
Elizabeth, 29; John, 29.

ROWERS (?):
Sarah, 65.

ROWLAND:
Ellen Harrison, 33; Thomas, 33.

ROWLES:
David, 33, 53; Elizabeth, 53; Jacob, 33; John, 33; Joseph, 33; Le-
rasia, 33; Nehemiah, 53; Rachel,
33; Rebecca, 53; Temperance, 53;
Thomas, 9.

RUMMELS:
Stephen, 30.

RUSSELL:
Benjamin, 15; James, 15; Jane, 15;
Jemima, 15; Keziah, 15; Mary, 15;

RUSSELL, continued:
Mary T., 94; Providence, 15; Richard, 15; Sarah, 15.

S___LEY:
Mary, 45.

SADLER:
Samuel, 6; Sarah Lewin, 6.

SANDERS:
Christina Shriver, 11; Eleanor, 70;
Elizabeth Gassaway, 26; Henrietta,
70; James, 14, 17, 46, 70; John, 26;
Julia, 70; Robert, 14, 17, 70; Samuel, 11; Sarah L., 70; William, 6,
17, 26.

SANDS:
Ann Maria, 40; Ariana, 40; Delilah,
40; Eleanor, 46; Eliza, 40; Eliza-
beth, 40; George, 40; Jane, 40;
John, 40, 46; Joseph, 38, 57, 61;
Mary Ann, 40; Sally Rawlings, 38;
Samuel, 40; Sarah, 27; Sophia, 40;
Susanna, 40; Thomas, 40; Washing-
ton, 40.

SANK:
George, 43; John, 34; Nicholas, 34,
65; Niel, 43; Rachel, 57.

SAPPINGTON:
Ann, 65; Caleb, 65; Caroline, 61,
65; Elizabeth, 65; Elizabeth Lewis,
5; John, 16, 65; Martha, 65; Nathan, 32; Nathaniel, 21; Polly, 29;
Rebecca, 61, 65; Thomas, 5; William,
61.

SARK:
Greenbury, 38.

SCHWARD:
George, 53; Margaret, 53.

SCOTT:
Ann, 40; Frederick, 28; Jane, 79;
Leonard, 30; Mary Ann, 69; Richard,
79; Sarah Cornish Wheeler, 30; Upton, 24; William, 83.

SCRIVENER:
Francis, 35; George, 35; John, 15,

SCRIVENER:
35, 56, 60, 62; Lewis, 35; Mary, 35; Mary Childs, 34; Mary Russell, 15; Thomas, 35; Vansant, 15.

SEBORN:
Benedict, 25.

SEEDERS:
Bennett, 8; James, 75; Martha, 8, 31; Mary, 8; Mary Ann, 31, 34; Ruth, 8, 31; William, 5, 8, 34; William W., 31, 75, 79, 83, 95.

SEFTON:
Charles, 21; Elizabeth, 21; James, 21; John, 21, 73, 81, 91; Maria, 21; Mary, 91; Richard, 21; Sarah, 21; Thomas, 21.

SELBY:
Ann, 2, 3; Benjamin, 2, 3; Deborah, 34; Elizabeth, 2, 3, 34, 52, 62; Harriet, 34, 52, 62, 68, 94-95; Jemima, 2, 3, 34; Jeremiah, 62; John, 34, 52; John S., 62, 68, 79, 80, 85, 94, 95; Jonathan, 42, 73; Joseph, 2, 3, 6, Joshua, 34; Lloyd, 94; Maria, 32, 52, 62; Mary, 3, 73; Polly, 2; Rebecca, 2, 3; Robert, 42; Sarah, 73; Susan, 73; Susanna, 42.

SELLMAN:
Alfred, 73, 74, 93, 94; Ann, 74; Betsy, 54; George C., 65; George M., 14, 59; Jannetta, 65, 70; John, 54, 71, 80, 81, 93; John H., 74; John S., 65, 70, 85, 87, 94, 96, 97; Jonathan, 32, 73; Leonard, 3, 4, 50; Lucinda M., 93; Mary, 70; Mary A.D., 65, 70; Nancy Chambers, 48; Richard, 74, 77, 81, 93, 94; Sally, 97; Thomas, 34, 46, 50, 52; Walter, 54.

SEVERN:
Vachel, 76, 85.

SEWELL:
Augustin, 57; Eleanor, 57; George, 57; John, 19; John M., 57; Lidia, 45; Nancy, 60; Nancy Swarmstadt, 50; William, 39.

SHAAFF:
Arthur, 44; John Thomas, 44.

SHAW:
George, 53, 83; James, 83; John, 6, 53, 83; Mary, 83; Thomas, 83.

SHECKELS:
Abraham, 9; Deborah, 31; Elizabeth, 9; Enoch, 92; Ezra, 92; Francis, 9, 82; John, 9; Levi, 82, 92; Mary, 9; Nancy, 35; Richard, 9, 17, 82; Samuel, 17; Sarah, 92; Sarah Smith, 55.

SHEETS:
Hannah, 67.

SHELHAMER:
Catherine, 21; George, 21; John, 21.

SHEPHERD:
Basil, 31, 34, 78, 80, 94; Eliza, 75; Elizabeth, 53, 75; John, 53, 75; Joseph, 75; Mary, 53, 75; Polly, 35; Richard, 46; Samuel, 75, 90; Susanna, 75; William, 75.

SHEREEN:
William, 66.

SHIPLEY:
Ann, 66; Denton, 64; Elias, 64; Elizabeth, 41; Enoch, 66; Enos, 79; James, 95; John, 11, 29, 41; Joshua, 64; Larkin, 37, 93; Nancy, 54; Rachel, 77; Robert, 64; Sarah, 77; Talbott, 24; Thomas, 64; Vachel R., 77; William, 52, 64, 79, 86, 90, 95.

SHORTER:
Charles, 77.

SHRIVER:
Christina, 11; Cornelius, 11; Elizabeth, 11; Frederick, 11; Henry, 11; Jacob, 11; Lawrence, 11; Lewis, 11.

SIBELL:
John, 26; William, 11.

SIDES:
Adelaide Maria, 94; Ann, 94; Jane Perry, 94.

SIFTON:
Charles, 46; Elizabeth, 46; James, 45; Richard, 46; Samuel, 46; Thomas, 46; William, 46.

SIMMONS:
Abraham, 32, 25; Achsah, 60; Agnes

SIMMONS, continued:
Hardesty, 30; Ann Childs, 8; Ann
Wyvill, 36; Barzilla, 16, 17; Benjamin Ward, 13; Bethridge, 21, 27;
David, 21, 45; Elizabeth, 13; Ezekiel, 60; Cassaway, 91; Gilbert,
32, 35, 58, 60; Isaac, 8, 9, 13;
Jeremiah, 32, 35, 58, 60; Jeremiah
Chapman, 13; John, 32, 35, 60;
Margaret, 13, 32, 35, 58; Mary,
15, 34, 46; Priscilla, 28; Richard,
13, 21, 32; Samuel G., 91; Susanna,
21, 32, 35; Thomas, 34, 36; William, 6, 9, 13, 21; William H., 60.

SIMPSON:
Basil, 60; Mary, 1; Mary Willson,
23; Mathilda Burgess, 31; William,
1.

SISCEL:
Isabella, 57.

SKIDMORE:
Sophia, 49.

SLEMAKER:
Jacob, 40, 57.

SLICER:
Andrew, 40, 62, 72.

SMALL:
Hellender, 8; Robert, 25; Sarah, 8;
Thomas, 8.

SMALLWOOD:
Ann, 59; Catherine, 59; Elizabeth,
59.

SMALLWOOD:
Evalina, 59; Jesse, 59; Philip, 59.

SMITH:
Abraham, 84; Ailcey, 88; Ann, 25, 82;
Ann Johnson, 50; Anthony, 56, 61;
Azariah, 55, 92; Basil, 20, 34, 63;
Daniel, 3, 10, 84; Edward, 76; Eliza,
61; Elizabeth, 55, 56, 69; Ellen,
82; Ellender, 73, 77, 81; Fielder B.,
47; Gustavus A., 76; Horatio, 69;
James, 67, 76, 82, 94; Jane, 61;
Jemima, 69; Jeremiah, 84; Jesse, 73;
Jethro, 82; John, 8, 25, 56, 61,
73, 77, 82; John T., 76; Joseph, 76,

SMITH, continued:
91; Margaret, 56, 61; Martha, 88;
Mary, 35; Mary Miles, 20; Milcah, 12;
Octavio O., 76; Philip, 56, 61; Rachel, 76, 82; Rachel A., 76; Richard,
55, 92; Robert John, 4, 10; Sabit, 82;
Samuel, 76; Sarah, 55, 92; Sarah Hunter, 43; Thomas, 34, 76; Thomas O.,
76; Toppin, 12; William, 20, 50, 51,
54, 55, 76, 88, 92.

SNOWDEN:
Ann, 29; Ann Maria, 51; Elizabeth,
82; Gerard, 51; John, 29, 51; John T.,
51; Louisa, 82; Margaret H., 51; Rachel, 51; Rezin, 51; Richard, 51, 82;
Richard P., 51; Thomas, 29.

SOLLARS:
Thomas, 30.

SOPER:
Ann, 27; James P., 28.

SOWARD:
Daniel, 8; Solomon, 8.

SPARKS:
Edward, 94; Sophia, 94.

SPURRIER:
Deborah Burgess, 31; Edward, 2; Re-
zin, 31, 57; Sally, 41; Sarah, 26;
Solomon, 16, 23; Thomas, 31.

STALKER:
Eleanor, 10; George, 10; John, 10;
Robert, 10.

STALLINGS:
Ann, 76; John, 72; Mary, 8; Thomas, 46.

STAMP:
Susan, 89.

STANSBURY:
Benjamin, 61, 62, 68; Betty, 62; Char-
ity, 13; Daniel, 13; Elizabeth, 13, 68;
Emanuel, 13; Ezekiel, 13; George, 68;
Isabella, 68; Joseph, 13, 62; Kitty, 62;
Rachel, 97; Rutha Ann, 68; Sarah, 68;
Sarah Swarmstadt, 50; William, 13.

STEELE:
Henrietta Lewin, 6; John, 6.

STEVENS:
Catharine, 26; Dennis, 1, 12; Elizabeth, 1; John, 7, 12; John Mercer, 17; Joseph, 3; Kitty, 1; Kitty Smith, 12; S____, 26; Vachel, 1, 3, 8.

STEWART:
Abraham C., 78, Alice Dove, 9; Ann, 19, 41, 57, 94; Ann Selby, 3; Benjamin, 84; Caleb, 84; Charity, 73; Charles, 1, 12, 14, 19, 59, 62, 67, 73, 82, 84, 86, 88, 91, 93, 95; Charlotte, 67; David, 17, 41, 85; Dorsey, 57, 89; Ebenezer, 12; Edward, 3, 17, 84; Elizabeth, 17, 19, 57; Elleanor, 19, 67, 73, 74, 84, 89; Ezekiel, 57, 67, 74, 84; Gassaway, 67, 73, 74, 89; Hannah, 14, 88; James, 9, 84; John, 84; John N.W., 73; Joseph, 81, 87, 91; Louisa, 91; Margaret, 59; Maria, 82, 91; Mark, 57; Mary, 41 59, 67, 73, 74, 84; Matilda, 91; Matilda Ann, 82; Mordecai, 16, 19, 50, 53, 54; Pamelia, 82, 91; Priscilla, 94; Rachel, 19, 41; Rebecca, 57, 87; Rhoda Hancock, 49; Rhoady, 41; Richard, 19, 73, 81, 87, 91; Sarah, 84, 88, 93; Sarah Ann, 89; Susan, 67, 73, 74, 84; Susanna, 19, 41; William, 84, 94.

STINCHCOMB:
Alfred, 82; Eliza Ann, 82; Henrietta R., 90; Margaret, 82; Nathan, 42; Nathaniel, 42, 90; Richard A., 90; Sarah, 42, 82, 90; Thomas, 8, 42, 82; Thomas W., 90; William, 42, 82; William H., 82; William V., 90.

STOCKETT:
Ann, 2; G____ L____, 76; George E., 79; John, 2, 24, 29, 46, 51, 53, 79; Joseph N., 51, 73, 74, 77, 79, 81, 91; Lewis, 2; Mary, 2, 73, 79; Nicholas A., 79; Noble, 24; Rebecca, 2; Richard, 2; R____ G____, 76; Richard G., 73, 85, 91; Richard L., 79; Thomas, 1, 2; Thomas J., 76, 83, 83-84; Thomas N., 79; Thomas Noble, 2; Wesley, 79; William Ijams, 2; William J., 29, 79; William Thomas, 24.

STODDERT:
Elizabeth Gwinn, 46, 47.

STONE:
Cassandra, 40.

STRINGER:
Elizabeth, 36; Ellen, 30; John, 39, 78.

SUDLER:
Charlotte, 61; Julian M., 61; William, 61.

SULLIVAN:
John, 39, 74, 78, 79; Julian, 74, 79; Lemuel H., 74, 78; Morgan, 54; Rebecca, 74, 78; Sarah, 34; Thomas, 16, 34; William 74, 79.

SUNDERLAND:
A____ F____, 74; Dorothy, 34; Eliza, 66; Elizabeth, 53, 54; Frances(Francis?), 46, 74; Jesse, 53; John, 66; Maria, 66; Maria A.G., 75; Maria Ann Francis, 54; Mary, 46, 66; Rebecca, 46; Richard, 66; Sarah, 46; Zachariah, 66, 74.

SWAIN:
Elizabeth, 45; Sarah, 69.

SWARMSTADT:
Levi, 50, 60, 75; Lorenzo, 50, 60; Luther, 50, 60; Mary, 60; Matilda, 50, 60; Nancy, 50; Nicholas, 40, 50; Samuel, 50, 60; Samuel L., 68; Sarah, 50, 60; Sidney, 50, 60.

SWEETSER:
Seth, 14, 48, 80.

TALBOTT:
Ann, 4; Benjamin, 4, 17, 18; Eleanor, 21; Elizabeth, 17, 18, 50; Elizabeth Green, 13; Lydia, 6; Mary, 17, 18; Mary Ann, 91; Odle, 73, 91; Sarah, 4, 17, 18; Thomas, 4, 6, 13.

TATE:
Joseph M., 86.

TAYLOR:
Benjamin, 4; Esther, 4; John, 30; Richard, 4; William, 4.

TAYMAN:
Elizabeth Talbott, 18; Henry, 18.

TELLOTT:
Sarah, 71.

TENAIN:
Eveline, 95.

TERRY:
William, 31.

TEVIS:
Robert, 1.

THERNEY:
Philip W., 44.

THOMAS:
Ann, 49, 71; Ann Boone, 31; Ann
C., 60, 90; Benjamin, 39, 43, 53,
54, 57, 58, 59, 60, 85; Benjamin
F., 90; Caroline, 71; Caroline M.,
90; Ebenezer, 31, 43, 45, 60, 61,
64; Eliza Boone, 59; Henry C., 60;
James E., 90; John, 71, 84; John
Chew, 36; John E_en, 42; John R.,
62, 76, 90; Julia, 71; Kinsey, 60;
Margaret, 71; Maria, 71; Mary, 71;
Mary Ann, 41; Matilda, 60; Philip,
1; Robert, 52, 71; Samuel, 82, 90;
Sarah A., 60; Susan, 71.

THOMPSON:
Alicia, 22, 69, 70; Ann, 54;
Charles, 22, 69; Edward, 22; Elea-
nor, 69, 75; Elizabeth, 19, 22,
70; Emily, 69; Henry, 22, 69, 70;
John, 22, 25, 51, 69; Mary, 25;
Mary A., 69; Matilda A., 70; Sarah,
20, 69; Thomas, 25.

THORP:
Sarah, 1.

TILLARD:
Emmeline, 74, 80; Jannetta, 74, 80,
86; John, 49, 74; John H., 61, 80,
86; Martha, 49; Mary E., 74, 80, 86;
Sarah, 61; William, 49; William S.,
61;

TILLY:
Horatio, 81; Lucretia, 81; Sarah,
81.

TIMMONS:
Edward, 1, 5, 7, 34; Sarah, 34.

TINGELL:
James, 43.

TODD:
Elizabeth, 6; John, 17; Lancelot, 17;
Mary, 17; Nathan, 6; Rezin, 17;
Sarah, 6, 10.

TOFT:
Eleanor, 9; John, 9; Mary, 9; Thomas, 9.

TONGUE:
James, 64, 86, 91; Thomas, 47, 69.

TOOTELL:
Ann, 37; Hellen, 37; James, 37; Rosanna, 37.

TOWNSEND:
Joseph, 26.

TRAVERSE:
Ann, 55; Rebecca, 55.

TRON:
Rebecca, 43; Ruth, 43.

TROTMAN:
John, 14.

TROTT:
Allison, 10; Elizabeth, 10; Ester,
10; James, 10, 33; Lewis, 35; Nancy,
10; Rebecca, 10; Samuel, 27, 58, 60;
Sarah, 10; Thomas, 10, 33.

TRUEMAN:
Elizabeth, 73, 77, 81.

TURNER:
Abraham, 20; Jane, 10; Johanna, 20;
John, 20; Richard, 20, 39; Sarah, 10;
Washington G., 96; William, 20, 40;
Zachariah, 20, 21, 23.

TUCKER:
Abel, 21, 48, 56, 61; Ann, 24, 48,
53; Charlotte, 61; Edward, 61; Eleanor Rawlings, 8; Eliza, 61; Elizabeth, 94; Enoch, 21, 48; Francis, 21,
48; Harriet, 45; Hellender Lusby, 14;
James, 21, 24, 30, 48, 53, 55, 72;
Jane, 57; John, 21, 24, 30, 37, 61,
72; Joseph, 21, 48; Lloyd, 84; Mary,

TUCKER, continued:
61; Mary Ann, 57; Mary Ann Lowe,
37; Nancy, 21, 48, 57; Rachel, 57;
Rebecca Fairbank, 37; Samuel, 21,
48; Sarah, 37, 57; Seley, 21, 24,
48; Susan, 24; Susanna, 30; Thomas,
10, 21, 24, 30, 57, 72; William,
21, 24, 30, 48, 56, 61; Zachariah,
8, 14.

TYDINGS:
Ann, 49; Artridge, 62; Catherine,
49; Elizabeth, 89; Ferdinando, 49;
Horatio, 49; 89; John, 49, 73, 88,
90, 91; Joseph, 62; Kinsey, 78;
Lewis, 91; Mary, 78; Rachel Riston,
56; Richard, 49, 73, 89; Sally, 89;
Samuel, 49, 74; Susan, 89.

TYVILLE:
Walter, 61.

URQUHART:
Maria Deford, 46; William, 46, 78.

VERNON:
Gabriel, 66.

VESSELS:
Ann, 38; Louisa, 38; Sarah, 38.

VIERS:
Catharine, 29.

VORE:
Benjamin, 26; Isaac, 26; Jacob, 26;
Rachel, 26; Rebecca, 26; Sarah, 26.

WALLACE:
Charles, 83; Joseph A., 54; Rebecca M., 54.

WALLER:
Susan, 88.

WALTERS:
James, 91.

WARD:
Cephas, 43; Eleanor, 19; Elizabeth,
30, 60, 61, 69, 78; Elizabeth Whittingham, 48, 59; John, 19, 48; Joseph, 82; Margaret A., 85; Mary,
60; Nathan, 30; Richard, 19; Robert, 19; Samuel, 13, 19, 23, 30;

WARD, continued:
Sarah, 19, 35, 60, 61; Sarah E., 60,
61; William, 19, 60, 61; Yate, 60, 61.

WARFIELD:
Achsah, 58; Alfred, 89; Allen, 60, 66;
Allen D., 56; Amelia, 41, 63; Amos,
67; Anderson, 32, 40, 54, 57, 60; Ann,
14, 41, 64, 65, 91; Ann Rogers, 14;
Anna, 89; Azel, 28, 57, 64, 65; B___,
71; Bala, 57; Bani, 89; Basil, 59, 73;
Beall, 43, 55, 63; Bela, 85; Benjamin,
55, 95; Caleb, 11, 95; Catharine, 55,
67; Catharine Ann, 93; Catharine D.,
75; Catharine Dorsey, 7; Charles, 7,
38, 41, 62, 64, 65; Charles A., 24,
28, 82; Charles Alexander, 28, 29, 31;
Charles C., 56; Charles D., 78, 89;
Charles M., 68; Daniel, 44, 89; Edward, 43; Eleanor, 34, 41, 60; Eli,
59, 60; Eli G., 60; Eliza, 64, 65;
Elizabeth, 29, 64, 65; Elizabeth A.,
68; Ellen, 95; Ellena, 56; Enoch, 95;
Ephraim, 20, 89; Frances, 60; George,
29, 59, 60, 62, 63, 64, 65; George A.,
93; George H., 68, 88; George W., 55,
75; Greenbury, 66; Gustavus, 82, 90;
Henry, 64, 65; Henry R., 82; James,
38; James H., 68; John, 14, 38, 66,
68, 79, 86; John D., 89; John H., 67,
88, 92; Jonathan, 95; Joshua, 14, 66,
86; Julia, 58; Kitty, 41, 63; Labon,
68; Lancelot, 25, 38; Lemuel, 38;
Levin, 43; Lloyd, 66; Lorenzo G., 92,
93; Louisa, 60; Lucretia, 58; Luke, 8;
Luther H., 68; Lydia, 33, 67; Margaret,
41, 89; Mary, 41, 43, 58, 64, 65, 67,
73, 91; Matilda, 64, 65; Nicholas, 57;
Nicholas D., 80, 89; Peregrine, 82;
Philemon, 55, 66; Rachel, 38, 58; Rachel D., 41; Reuben, 60, 89; Richard,
64, 65, 95; Robert, 43, 89; Roderick,
73; Rufus, 60; Samuel, 17; Sarah, 2,
9, 13, 17, 38, 41, 43, 58, 64, 65, 67,
88; Sarah A., 93; Seth, 60; Seth W.,
67, 88, 92; Silvanus, 44; Susanna, 17,
29; Theodrick, 91; Thomas, 11, 21, 23,
88, 95; Thomas J., 64; Tilghman D., 85;
Vachel, 33, 56, 66; Vachel H., 56; Walter, 29; William, 56, 61, 62, 63, 84,
95; William R., 55, 75; William W.,
64, 65; Zachariah, 29.

WARREN:
Basil, 85.

-130-

WATERS:
Ann Janetta, 81; Ann L., 93; Arnold, 13, 27; Artridge, 93; Asa, 42; Azel, 72, 83; Cephas, 11; Charles, 3, 25, 36, 49, 88, 95; Charles A., 93; Elizabeth, 3, 42, 42-43, 72; Elizabeth Ann, 86; Franklin, 93; Harriet, 69, 95; Horace W., 84; Isabella E.O. Madden, 81; Jacob, 3, 72, 93; James L., 68; James W., 93; John Willson, 81, 92; Jonathan, 17, 68; Joseph Howard, 81; Julianna, 68; Margaret, 92; Maria, 81; Maria Louisa, 92; Martha, 27; Martha E., 93; Mary, 3; Mary Ann, 42, 81; Mary Edwards, 11; Mary Louisa, 93; Nancy, 29; Nathan, 93; Nicholas, 81; Nicholas R., 68; Philip A., 43; Plummer, 54, 57; Rachel, 43, 93-94; Rachel Howard, 81; Ramsay, 81, 86, 92; Rebecca, 81; Richard, 37; Richard B., 42; Sally, 29; Samuel, 93; Sarah, 57; Sarah A., 68; Sarah Ann Mayo, 17; Sarah Deaver, 18; Susanna, 62; Thomas, 54, 57; Thomas G., 68, 86, 90, 96; Washington, 81; William M., 81; Willso, 35, 44, 81, 86, 92; Zebulon, 42.

WATKINS:
Ann, 32, 59, 73, 81, 87, 91; Benjamin, 17, 87; Eleanor, 55, 73, 81, 82, 87, 91; Elizabeth, 42, 55, 59, 77, 81, 87; Gassaway, 23, 24, 29, 44, 46, 49, 54, 78, 80, 81; George, 82, 91; George W., 87; Harriet, 80, 81; Harriet Ann, 80; James, 4; James H., 94; John, 32, 37, 42, 55; Joseph, 19; Julia, 81; Juliana, 32; Lafayette, 80; Manella, 80; Manella E., 81; Margaret, 49, 73, 81, 82, 87, 91; Nicholas, 4, 6, 7, 32, 55, 66, 79, 80, 86; Nicholas G., 82, 87, 91; Nicholas J., 48, 61, 62; Oliver P., 80, 81; Rachel, 32; Rachel Sprigg, 55; Rezin, 74; Richare, e; Ruth, 5; Samuel, 33, 74; Samuel C., 45, 58; Sarah, 4; Stephen, 55; Surene W., 73, 91; Thomas, 32, 55; Thomas W., 79, 81; Walter, 74; William, 55, 74; William P., 66, 81; William Pitt, 80; William T., 80, 81.

WATSON:
Charles, 11, 42, 53, 71; Elizabeth, 96; Elizabeth H., 96; Emily, 96; Julianna, 96; Maria L., 96; Mary, 11, 71; Rachel, 96; Richard, 71; Rutland, 96; Thomas, 96; William, 11, 71, 96.

WATTS:
Eliza, 47; George, 34, 47, 55, 59; Henry, 94; Philip, 15, 31, 47; Philip Key, 47; Rebecca, 5, 47; Richard B., 57; Sarah, 47.

WAYBILL:
Adam, 28, Elizabeth, 28; Hannah, 28; Mary, 28; William, 28.

WAYMAN:
Ann, 41; Edmund, 10; Henry, 20, 41, 63; Joseph, 77; Mary, 96; Milcah, 41; Thomas G., 96.

WEAVER:
John, 78.

WEBB:
Eliza, 95; George R., 94; Levi, 95.

WEEDER:
William S., 95.

WEEDON:
Ann, 5; Caroline, 34; Cloudsberry, 44; Daniel, 5; Eli, 44; Eliza, 26; Elizabeth, 79; Harriet, 79; Helen, 44; John, 5, 31, 34; Jonathan, 26; Julian, 26; Martha, 34; Martha Seeders, 31; Mary, 79; Richard, 5, 8, 26, 79; Samuel, 5, 44; Sarah, 26; Thomas, 31, 34.

WEEKS:
Alfred, 85; John, 77; John Francis, 85; Mary E., 85; William H., 85.

WEEMS:
Elijah, 55; Elizabeth, 28; James, 64; James N., 38; John, 64; John B., 43, 51; John Beall, 28; John W., 94; Margaret, 51; Margaret H., 51; Mary, 28, 51; Mary D., 51; Nancy, 28; Philip P., 92; Rachel, 64; Richard, 64; William, 28, 51, 80, 86, 92.

WEIR:
Elizabeth, 91.

WELCH:

_____, 92; Aaron, 22, 75; Ann, 47;
Benjamin, 3, 16, 22, 33, 36, 43,
49, 54, 56, 58, 75, 87, 89, 90, 92;
Catherine, 22; Charles, 47, 75;
Elizabeth, 22, 46; Francis, 46, 81;
Henry, 75; Henry James, 47; John,
4, 13, 16, 19, 21, 22, 23, 32, 37,
43, 47, 49, 72, 75; John M., 83;
John Warren, 47; Joseph, 75; Mary,
75, 90; Matilda, 92; Nimrod, 89;
Priscilla, 32, 49, 73; Rachel, 22;
Reason, 47; Robert, 19, 22, 23, 33,
36, 38, 40, 45, 47, 49, 54, 56, 58,
87, 89, 90; Samuel, 47; Sarah, 47;
Singleton, 47; Susanna, 49; Thomas,
70, 74; Upton, 64, 82, 83; Walter,
47; Warner, 77, 88; Warren, 67.

WELLHAM:
Ann, 43, 44, 45; Hezekiah, 64, 72;
John, 39, 43, 44, 45, 64, 72, 95;
Nelson, 44, 45, 72; Wallace, 44, 45;
72; William, 43, 44, 45, 50, 64.

WELLING:
Henry, 55, 71, 75, 80, 81, 93;
James W., 93; Mary, 93; Polly, 93;
Sarah, 75; Willian, 71, 75, 93.

WELLS:
_____, 71; Artridge, 56; Benjamin,
51, 85; Daniel, 37, 72; Elizabeth,
51, 55; Floyd, 71; Frederick, 72;
George, 71, 85, 96, 97; James, 71;
John, 72, 87; John B., 85; Matilda,
71; Nathan, 71; Onerah, 51; Richard, 10, 70, 72, 87; Sarah Lee, 16;
Sarah Tucker, 37; Susan, 72; Susanna Gaston, 16; William, 72, 91.

WELSEY:
William, 51.

WEYLIE:
Ann, 53; Eleanor, 53; John V., 53;
Martha J., 53.

WHALLEN:
Henry, 67.

WHARFE:
Eleanor Brewer, 25; James, 25.

WHEELER:
Baruch, 84; Caroline, 78, 85;
Mary, 75; Sarah Cornish, 30.

WHIPS:
Benjamin, 12; George, 12; John, 12;
Samuel, 12; Sarah Lucrese, 12.

WHITE:
Alfred, 2; Caleb, 21; Charles, 24;
Delilah, 32, 65; Elisha, 21; Elizabeth, 21, 24, 42; Frances, 2; Frances Freeland, 2; Francis, 21; George, 42; Gideon, 21, 33, 38, 48, 56,
60, 65, 72, 78; Griffith, 2; Isaac,
21; John, 39, 40, 42; Jonathan, 42;
Joseph, 2, 42; Margaret, 42; Mary
Ann, 42; Nacky, 24; Otho, 39; Polly,
24; Regancy, 24; Reuben, 21; Richard, 25, 32; Richard Thomas, 32;
Roena, 2; Ruthy, 21; Sarah, 21, 24;
Sarah Ann Ridgely, 78.

WHITELOCK:
Elizabeth, 73, 75.

WHITTINGHAM:
Eleanor, 59; Elizabeth, 59; Mary,
59.

WHITTINGTON:
Ann, 61; Catherine, 76; Eleanor, 48;
Elizabeth, 35, 48; James, 48; John,
56; John A., 69, 78; Joseph, 15; Mary,
23, 34, 48; Sarah, 69, 78; Sarah Russell, 15; Susanna, 34; Thomas, 7.

WHITTLE:
Ann, 31; David, 31; Elizabeth, 31;
Mary, 31; Nancy, 31; Nicholas, 31;
William, 31.

WHITWRIGHT:
Jacob, 63.

WIGGINS:
Harriet W., 68; Jemima Cross, 62;
Rebecca, 30.

WILKENS, WILKINS:
William, 1, 38;

WILLIAMS:
Abraham, 7; Allison, 49; Ann, 41;
Basil, 35, 37; Bryan, 7, 35, 37, 39,

WILLIAMS, continued:
41, 61, 64; Charlotte, 49; Delilah, 49; Editha, 95; Edward, 62; Edward C., 95; Eleanor, 17; Elijah, 56, 61, 64, 73, 85; Elizabeth, 49, 61, 64; Ennion, 26; Francis, 79; Henry, 58, 59, 61, 64, 85; Jacob, 46-47, 55, 56, 58, 61, 64; Jesse, 49; John, 7, 35; John S., 88; John W., 95; Joseph, 35, 46, 76; Joseph S., 95; Louisa, 85; Maria A., 95; Marmaduke, 7; Mary, 31; Mary A.W., 95; Mary Ann, 49; Mary E., 85; Minty, 7; Nathan, 49; Nicholas, 35; Oliver H., 85; Osborn, 56, 61; Philip, 14; Rachel, 74; Richard, 72, 76; Sally, 41; Sarah, 7, 49; Sarah A., 85; Thomas, 46.

WILLIAMSON:
James, 84, 85; Sarah, 38.

WILLINGMAN:
Catherine, 85; Mary Swarmstadt, 50.

WILLSON, WILSON:
Alethea, 46; Ann, 23, 46; Drusilla, 23; Elizabeth, 23, 95; Fielder, 23, 46, 88, 92; Henry, 23, 46; John, 70; John T., 71; Juhan, 70; Letha, 23; Mary, 23, 70; Oliver, 23, 46; Susanna, 23, 46; William, 23, 46.

WINTERSON:
Ann, 30; Benjamin, 30, 46, 48, 51, 53, 55, 72, 85, 89; Gassaway, 81, 84, 85, 89.

WOOD:
Ann, 13, 40; Arimenta, 95; Barbara, 27; Cassandra, 16; Elizabeth, 16; Henry, 34; Hopewell, 40; James, 34; Hopewell, 40; James, 34; James P., 33, 34, 37; John, 27, 34, 56, 63, 72; John Jonas, 27; Margaret, 16; Mary, 56; Mary Ann, 18; Matilda Burgess, 27; Morgan, 16; Rebecca, 62; Richard, 56; Robert, 34; Samuel, 34, 62, 87, 95; Sarah, 61; William, 16, 34; William H., 87; Zebedee, 13, 40.

WOODFIELD:
Eleanor, 42; Elizabeth Norman, 6; John, 6, 38; Mary Simmons, 34;

WOODFIELD, continued;
Thomas, 17, 24, 36, 37.

WOODWARD:
Abraham B., 35; Achsah, 18; Harriet, 18, 37; Henry, 37; Margaret, 37; Mary Ann, 37; Mary Orme, 37; Priscilla, 35; Rebecca, 18; Thomas, 37; William, 7, 37.

WOOTTEN:
Arah Ann, 69; Araminta, 69; Arthur, 25; Elizabeth, 25; Elizabeth Jane, 69; John, 25; Richard, 25, 69; Richard Arthur, 69; Samuel, 25; Thomas, 25; Willa Maria, 69; William, 25; William Thomas, 69.

WORTHINGTON:
Achsah Ann, 79; Ann, 68, 70, 71; B____, 60; B____ J____ G____, 60; Brice J., 59; Brice J.C., 70, 71, 79; Charles, 59; Charles C., 70, 71, 79, 84; Elizabeth, 59, 60; John, 16, 30, 35, 59, 60; J____ G____, 84; John G., 70, 71, 88, 96; John T., 60; John Tolley Hood, 14; Julia, 57; Mary, 79, 84; Nicholas, 30, 51, 59, 68, 70, 71; Sarah, 14, 24, 52; T____ B____, 60; Thomas, 30, 51, 57, 59, 68, 70, 71; Walter T., 14; Walter Tolley, 14, 24; William H., 79.

WRIGHT:
Ann, 58, 65, 88; George, 48, 58; Isaac, 58; Joshua, 17.

WYVILL:
Ann, 36; Edward, 87; Elizabeth, 36, 39; Hail, 36; Harriet, 39; Jane, 36; Marmaduke, 35, 39; Mary, 36; Priscilla, 36; Susanna, 35, 36; Walter, 39.

YATES:
Vachel, 5.

YEALDHALL:
Aaron, 39; Ann Eliza, 50; Aquila, 40, 50; Benjamin, 34, 39; Elijah, 39, 40, 50, 69; Eliza, 62; Elizabeth, 2, 7, 40, 69; Frances, 7, 26, 40; Francis, 69; Frederick, 40, 69; Gassaway, 34; Gilbert, 7; Harriet, 39, 43; Henri-

YEALDHALL, continued:
etta, 50; Henry, 40; John, 43, 62;
Joseph, 43; Joshua, 40; Louisa, 43;
Mary, 43, 45, 50, 57, 69; Samuel, 7,
24, 39, 51, 63, 82; Sarah, 7; Susanna, 39; William, 8, 34, 40.

YEWELL:
Basil, 75, 83; Eliza, 83; Henry, 75;
James T., 83, 95; John, 75; Thomas,
83.

YOUNG:
Benjamin, 24; Charlotte, 39; Comfort,
24; Elizabeth, 93; Henrietta, 76;
Jason, 96; John, 25, 56; Joshua, 24,
42, 62, 87, 96; Levi, 93; Lurana, 24;
Mary, 24; Nathan, 24; Orpha, 39, 96;
Rachel, 24; Rebecca, 18, 29; Richard,
24; Ruth, 39; William, 23, 24, 96.

ZIGLER:
Elizabeth, 42.

www.ingramcontent.com/pod-product-compliance
Lightning Source LLC
Chambersburg PA
CBHW071810090426

42737CB00012B/2020

*9 7 8 1 5 8 5 4 9 0 8 6 8 *